AVOIDING WAR WITH CHINA

OTHER BOOKS BY AMITAI ETZIONI

Foreign Policy: Thinking Outside the Box (2016)

The New Normal (2014)

Hot Spots: American Foreign Policy in a Post-Human-Rights World (2012)

From Empire to Community: A New Approach to International Relations (2004)

Security First: For a Muscular, Moral Foreign Policy (2006)

Political Unification Revisited (2001)

The New Golden Rule (1996)

The Active Society (1968)

Winning without War (1964)

The Hard Way to Peace (1962)

A Diary of a Commando Soldier (1952)

AMITAI ETZIONI

AVOIDING WAR WITH CHINA

TWO NATIONS, ONE WORLD

University of Virginia Press
CHARLOTTESVILLE AND LONDON

University of Virginia Press
© 2017 by the Rector and Visitors of the University of Virginia
All rights reserved
Printed in the United States of America on acid-free paper

First published 2017

ISBN 978-0-8139-4003-8 (cloth)
ISBN 978-0-8139-4004-5 (ebook)

9 8 7 6 5 4 3 2 1

Library of Congress Cataloging-in-Publication Data is available from the
Library of Congress.

For peacemakers, whatever their affiliation

CONTENTS

AVOIDING WAR WITH CHINA

INTRODUCTION

The change of administration following the 2016 election in the United States provides an opportunity to reexamine US foreign policy in general and regarding China in particular. We shall see shortly that there are good reasons to fear that the United States and China are on a collision course. Before we move further down this road, the public—and not just policymakers—should closely study whether such a confrontation is avoidable, without either side sacrificing its core values or interests. This book is meant to provide a dialogue starter for such a much-needed public discourse.

If you are the betting type, I have a promising bet for you. Wager that the United States and China will engage in a major war in the foreseeable future. Some scholars who specialize in international relations, such as John Mearsheimer, contend that a war between the United States and China is more likely today than a "hot" war between the United States and the USSR ever was.[1] Timothy Garton Ash, a British historian and commentator, states that the United States and China will "probably" go to war if they do not carefully manage the slew of points of tension between them.[2] Michael Pillsbury, an expert with four decades of experience studying US-China relations, observes that China's lack of military transparency practically guarantees inadvertent escalation, leading to war.[3]

Others consider a war with China inevitable because of an "iron law" of history, according to which prevailing superpowers such as the United States necessarily fail to yield power quickly enough to a new power such as China, thereby causing rising tensions and, eventually, war. Graham Allison writes: "The defining question about global order for this generation is whether China and the United States can escape Thucydides's trap. The Greek historian's metaphor reminds us of the attendant dangers when a rising power rivals a ruling power. . . . [Avoiding war] required huge, painful adjustments in attitudes and actions on the part not just of the challenger but also the challenged."[4] Even optimists,

I

against whom you'd be betting, give the United States and China only a one in four chance of avoiding war. According to Allison's report, superpowers adjusted and avoided war with rising powers in four out of sixteen cases since 1500.[5] (In one of these cases, Great Britain yielded to the United States during the late 1800s and early 1900s.)

This book hopes to sour your bet (with due apologies) by outlining several policies that may allow us to achieve a peaceful transition of power without endangering the United States' core interests in Southeast Asia—or undermining the United States' position as a global power. To find a peaceful way, both the United States and China need to change their foreign policies. Scores of books and articles argue what China must do: stop its military buildup, improve its transparency, bring its military more under the control of the government rather than the Communist Party, and transition to a liberal democracy, among other recommendations. This book, in contrast, is written by an American for Americans; it focuses on the actions the United States could take to reduce the probability that the world will face another major war.

I cannot stress enough that when I point in the following pages to flaws in the ways that the United States is currently dealing with China (for instance, by excluding it from the Trans-Pacific Partnership), this does not mean that China has conducted itself better or does not need to mends its ways. It simply means that China's warts have been amply charted and dissected; this book focuses on what the United States could do better.

To proceed, Americans need to engage in a national dialogue, a public debate about what the United States' China policy is and should be. The United States often engages in such debates about other subjects, such as same-sex marriage, climate change, dealing with ISIS and with Iran. Such a national debate about China policy has not yet happened.

Indeed, during the most recent presidential primary season, both Republican and Democratic presidential candidates have mainly avoided the subject, though Donald Trump argued that China is out to "eat our lunch."[6] Now that the elections are over, and a new administration is coming in, this is a particularly opportune time to engage in such a public debate. This book seeks to serve this overdue give-and-take.

Going to or sliding into war with a rising China is especially tragic because—as I see it—China and the United States share many complementary interests and have surprisingly few substantive reasons to come to blows.[7] (By "substantive" I mean those issues that are distinct from symbolic or hyped-up ones, such as the question of who owns a pile of rocks somewhere difficult to find on a map.)

Some use the terms "panda huggers" and "dragon slayers" to categorize analysts and public leaders in the West according to the approaches they recommend adopting toward China; these terms replace the "doves" and "hawks" of the Cold War. (I sometimes refer to them as "Engagers" and "Adversarians.")

Some might consider this book to fall on the dovish side. However, I am not a "panda hugger," but rather someone who has been to war. This experience left me with a strong commitment to seeking peaceful resolutions to international conflicts.[8]

The overdue public debate about America's China policy will not take place in a vacuum. The US military, in the course of carrying out its duty to secure the United States, has identified China as a major strategic threat. Accordingly, it has made the case in the media, in congressional hearings, and in presentations to the White House that the United States should take a tougher approach to China and should build up its military in order to prepare for a war with China. The defense industry supports the same charge for its own reasons. To digress, I do not claim that there exists a military-industrial complex in the sense of a solid military-corporate bloc whose representatives meet at night in a motel in Arlington to plot how to gain glory and profit by pushing the United States into war with China. As a matter of fact, the US military's various services compete with each other; thus the US Army is much less inclined to target China than the US Air Force and Navy are. And many corporations that make money out of peaceful pursuits compete with defense-focused ones, and defense corporations compete with each other. However, as we shall see, major segments of the military and corporations do have strong, vested interests in preparing for war with China for reasons that do serve their constituents, but not necessarily the good of the United States (chapter 1).

The White House and Congress have neither systematically examined these pressures to prepare for war with China, nor squared them with other assessments of China's threat, especially those of the Department of State and the intelligence community. It is up to leading civilian authorities—the president of the United States and members of Congress—to make the ultimate decisions in these matters.

So far, the president and Congress have muddled through, which has allowed the United States and China to drift closer to war. To provide but one small example, on December 16, 2015, the *New York Times* ran a story under the headline "U.S Admiral Assails China's 'Unilateral' Actions at Sea." While the admiral did not mention China by name, there was no doubt about which nation he charged with interfering in the freedom of navigation in the region by diverting ships that were traveling too close to the artificial islands recently built by China. The admiral also stated that China was subjecting commercial and military operations in the area to various warnings, and that fishermen—who have been fishing in the region for generations—have been intimidated. The tone of the speech, the *Times* reported, was "tougher" than previous ones. When the admiral was asked for specific examples of such actions by China, his staff did not provide any, and stated that these needed to be researched. As these lines go to press, the admiral and his staff have still not provided a single example of the highly aggressive moves he attributed to China. And—the White House and Congress have continued to be mum about a military official making such provocative statements. If this had been an isolated incident, I would agree that no one should make much of it, but this is not the case (chapter 1).

Sociological and psychological factors as well as special interests drive a tendency to view China as an adversary approaching an enemy. Developed nations tend to be communities in which the people become deeply involved in the ways their nation is treated and viewed. They are personally offended if a foreign leader mocks or otherwise seems to slight their nation, and they feel proud when their flag is raised at the Olympic Games. They are quick to see the world in terms of "us" versus "them," and to split their feelings by attributing worthy motives to their nation and unworthy motives to other nations. During the Cold War, Americans had many good reasons to view the United States as the promoter of liberty and human rights, and the USSR and China as nations that enslaved their citizens. Indeed, when China and the USSR broke up, many Americans refused to believe that such a breakup took place. Since then China has slowly changed its economy into a semicapitalist one, ceased to promote communist regimes in other countries, and focused on providing its people with American-like affluence. However, many Americans still hold on to their old image of China. That China's political system has changed much less than its economy feeds into this troubled view of China. What deserves a reexamination remains: How much of an adversary is this new, partly transformed China? Is it a powerful, military nation? Is its economy about to overtake the United States' own? Is China set on dominating the world? Chapter 2 addresses these questions.

The book next turns to asking how aggressive China's conduct has been in the past decade. The answer turns out to be far from obvious, because it hinges in part on the definition of "aggressive." This may seem like a typical academic exercise in hairsplitting, but it is not; instead, the definition plays a key role in determining whether the United States will view China as a world-class bully or as a newly assertive regional power that is moving cautiously. To proceed, the chapter introduces a distinction among three layers of international relations: symbolic, economic, and coercive. The symbolic sphere deals with declarations, planting flags, and propaganda. The economic sphere involves trade, investment, and sanctions. The coercive sphere involves the use of military or paramilitary forces, as well as terrorism. By drawing on this distinction, we will see that most who characterize China as "aggressive" do so not on the basis of cases in which China has used actual force (very rare in the past decade and on a very low scale)—but often on the basis of China's economic investment in other countries, of verbal statements made by China claiming sovereignty over parts of the South China Sea or piles of barren rocks, and other such actions. These views of China ignore the difference between moves such as Russia invading Ukraine with troops and tanks or annexing Crimea, and moves such as China declaring portions of the South China Sea as part of its air defense identification zone (ADIZ). These claims are typically ignored by other states, and when China does respond to the violations of its ADIZ, it does so with more declarations, that is, with words. It seems less confusing and more conducive to sound analysis of limits to apply the term "aggressive" to the use of force and to view other actions as merely assertive. Chapter 3 applies this criterion to China's foreign policy over the past ten years in order to determine whether and to what extent China has been aggressive. It also points out the benefits that the United States and the international community will accrue if they meet assertive acts with assertive responses rather than with aggressive countermoves.

Several leading international relations scholars have asked whether China, far from using force to settle international differences, lives up to a much higher standard of conduct, namely, that of a "good citizen" or a "responsible stakeholder" in the international community. To answer this question, chapter 4 outlines the characteristics of a good citizen and asks whether many nations, the United States included, meet these criteria. The examination reveals that many of the criteria according to which international relations scholars assess a nation's good citizenship are "aspirational." That is, many people wish that nations would be good citizens, but most are not most of the time. Chapter 4 then turns to assessing where China stands from this exacting viewpoint.

If the United States is to avoid Thucydides' trap and stop sliding toward war with China, American policymakers and experts must abandon the notion that every change to the status quo amounts to appeasement that will "reward" China's "aggression" and thereby further embolden it. Americans ought to take into account that China has been occupied by foreign powers that have treated China's citizens horribly, and note that China—which has a rich legacy as a great civilization— was humiliated for centuries by Western powers. In the past few decades, China has finally "found its legs." Its economic development took off; indeed, its rapid economic growth outpaces every other major nation, including the United States, other Western nations, and India. It has lifted hundreds of millions of people out of poverty. Its bullet trains, modern airports, and skyscrapers surpass Western ones, and it has substantially modernized its military, even though it is still rather weak compared to the United States' armed forces. The newly empowered China is seeking some changes in the international agreements that were made when China was weak and subject to other powers' whims. To block any and all of these initiatives is to invite a confrontation. At the same time, accommodations to the new China cannot require that the United States and its allies abandon arrangements they consider essential for their own "core interests."

We need to learn to differentiate between truly "core" interests and other ones. Defending Japan, which is the United States' foremost ally in the region, is a core interest; defending the Philippines' claims for an exclusive economic zone (EEZ) in the South China Sea, on the other hand, may not qualify. Similar demands by Vietnam may be even less critical. More important accommodations to the new China must be reached through diplomatic means such as negotiations, appeals to international courts, international mediation, and arbitrations—and not through the use of force by either side. Chapter 5 discusses the set of accommodations the United States and China could make. These suggestions differ from those made in previous chapters in that while they could be initially advanced by the United States making unilateral moves, significant progress in reducing tensions and working out differences between the United States and China will only occur if China cooperates. Thus, chapter 5 addresses not merely American citizens and policymakers but also those in China who care about a peaceful world.

To return to my call for a public debate about what American China policy ought to be, one notes that currently there is a lack of clarity—to put it gently—about what that policy is.[9] Often the United States' representatives speak about the importance of collaborating and sharing responsibilities with China, but the United States often behaves as if it intends to contain and isolate China. This discrepancy is evident in the case of the United States' establishment of new military bases in the Asia-Pacific region along China's land borders, its encouragement of Japan's military buildup, and its continued, almost daily reconnaissance flights up and down China's coastlines. Repeatedly, the United States has called upon China to join international institutions and to adhere to international rules (established by the United States and its allies, mainly at the end of World War II), but when China has moved to respond to such exhortations, the United States has impeded its efforts, as the first section of chapter 6 describes. The United States regularly calls on China to shoulder more of the international responsibility to provide peacekeeping and human rights assistance, but it attempted to block China's creation of an international development bank (much of chapter 6).

These findings that suggest the United States ought to reconsider its approach to China imply neither that China's policy is beyond reproach nor that it need not reexamine the course it follows. However—as I mentioned at the outset of this discussion—many American scholars have often and clearly pointed out China's flaws, including its human rights violations, its massive disregard for property rights, its censorship, and its attempts to bully its allies. The focus of this book is to establish what the United States could do differently to improve its relationship with China without sacrificing any American core interests.

Moreover, it seems that focusing the United States' military budget and strategic planning on a war with China distracts from facing what is turning out to be the spread of jihadists into more nations in Africa, Asia, and elsewhere. Theoretically, a global superpower should be capable of facing challenges on multiple fronts; however, budgets are in reality limited and force tradeoffs. To illustrate: training additional sailors for more ships and submarines diminishes the funds available for training more Special Ops forces that are suitable for fighting jihadists. Buying more F-35 jets suitable for wars with major powers is useless in fighting terrorists and cuts into the funds needed for A-10s—slow-flying aircraft well suited for close support of ground forces. Ordering more nuclear submarines does nothing to degrade ISIS, a mission more suited for attack helicopters. There has been very little public discussion as to what the United States' priorities ought to be in the near future—investing ever more in preparing for a war with China or facing up to the spread of Islamic terrorism. It is a discussion that should not be delayed, given that in effect the Pentagon and lobbyists representing select major corporations act as if such a discourse took place and China was chosen as the most pressing target (see chapter 7.)

The United States, China, and most nations in the world agreed to downgrade sovereignty and consider armed interventions in the internal affairs of nations by outside powers as legal only if these interventions seek to stop genocide (sometimes broadly defined). This new normative tenet is commonly referred to as R2P or RtoP, which stands for "Responsibility to Protect." However, this shared understanding has been undermined when the United States and its allies seemed to or actually did use RtoP to justify armed interventions that led to regime change. I suggest that limiting the grounds for intervention and establishing a clearer understanding of which authority can determine that an armed intervention is justified could restore the US-China consensus in this important matter. I suggested that another downgrading of sovereignty is called for, namely, the responsibility to prevent transnational terrorism (see chapter 8).

Freedom of navigation assertions (FONA) are little-known military operations the United States carries out worldwide. However, since the beginning of 2015 they serve as a major way for the United States to demonstrate its disapproval of China's island building in the South China Sea. On the one hand, these operations avoid outright military confrontations and show China, the world, and the public at home that the United States is not sitting by idly, is "doing something," and is not accepting China's claims about its rights in the region. On the other hand, these moves militarize the conflict, as even the US Department of State pointed out, and could lead to accidental conflagration, of the kind that started World War I.

More generally, an examination of the FONA serves to examine the United States' self-assigned role as "the world's policeman." In effect, the United States often acts as a global prosecutor, judge, and executioner (chapter 9).

1

WHO AUTHORIZED PREPARATIONS FOR WAR WITH CHINA?

The United States is preparing for a war with China, a momentous decision that so far has failed to receive a thorough review from elected officials, namely, the White House and Congress. This important change in the United States' posture toward China has largely been driven by the Pentagon. There have been other occasions in which the Pentagon has framed key strategic decisions so as to elicit the preferred response from the commander in chief and elected representatives. A recent case in point was when the Pentagon led President Obama to order a high-level surge in Afghanistan in 2009, against the advice of the vice president and the US ambassador to Afghanistan. The decision at hand stands out even more prominently, because (a) the change in military posture may well lead to an arms race with China, which could culminate in a nuclear war; and (b) the economic condition of the United States requires a reduction in military spending, not a new arms race. The start of a new term, and with it the appointment of new secretaries of state and defense, provide an opportunity to review the United States' China strategy and the military's role in it. This review is particularly important before the new preparations for war move from an operational concept to a militarization program that includes ordering high-cost weapons systems and force restructuring. History shows that once these thresholds are crossed, it is exceedingly difficult to change course.

In the following pages, I first outline recent developments in the Pentagon's approach to dealing with the rise of China; I then focus on the deliberations of the highest civilian authorities. These two sides seemed to operate in parallel universes, at least until November 2011 when the pivot to Asia was announced by the White House—though we shall see that their paths hardly converged even after that date. I conclude with an outline of what the much-needed civilian review ought to cover.

I write about the "Pentagon" and the "highest civilian authorities" (or our elected political representatives), rather than contrast the view of the military and that of the civilian authorities, because the Pentagon includes civilians, who actively participated in developing the plans under discussion. It is of course fully legitimate for the Pentagon to identify and prepare for new threats. The question that this chapter raises is whether the next level of government—which reviews such threats while taking into account the input of the intelligence community (which includes nonmilitary agencies such as the CIA and NSA) and other agencies (especially the State Department)—has adequately fulfilled its duties. Have the White House and Congress properly reviewed the Pentagon's approach and found its threat assessment of China convincing? Have they approved the chosen response? And if not, what are the United States' overarching short- and long-term political strategies for dealing with an economically and militarily rising China?

In the Pentagon

Since World War II, the United States has maintained a power-projection military built upon forward deployed forces with uninhibited access to the global commons—air, sea, and space. For more than six decades the United States' unrivaled naval and air power has underwritten the maritime security of the Western Pacific. However, starting in the early 1990s, Chinese investments in sophisticated but low-cost weapons—including antiship missiles, short- and medium-range ballistic missiles, cruise missiles, stealth submarines, and cyber- and space arms—began to challenge the United States' military superiority, especially in China's littoral waters. These "asymmetric arms" threaten two key elements of the United States' force-projection strategy: its fixed bases (such as those in Japan and Guam) and aircraft carriers. Often referred to as anti-access/area denial capabilities (A2/AD), these Chinese arms are viewed by some in the Pentagon as raising the human and economic cost of the United States' military role in the region to prohibitive levels. To demonstrate what this new environment means for regional security, military officials point out that in 1996, when China conducted a series of missile tests and military exercises in the Strait of Taiwan, the United States responded by sending two aircraft carriers to the South China Sea, a credible display of force that reminded all parties of its commitment to maintaining the status quo in the region.[1] However, these analysts point out, if in the near future China decided to forcefully integrate Taiwan, the same American aircraft carriers that are said to have once deterred Chinese aggression could be denied access to the sea by the People's Liberation Army (PLA) antiship missiles. Thus, American interests in the region, to the extent that they are undergirded by superior military capabilities, are increasingly vulnerable.

Two influential American military strategists, Andrew Marshall and his protégé Andrew Krepinevich, have been raising the alarm about China's new capabilities and aggressive designs since the early 1990s. Building on hundreds of war games played out over the past two decades, they gained a renewed hearing for their concerns following Pacific Vision, a war game conducted by the US Air Force in October 2008. The game was financed in part by Marshall's Office of Net Assessment, a division of the Pentagon focused on identifying emerging security threats to the United States. The *Air Force Magazine* reported at the time that the simulation convinced others in the Pentagon of the need to face up to China, and "when it was over, the PACAF [Pacific Air Force Command] staff set about drawing up its conclusions and fashioning a framework for AirSea Battle"—a plan to develop the new weapons and operation capabilities needed to overcome the challenges posed by A2/AD.[2]

With Marshall's guidance, Secretary of Defense Robert Gates instructed the Chiefs of Staff to begin work on the AirSea Battle (ASB) project and, in September of 2009, Air Force Chief of Staff Gen. Norton Schwartz and Chief of Naval Operations Admiral Gary Roughead signed a classified memorandum of agreement endorsing the plan.[3] ASB received Gates's official imprimatur in the 2010 Quadrennial Defense Review, which directed the United States military to "develop a joint air-sea battle concept . . . [to] address how air and naval forces will integrate capabilities across all operational domains—air, sea, land, space, and cyberspace—to counter growing challenges to U.S. freedom of action."[4] In late 2011 Gates's successor, Secretary of Defense Leon Panetta, also signed off on the ASB and formed the new Multi-Service Office to Advance AirSea Battle. Thus, in only a few years, ASB was conceived, born, and began to grow.

ASB called for "interoperable air and naval forces that can execute networked, integrated attacks-in-depth to disrupt, destroy, and defeat enemy anti-access area denial capabilities."[5] The hypothetical battle would begin with a campaign to reestablish power-projection capabilities by launching a "blinding attack" against Chinese anti-access facilities, including land- and sea-based missile launchers, surveillance and communication platforms, satellite and antisatellite weapons, and command and control nodes. American forces could then enter contested zones and conclude the conflict by bringing to bear the full force of their material military advantage.

At the time the Pentagon proposed ASB, contemporary US technologies and force structures were unprepared to carry out such a hypothetical campaign; its architects urged investments in penetrating, long-endurance ISR (intelligence, surveillance, and reconnaissance) and strike capabilities; aerial tankers; and forward base hardening. Strategists also encouraged the navy to "develop and field long-range/endurance UUVs [unmanned undersea vehicles] for multiple missions germane to intelligence preparation of the undersea battlespace" and recommended that the air force and navy stockpile precision-guided munitions "in sufficient quantities to execute an ASB campaign."[6] ASB also involved a considerable shift of budgetary priorities from the army and marines to the navy and air force.

Some argue that ASB is merely a limited "operational concept." However, it has already shaped acquisition decisions and decisions about Pentagon force structure. General Schwartz wrote in 2012, "The first steps to implement Air-Sea Battle are already underway here at the Pentagon. In our FY 2012 and FY 2013 budgets we increased investment in the systems and capabilities we need to defeat access threats."[7] Admiral Greenert points to the investments in antisubmarine warfare, electronic warfare, air and missile defense, and information sharing that were included in the president's 2012 budget as one aspect of ASB's implementation, and he notes that the 2013 budget "sustains these investments and really provides more resilient C4ISR [Command, Control, Communications, Computers, Intelligence, Surveillance and Reconnaissance] investments."[8] The *New York Times* reported that the new Littoral Combat Ship, which is able to deftly navigate shallow coastal seas, is "central to President Obama's strategy of projecting American power in the Pacific."[9] So far, two of the planned fifty-five ships have been completed, and the first were deployed in Singapore in 2013. A press report in August 2012 stated that "the Air-Sea Battle concept has prompted Navy officials to make significant shifts in the service's FY2014–FY2018 budget plan, including new investments in ASW [antisubmarine warfare], electronic attack and electronic warfare, cyberwarfare, the F-35 Joint Strike Fighter (JSF), the P-8A maritime patrol aircraft, and the Broad Area Maritime Surveillance (BAMS) UAV [unmanned aerial vehicle]."[10] Some point out that many of these weapons would have been ordered even if there were no ASB, and that some purchases merely constitute technological updates. However, it is also true that a smaller defense budget means making choices about the allocation of resources, and evidence suggests that the Pentagon has made the hardware of ASB a high priority. In addition, a 2012 report by the Congressional Research Service on the implications of Chinese naval modernization disclosed that there has been a "redeployment of various advanced U.S. nuclear submarines and Aegis SM-3 based missile defense vessels to the Pacific in close cruising distance to China and North Korea. Other vessels in the Pacific were recently moved to Guam and Hawaii to presumably cut transit time to areas of possible conflict. All of this would be helpful if AirSea concepts are employed."[11]

In January 2015, the Joint Chiefs of Staff released a memo announcing the "development, evaluation, and implementation" of a Joint Concept for Access and Maneuver in the Global Commons (JAM-GC), which the memo stated was a new name for the concept "formerly known as AirSea Battle."[12] The AirSea Battle Office is responsible for "support[ing] and oversee[ing] the writing and development of the new JAM-GC concept," and will dissolve when the Joint Staff approves the concept, at which point "the ASB Office will become the JAM-GC Office," a representative of the AirSea Battle Office stated.[13] A number of experts agree that JAM-GC is virtually indistinguishable from ASB, and that the decision to rename the concept without substantially revising the concept itself suggests the Department of Defense was motivated by "getting the topic out of the daily headlines" and "engender[ing] little scrutiny or debate."[14] Navy Captain Terry Morris, the deputy director of the AirSea Battle Concept program, however, contests this suggestion; he says that JAM-GC is meant neither "to replace Air-Sea Battle [. . . nor to] throw the Air-Sea Battle concept out and start all over again." He characterizes JAM-GC as an expansion of the ASB concept's focus in response to new regional threats and intra-armed forces issues.[15] Jacek Bartosiak of the Potomac Foundation supports this assessment, saying that a wide variety of A2/AD threats have emerged since ASB was first proposed, and that JAM-GC will be developed with an eye to each of them, whereas ASB was focused exclusively on China.[16] However, it is a safe assumption that JAM-GC is dedicated to the same objectives and approaches as the original ASB concept, even if it incorporates additional elements.

One should note that several officials also maintain that ASB is not aimed at China. At a background briefing on ASB, one Pentagon official stated, "It is not about a specific actor. It is not about a specific actor or regime."[17] General Norton Schwartz has said that questions about China's place in the concept are "unhelpful."[18] However, the consensus of most observers is that "Air-Sea Battle is billed as the answer to growing anti-access/area-denial capabilities generically, but as everyone knows, specifically China," as former Marine Corps officer J. Noel Williams put it.[19] And according to a senior navy official overseeing the forces modernization efforts, "Air-Sea Battle is all about convincing the Chinese that we will win this competition."[20]

Indeed, as far as one can determine, the Pentagon decided to embrace the ASB concept over alternative ways for sustaining American military power in the region that, critically, are far less likely to lead to escalation. One such is the "war-at-sea" option, a strategy proposed by Jeffrey Kline and Wayne Hughes of the Naval Postgraduate School which would deny China use of the sea within the first island chain (which stretches from Japan to Taiwan and through the Philippines) by means of a distant blockade, the use of submarine and flotilla attacks at sea, and the positioning of expeditionary forces to hold at-risk islands in the South China Sea. By forgoing a mainland attack, the authors argue that the war-at-sea strategy gives "opportunities for negotiation in which both sides can back away from escalation to a long-lasting, economically-disastrous war involving full mobilization and commitment to some kind of decisive victory."[21] In the same vein, the "Offshore Control Strategy" put forward by National Defense University's T. X. Hammes "seeks to use a war of economic attrition to bring about a stalemate and cessation of conflict" by establishing a distant blockade and a maritime exclusion zone within the first island chain, while dominating the surrounding waters "to ensure the continued flow of trade to our allies while tightening the blockade against China."[22] This would not bring a decisive victory, but would allow the United States to achieve its objectives of protecting its allies and maintaining free access to sea-lanes, while giving China space to back down. Indeed, even Krepinevich in 2015 advocated a strategy he called "Archipelagic Defense," which was closer to Offshore Control than to ASB.[23]

Several defense analysts in the United States and abroad, as well as in China, see ASB as highly provocative. General James Cartwright, former vice chairman of the Joint Chiefs of Staff, stated in 2012 that "AirSea Battle is demonizing China. That's not in anybody's interest."[24] An internal assessment of ASB by the Marine Corps commandant cautions that "an Air-Sea Battle–focused Navy and Air Force would be preposterously expensive to build in peace time" and if used in a war against China would cause "incalculable human and economic destruction."[25]

Several critics point out that ASB is inherently escalatory and is likely to accelerate the arms race in the Asia-Pacific. China must be expected to respond to military acquisitions and deployments that are needed for the implementation of ASB by accelerating its own military buildup. Chinese colonel Gauyue Fan stated, "If the U.S. military develops AirSea Battle to deal with the [People's Liberation Army], the PLA will be forced to develop anti-AirSea Battle."[26] Moreover, Raoul Heinrichs, from the Australian National University, points out that "by creating the need for a continued visible presence and more intrusive forms of surveillance in the Western Pacific, ASB will greatly increase the range of circumstances for maritime brinkmanship and dangerous naval incidents."[27]

Other critics argue that ASB operates in a strategic vacuum. Hammes maintains that "ASB is the antithesis of strategy. It focuses on the tactical employment of weapons systems with no theory of victory or concept linking the Air-Sea approach to favorable conflict resolution."[28] Dan Blumenthal of the American Enterprise Institute agrees: "ASB is an operational concept detached from a strategy. . . . As a result, the U.S. is both making commitments to Asia that it may not be able to afford and articulating a high-risk operational doctrine that does not answer basic strategic questions."[29]

As I see it, the implied strategy is clear: ASB planners aim to make the United States so clearly powerful that not only would China lose if it engaged militarily but it would not consider engaging because the United States would be sure to win. Krepinevich holds that ASB achieves both deterrence through denial, "designed to convince a would-be aggressor that he cannot achieve his objective, so there is no point in trying," and deterrence through punishment, "designed to persuade him that even though he may be able to achieve his objective, he will suffer so much as a result that his anticipated costs will outweigh his gains."[30] The imagined result of ASB is the ability to end a conflict with China in much the same way the United States ended World War II: the American military defeats China and dictates the terms of surrender.

This military strategy, which involves threatening to defeat China as a military power, is a far cry from containment or any other strategies that were seriously considered in the context of confronting the USSR after it acquired nuclear arms. The essence of the Cold War was mutual deterrence, and the conflict was structured around red lines that not only were meant to prevent Warsaw Pact forces from moving into NATO-controlled areas but also bound NATO forces to respect the territorial sovereignty of the Soviet realm, including Eastern Europe and East Germany. (This is the reason the United States did not help the freedom fighters who rose against the Communist regimes in Hungary and Czechoslovakia.) First-strike (nuclear) strategies were forsworn, and steps were taken to avoid a war precipitated by miscommunications, accidents, or miscalculations. In contrast, ASB requires that the United States be able to take the war to the mainland with the goal of defeating China, which quite likely would require striking first. Such a strategy is nothing short of a hegemonic intervention.

When Andrew Krepinevich suggested that ASB is simply seeking to maintain stability in the Asia-Pacific, he was asked if this "stability" really meant continued American hegemony in the area. He chuckled and responded, "Well, the nations in the area have a choice: either we are number one or China [is]—and they prefer us."[31] Actually, most of the nations in the region tend to play the big powers against each other rather than join a particular camp. They greatly benefit from trade and investment from China and, at the same time, are quite willing to receive security backing from the United States. And they realize that in a case of conflict between the United States and China, they stand to lose a great deal. (A common saying in the area: "When the elephant and tiger rumble, the grass gets trampled.") Most important, one must ask whether there are other strategies that do not operate on the assumption that our dealings with China represent a zero-sum game. For instance, one should consider whether there are strategies in which the superpower pursues its interests by accommodating a rising power— especially when this power is mainly a regional one—by allowing it an increased sphere of influence. This is how Britain, once a superpower that relied greatly on naval power, accommodated a rising upstart—the United States.

The White House and Congress

To judge by several published reports that will be discussed in greater detail below, including those by government "insiders," there is no indication—not even a passing hint—that the White House has ever considered earnestly preparing the nation for a war with China. Nor is there any evidence that the White House has compared such a strategy to alternatives, and—having concluded that the hegemonic intervention implied by ASB is the course the United States should follow—then instructed the Pentagon to prepare for such a military showdown. Indeed, as far as one can determine at this stage, the White House and State Department have engaged in largely ad hoc debates over particular tactical maneuvers, never giving much attention to the development of a clear underlying China strategy. True, some individuals in the State Department and White House pursued engagement and cooperation, and others advocated "tougher" moves that seem to reflect a vague preference for containment. However, neither approach was embraced as an overarching strategy. The November 2011 presidential announcement that the United States was beginning a "pivot" from the Near to the Far East may at first seem to suggest that a coherent stance on China eventually coalesced within the administration. We will see shortly that this is not the case.

One major source of information regarding the development of China policy in the Obama White House is an insider's report fully dedicated to the subject at hand, entitled *Obama and China's Rise*, by Jeffrey A. Bader. Having served as senior director for East Asian affairs on the National Security Council from January 2009 to April 2011, Bader reports in great detail on how the Obama administration approached China policy. When Obama was still a senator campaigning in the 2008 election—at the same time that the Pentagon was launching the ASB mission—his philosophy was to engage the nations of the world rather than confront them; to rely on diplomacy rather than on aggressive, let alone coercive, measures; and to draw on multilateralism rather than on unilateral moves. Following his election, the president's key staffers report that, with regard to China, containment was "not an option," nor was the realpolitik of power balancing embraced. Instead, the administration pursued a vague three-pronged policy based on "(1) a welcoming approach to China's emergence, influence, and legitimate expanded role; (2) a resolve that a coherent stance on China eventually coalesced to see that its rise is consistent with international norms and law; and (3) an endeavor to shape the Asia-Pacific environment to ensure that China's rise is stabilizing rather than disruptive."[32]

Once in office, the administration's main China-related policy questions involved economic concerns (especially the trade imbalance, currency manipulation, and the dependence on China for the financing of

American debt), North Korea's development of nuclear arms and missiles, sanctions on Iran, Tibet and human rights, and counterterrorism. The fact that China was somewhat modernizing its very backward military is barely mentioned in the book-length report. There is no reference to ASB or to the strategy it implies being considered, questioned, embraced, or rejected—let alone to how it fits into an overarching China strategy, which the Obama administration did not formulate in its first term.

Moreover, Bader's account leaves little doubt that neither the Obama White House nor the State Department ever developed a coherent China strategy. In effect, key staff members scoffed at the very idea that such overarching conceptions were of merit or possible (as opposed to reactive responses to ongoing developments). The Obama team, Bader notes, "fine-tun[ed] an approach" that avoided the extremes of, on the one hand, relying "solely on military muscle, economic blandishments, and pressure and sanctions of human rights" and, on the other, pursuing "a policy of indulgence and accommodation of assertive Chinese conduct."[33] Not too hot, not too cold makes for good porridge, but is not a clear guideline for foreign policy.

A closer reading of these lines, as well as similar statements issued by the administration that were often fashioned as strategic positions, reveals them to be vague and open to rather different interpretations. They seem more like public rationales than guidelines capable of coordinating policies across the various government agencies, let alone of reining in the Pentagon. The overarching ambiguity is captured by Bader, who first reports, "For China to directly challenge America's security interest, it would have to acquire ambitions and habits that it does not at present display. The Unites States should not behave in a way that encourages the Chinese to move in that direction." Then, just pages later, he concludes that "the United States needs to maintain its forward deployment, superior military forces and technological edge, its economic strength and engagement with the region, its alliances, and its enhanced relationships with other emerging powers. Chinese analysts are likely to consider all these traits to be hostile to China."[34]

Another book describing the same period, *The Obamians: The Struggle inside the White House to Redefine American Power,* by James Mann, reveals that although President Obama sought to engage China, his administration was increasingly "irked" by various Chinese moves, from its assertive declarations about the South China Sea to the cyber-attacks assumed to originate from within its borders. In response, the Obama administration is reported to have "stiffened" both its rhetoric and diplomatic stance toward China. For example, in response to Beijing's pronouncement that the South China Sea represented one of China's "core interests," Secretary of State Hillary Clinton told an audience at the 2010 Association of Southeast Asian Nations (ASEAN) meeting that freedom of navigation in the seas was a "national interest" of the United States. She also delivered a speech criticizing China's abuse of Internet freedom and argued that such nations "should face consequences and international condemnation." It is reported that State Department officials, who generally sought to avoid conflict with China, "absolutely hated" the speech.[35] If such a speech caused tensions to flare up in the department, it is not hard to imagine the outcry that would have followed had the administration approved ASB—that is, if it was considered in the first place. Yet in Mann's account of the period under study there is no reference to either ASB or the strategy it implies—or to what a former Pentagon official called a White House "buy-in."[36]

A third book covering the same era, *Bending History: Barack Obama's Foreign Policy*, confirms with much nuance what the other two books report. It discusses the White House "toughening" its reaction to what were viewed by many as assertive moves by the Chinese, such as its aggressive action in the South China Sea in 2010, and President Hu Jintao's refusal to condemn North Korea's torpedo attack on a South Korean warship.[37] Here again, it is reported that the White House and State Department reacted by changing the tone of the speeches. For instance, in a thinly veiled criticism of China, Obama stated in 2011 that "prosperity without freedom is just another form of poverty."[38] The administration also intensified the United States' participation in ASEAN and the East Asia Summit (EAS) and encouraged—but only indirectly and cautiously—countries in the region to deal with China on a multilateral rather than bilateral basis in resolving territorial disputes. The Obama administration also ramped up the United States' participation in the Trans-Pacific Partnership negotiations, a free trade agreement that at least initially would exclude China and is thought by many to be a counterbalance to China's extensive bilateral trade relationships in the region. Furthermore, the president paid official visits to both Burma and

Cambodia—two nations that have distanced themselves from China in recent years.

In his book *Confront and Conceal,* David E. Sanger confirms what these three accounts suggest: the Obama administration never formulated a coherent, consistent, proactive China strategy and its policies were primarily reactive.[39] Sanger's book, too, lacks any mention of a review of ASB and the military strategy it implies.

Congress, meanwhile, held a considerable number of hearings about China in 2008 and in the years that followed. However, the main focus of these hearings was on economic issues such as trade, job losses due to companies moving them overseas, American dependence on China for financing the debt, Chinese currency controls, and Chinese violations of intellectual property and human rights. In his testimony before the Senate Armed Services Committee in February 2012, Admiral Robert F. Willard spoke of the potential challenges posed by China's A2/AD capabilities, but made no mention of ASB. Rep. Randy J. Forbes (R-VA), founder and cochair of the Congressional China Caucus, wrote to Secretary of Defense Panetta in November 2011 that "despite reports throughout 2011 [that] AirSea Battle had been completed in an executive summary form, to my knowledge Members of Congress have yet to be briefed on its conclusions or in any way made a part of the process."[40] In the same month, Senator Joseph Lieberman (I-CT) cosponsored an amendment to the Fiscal 2012 Defense Authorization Bill that required a report on the implementation of and costs associated with the ASB concept. It passed unanimously, but as of April 2013, such a report has yet to be released.[41]

In the public sphere there was no debate on ASB—led by either think tanks or public intellectuals—like that which is ongoing over whether or not to use the military option against Iran's nuclear program, or the debate surrounding the 2009 surge of troops in Afghanistan. ASB did receive a modicum of critical examination from a small number of military analysts. However, most observers who can recount the ins and outs of using drones or bombing Iran have no position on ASB or its implications for US-China relations and the world order, simply because they do not know about it. A December 11, 2012, search of Google brings up 15,800,000 hits for "US drone strikes"; a search for "AirSea Battle," less than 200,000. In Googlish, this amounts to being unknown, and suggests the significant military shift associated with ASB is simply not on the wider public's radar.

Subterranean Interests

The structural civilian inattention to the adoption of ASB is also driven by subterranean forces. The situation is akin to a medical specialist who reads an x-ray and concludes that it justifies a costly operation, which is driven both by his legitimate interpretation of the x-ray (despite the fact that the situation can also be read as benign) and by the fact that he benefits financially from such interventions. Threat assessments can be legitimately read to suggest that China might pose a threat to American interests, especially if what constitutes such a threat is broadly defined; and at the same time, decisions as to how to react to them can be influenced by various special interest considerations.

Before discussing an outline of the subterranean forces, it is useful to point out that some have argued that ASB is "more rhetorical than material"[42] or even a "fantasy."[43] Actually, although at an early state of implementation, ASB is becoming an "operational reality"[44] that deeply affects numerous vested interests.

One factor is what sociologists have found as the tendency of organizations to engage in goal succession. That is, when the goals assigned to an organization are accomplished, the organization, rather than disbanding or greatly scaling back, often formulates new missions. Famously, after the highly successful March of Dimes foundation helped eradicate polio in the United States, it adopted the new mission of preventing birth defects.[45] Goal succession helps account for ASB. After the winding down of two major wars in the Middle East—with no other major war in sight, a president who declared that the war against terror was largely won,[46] a public very weary of military engagements overseas and antiterrorist measures at home (as revealed in the reaction to revelations about the actions of the NSA), and growing political pressures to reduce the budget (even of the military), the Pentagon has an objective need for a new mission. ASB is an answer to this need, irrespective of the need's influence over ASB's formulation as an operational platform.

Another factor working to advance ASB's agenda is the large outlays involved. Some reliable estimates indicated that ASB would entail spending $524 billion in military R&D and procurement through 2023.[47] The required weapons, according to Congressman J. Randy Forbes and analyst Elbridge Colby, would include additional Virginia-class submarines and new technologies designed to "sustain our undersea-warfare advantage"; future aircraft with novel capabilities designed to meet "emerging threat environments in the Western Pacific," including additional long-range bombers that would improve on the B-2; new "credible kinetic and non-kinetic means to deter potential adversaries from extending a conflict into space"; a "new generation of offensive munitions"; and greater spending, generally speaking, on "cutting-edge and next-generation technologies."[48]

Mark Gunzinger, who agrees with Forbes and Colby, coauthored a document with Jan Van Tol, Andrew Krepinevich, and Jim Thomas on ASB in which the authors recommended a host of military expenditures, including "long-range penetrating and stand-off [electronic warfare]-capable platforms (manned and/or unmanned)"; "quantity obscurants, decoys, and false target generators for both offensive and defensive [electronic warfare] missions"; alternatives to GPS navigation [to reduce] US reliance on GPS for its "precision guided weapons"; directed-energy weapons (DEW); additional unmanned undersea vehicles for intelligence purposes; new mobile mines "deployable by submarines and stealthy Air Force bombers"; "stockpiling" precision-guided weapons; and additional air tankers.[49] Considerations related to ASB have also led the navy to prioritize building new missile destroyers.[50] Finally, though Van Tol et al. warn against dependence on "relatively short-ranged land- and sea-based tactical aircraft,"[51] the F-35 fighter in particular has become a pillar of ASB, making up the largest part of projected related spending.[52]

Corporations that specialize in serving the military find themselves in a similar situation as the Pentagon, as the wars in the Middle East are ending. They too have objective interests in new missions and outlets for their production capacities. ASB's long shopping list provides for such outlets.

There is no single military-industrial complex or iron triangle in the United States, as some critics from the left hold. There is no one power elite that meets at night in a motel in Arlington to decide what the military should purchase and how to divide the spoils, or how to promote a strategy that favors its interests. There are, though, a number of military-industrial-congressional alliances that, although competing with each other, do jointly affect American foreign policy and tilt it toward the Far East and away from the Middle East.

A major reason the focus on the Far East is preferable from the viewpoint of such major alliances is that preparing for war in this region is capital intensive, while wars in the Middle East—fighting terrorists and insurgents—are labor intensive. Counterinsurgency operations like the Iraq and Afghanistan wars require high troop levels.[53] The main forces used were the army (Special Forces included), marines, and CIA. These forces spend a greater part of their budget on personnel costs (salaries, benefits) and use relatively low-cost equipment.[54] Although some corporations specialize in service provisions to these troops and in supplementing them with private contractors, large defense contractors like Lockheed Martin gain little from funds allotted to military salaries and benefits.

By contrast, the major forces to be used in the Far East are those of the air force and navy. These are capital-intensive[55] services that use relatively little labor and buy aircraft carriers, nuclear submarines, fighters and bombers, all of which are manufactured by the private sector at a high cost. The business model of major defense contractors, including Lockheed, Boeing, Northrop Grumman, and General Dynamics, relies on capital-intensive rather than labor-intensive expenditures.[56]

Next, corporations can gain a monopoly or at least a duopoly in the production of many of these so-called big-ticket items because the nature of the market discourages competition. The market for major weapons systems is characterized by high entry costs, technical complexity, "winner-takes-all" competitions, and increasing emphasis on versatility rather than diversity of platforms, which facilitates consolidation and even monopolies among producers of such systems (particularly aircraft).[57] For example, by winning the contract in 2001 to design and manufacture the Joint Strike Fighter, Lockheed Martin positioned itself as the monopoly player in advanced fighter aircraft. Along the same lines, Huntington-Ingalls has a monopoly on building and servicing US aircraft carriers, and a duopoly (along with General Dynamics) on navy submarines. Such a position gives producers of major systems certain advantages, since it is difficult for the government to cancel a program if there is no alternative. For instance, despite the technical issues, delays, and cost overruns associated with Lockheed's F-35 stealth fighter, the Pentagon has little choice but to work with Lockheed for a weapon system that officials consider indispensable.[58]

One should note in this context that although corporations always played a role in these matters, their leverage over Congress has increased in recent years following several major decisions by the Supreme Court that allowed corporations, in effect, to give unlimited campaign contributions to members of Congress.[59] Political scientists differ a great deal in their conclusions about the effects of such campaign contributions. It would take us far afield to sort out, in the context of this chapter, what the "true" answer is, if there is one. However, one should note that some highly regarded scholars find a "robust relationship between defense earmarks and campaign contributions from defense political action committees,"[60] and "even after controlling for past contracts and other factors, companies that contributed more money to federal candidates subsequently received more contracts."[61]

In short, the kind of military procurement and force structure entailed by ASB are one in the same as those favored by major corporations. This was confirmed by an interview with a high-ranking Pentagon official from the Bush administration, with an official of the Clinton administration (who has since dedicated his work to the study of the military), and with a designer of ASB.[62]

Furthermore, the military's model of weapons acquisition often benefits large defense manufacturers. In his insightful essay "Silicon, Iron, and Shadow," retired US Army lieutenant general David Barno shows how the US military's strategic focus on "iron" kinds of war serves to encourage the sort of capital-intensive services favored by vested interests and required for the development of ASB.[63] He points out that the US military strongly prefers to fight World War II–style conflicts in which the naval, air, and land forces of one nation are clearly arrayed against another—what Barno calls "iron wars." In the words of former defense secretary Gates, conventional war is in the military's "DNA," leading to a misconception that "if you train and equip to defeat big countries, you can defeat any lesser threat"—ignoring the lessons of Iraq, Afghanistan, and Vietnam.[64] Thus, the military, defense contractors, and Congress fight to retain "the big procurement programs initiated during the Cold War" and drag their feet in preparing for asymmetric conflicts against terrorists and insurgents, or what Barno calls "shadow wars." It was in this sense that, in February 2014, Undersecretary of Defense Frank Kendall referred to the US military as "distracted" by counterinsurgency and at risk of losing its technological superiority.[65] This proclivity further reinforces the preferences for fighting in the Far East over the Middle East. ASB is a form of iron war suited to the Far East.

The Pivot: An Exception That Proves the Rule

In November 2011 President Obama announced that, with the wars in the Middle East coming to a close, his national security team was to make the United States' "presence and mission in the Asia-Pacific a top priority."[66] The State Department called for a "pivot" to Asia, widely understood to mean facing up to China. When US allies in Europe were troubled by these announcements, which they understood as pivoting away from the "Old World," and when others feared that the United States was provoking China, the White House and the State Department started to refer to the reallocation of forces and change in focus as an act of "rebalancing." The United States was said to merely be restoring to Southeast Asia forces that were removed to fight the wars in the Middle East, now said to be winding down. Soon it became clear, though, that the force buildup, the budget reallocations, and the new military alliances in the region greatly exceeded the previous "balance." According to a 2015 report by the Congressional Research Service, the pivot—now called the "rebalance"—has entailed "increased rotational deployments to Australia, the Philippines, and South Korea, . . . deepened engagement with allies and partners in the region, and a concurrent effort to knit strong bilateral ties into a web of regional security cooperation." In addition, the United States now encourages regional allies to increase their own military capabilities.[67] Moreover, 60 percent of the navy would be positioned in the Pacific by 2020—up from 50 percent. Also particularly relevant is that Japan—which occupied, brutalized, and humiliated China and never properly acknowledged its war crimes—is under pressure by the United States to increase its share of "burden sharing" of the military costs that containing China entails.

In conclusion, I am not arguing that the US military is seeking out war or intentionally usurping the role of the highest civilian authorities. Information about the rise of China as an economic and military power is open to a range of interpretations. And the Pentagon is discharging its duties when it identifies new threats and suggests ways to respond to them. Moreover, civilians—including two secretaries of defense—have endorsed ASB and by implication the strategy it entails.

While it would be a serious mistake to dismiss ASB on the grounds that it is merely an attempt to secure a mission and funds for the military, there is room to question whether the threats have been overstated and to ask whether the Pentagon-favored response is the right strategy. The start of a new administration in Washington invites the White House and Congress to reassess both the threat of China and the suggested response—and for the public to join the debate.

Three areas ought to be considered in such a review process:

(i) Although the economy of China does not by itself determine its military strength, it does constrain its options. One would be wise to take into account that China's per capita GDP is far below that of the United States, and that to maintain public support, the Communist Party needs to house, feed, clothe, and otherwise serve a population that is approximately four times as big as that of the United States. This is on top of dealing with major environmental strains, an aging population, high levels of corruption, and growing social unrest.

(ii) The military modernization of China often provokes concerns that it is "catching up" with the United States. Although it is true that China has increased military spending, the budget for the PLA started well behind that of the US military, and China's defense spending is still dwarfed by that of the United States.

(iii) Moreover, whatever its capabilities, China's intentions are relevant. For the last two decades China has shown little interest in managing global affairs or imposing its ideology on other nations. Instead, China has shown a strong interest in securing the flow of raw materials and energy on which its economy depends. The United States can accommodate this core interest without endangering its own security by facilitating China's efforts to secure energy deals in the global marketplace and pathways for the flow of resources (for instance, by constructing pipelines, railways, and new ports in places such as Pakistan)—rather than seeking to block such efforts.

It is up to the responsible media, think tanks, public intellectuals, and leaders of social and political movements to launch and nurture a comprehensive review of US-Sino policies, and to counter the gradual slide toward war that the Pentagon is effecting—even if its intention may well be to promote peace through strength.

2

CHINA: MAKING AN ADVERSARY?

At the end of the first decade of the twenty-first century, the *Economist* issued a report that asked, "China—friend or foe?" However, the cover of that same issue, referring to the same report, was more direct: "The danger of a rising China."[1] Many others in the Western media, the US Congress, and academia increasingly contend that China is on its way to becoming a threatening global force, an adversary, and potentially an enemy. This chapter examines whether viewing China as an adversary is justified and explores alternative American responses to China's rising power.

Adversarial Predispositions

There are strong a priori reasons to critically examine all claims that a nation is turning into an adversary, because there are considerable political, sociological, and psychological forces that push nations to find adversaries and make enemies where there either are none—or when the evidence is ambiguous. This phenomenon is widely known, having found its way into popular literature and movies, such as *Wag the Dog*. It is particularly relevant that those who frame a nation as an opposing force achieve several "secondary gains," that is, benefits one derives from what is otherwise a loss. A nation whose people (at least the majority of them, the elite, and the mainstream media) have come to regard other nations as a threat is more likely to be able to suppress differences and achieve national unity, and its populace will be more likely to be willing to fight and make sacrifices for the common good than a nation without an adversary. Thus, a typical headline reads, "Poland, Lacking External Enemies, Turns on Itself."[2] Moreover, finding an adversary rewards special interests, such as the defense community, arms manufacturers, and those who oppose free trade. And politicians who champion the view that another nation is an adversary are often more successful than those who seek to refute said view, at least in the United States.

One must also take into account the limited capacity of futurists and other scholars to foretell the course of a nation. Several highly influential predictions about the rise and fall of global powers turned out to be far off the mark. These include the well-known forecasts by Paul Kennedy and Ezra Vogel that Japan would rise to global preponderance.[3] For decades, American estimates of the military power and political stability of the Soviet Union were vastly inflated. And the misjudgments concerning Saddam Hussein's weapons of mass destruction are well documented. Ergo, one ought to take predictions that we have entered a "Chinese century"[4] or that China is poised to "rule the world"[5] with considerable caution.

No less important is the fact that characterizing China as an adversary is one factor that can make it into one. As Joseph Nye says: "If we treat China as an enemy, we can guarantee enmity. If we treat China as a friend, we cannot guarantee friendship, but we at least keep open a much wider range of possible futures."[6]

Social scientists have shown that nations respond to being defined and treated as an adversary with moves that confirm the initial claims of the adversary makers, leading to a vicious cycle.[7] Already, military, economic, and political moves by the United States and by China reveal some early signs of this self-fulfilling prophecy. For example, China responded to the US-India nuclear deal by implementing a deal to supply Pakistan with two nuclear reactors.[8] And China responded to close surveillance by harassing American surveillance ships and warplanes, leading to incidences that made the United States see China as belligerent.[9] In other situations, moves by China led to American responses, such as in the mid-1990s, when Chinese missile tests over the Taiwan Strait caused the United States to respond by deploying aircraft carriers to the region.

The Debate, by Sector

The significance of subjecting adversarial predispositions to critical analysis has thus been established, but there remains the question of whether, in the case of China, there is an emerging adversary. This examination proceeds by summarizing the arguments of those who consider China an adversary in the making, if not an enemy, and the responses of those who hold that China is leaning toward a peaceful development and should be engaged by the United States. As mentioned previously, I refer to the former as Adversarians and to the latter as Engagers. The first group tends to consider the rise of China as threatening to the United States' interests and to the world order, although they do not rule out the possibility of "socializing" China into the prevailing international institutional framework. The second group tends to consider China as a nation that seeks to focus on its own development and can be engaged to work with the United States and other nations to advance shared interests and the common good, although they do not rule out that China may turn into a formidable adversary. As the following analysis indicates, one can, as a rule, discern whether the basic outlook of the various scholars, think tanks, and public leaders who comment on China's rise falls into the Adversarian or Engager camp.

The following discussion is organized into three segments, with regard to different sectors of power: military/geopolitical, economic, and ideational; within each segment, we will look at the debate between the two camps. This tripartite categorization is based on a study of power, initially undertaken with reference to domestic politics,[10] which was then applied to China in a seminal essay[11] and later used as the basis of a major book on China.[12]

Though all forms of power have been invoked in the popular debate over whether or not China is becoming an adversary, military power is widely regarded as the most threatening and influential in deliberations over China's rise, and is thus accorded the most detailed analysis. However, even in dealing with this kind of power, I provide merely what I consider several very telling assessments, rather than attempt a full review. It would take a volume larger than this one to carry out such a review, and it already has been done, although hardly from the viewpoint advanced here.[13]

Military and Geopolitical Assessments

Defense Budget. Adversarians point to China's surge in military spending from 2005 to 2014, during which time the budget grew by an inflation-adjusted average of 9.5 percent per year.[14] Elbridge Colby warned in 2015: "Whatever the inherent justifiability of China's intentions, the brass tacks reality appears to be that Beijing will continue to move towards fielding a military increasingly capable of contesting America's primacy in the Asia-Pacific."[15] Yet while military spending in China has steadily increased, it still remains far behind that of the United States.

The $216 billion appropriated to the PLA in 2014 is just over a third of the $610 billion that the United States spent on military expenditures in the same year.[16] As a percentage of GDP, China spends slightly less (approx. 2.1 percent) on its military than the global average of 2.3 percent. Ted Galen Carpenter of the Cato Institute writes, "China already is a major global economic and diplomatic player, and it is now a serious regional military power as well. But the PRC is still decades away from competing with America's military clout on a global basis, if such a challenge ever emerges. Beijing's latest defense budget does not change that reality in any meaningful way."[17]

Engagers also note that the Chinese rise in military expenditures coincided with a period of rapid overall economic growth in China. As China's economic growth has slowed, so too has its defense spending. The recently released 2016 budget revealed the smallest increase in defense spending since 2010; military expenditures will grow by only 7–8 percent in 2016, far less than the double-digit increase that some Chinese analysts had predicted.[18]

Naval Capabilities. Much of the attention to China's growing naval capabilities centers on the launching of its first aircraft carrier in 2012.[19] This number should be compared with the United States' eleven Nimitz America-class carriers and eight other Wasp-class carriers that, Robert Farley argues, "We would refer to as aircraft carriers if they served in any other navy."[20]

Still, for Adversarians, the Chinese aircraft carrier is a significant step in China's military development, and an unmistakable sign of China's attempt to project power far beyond its neighborhood. Bryan McGrath and Seth Cropsey of the Hudson Institute argue that, "put another way, the strategic target of the PLAN in building a carrier force is not the U.S. Navy, but the network of alliances that longstanding U.S. economic and security interests in the region aim to preserve. Creating uncertainty and doubt in the minds of regional governments that the United States can continue to assure their security is at the heart of China's desire to see the U.S. diminished in the region."[21]

An Engager notes that, aside from the United States' considerable numerical advantage in carriers, the Chinese Liaoning aircraft carrier was built from the hull of a Soviet-era carrier purchased from Ukraine in 1998. The Liaoning is significantly smaller than the United States' Nimitz-class aircraft carrier. Andrew Erickson, Abraham Denmark, and Gabriel Collins of the Naval War College stop just sort of derision, observing that Liaoning "is of very limited military utility; it will serve primarily to confer prestige on a rising great power."[22] China is working on building a second aircraft carrier, but it too will be much smaller than Nimitz-class carriers.

The broader modernization of China's navy encompasses a variety of new weapons and platforms, including antiship ballistic missiles, antiship cruise missiles, and submarines.[23] Among these missiles, the most noteworthy is the anti-access DF-21D missile, sometimes called the "carrier killer." These kinds of missiles are troubling to the Adversarians because aircraft carriers are a significant tool for projecting American power and protecting allies. In 1996, as China carried out threatening military exercises just off the coast of Taiwan—meant to influence the latter's presidential elections to the detriment of proindependence candidates—the United States dispatched two aircraft carriers to the region; the mere presence of these carriers sufficed to bolster the credibility of the United States' promise to defend Taiwan in the case of an attack, and forced the PLA to reconsider its aggressive posture toward Taiwan.[24] Given the importance of aircraft carriers to American power projection, antiship missiles have the potential to substantially limit US naval power in the areas close to China. However, Harry Kazianis writes that Chinese antiship missiles have only been tested over land, and never against a target moving at combat speed.[25]

China's naval modernization includes significant growth of its submarine fleet, with the introduction of both nuclear-powered and diesel electric submarines. In fact, US vice admiral Joseph Mulloy, testifying before the House subcommittee that oversees the navy and marine corps, warned that China now has more commissioned submarines than the United States does.[26] Moreover, a RAND assessment found that "Chinese submarines would present a credible threat to U.S. surface ships in a conflict over Taiwan or the South China Sea."[27] Engagers respond that while China may have surpassed the United States in quantity of submarines, it has not done so in quality; Mulloy noted in the same hearing that China most likely does not equip its submarines with nuclear missiles. Additionally, of the sixty-two PLA Navy submarines accounted for in the Pentagon's 2015 report, only nine were nuclear powered. Diesel submarines have a short range and are usually limited to operations close to shore.[28] Additionally, most of China's submarines are rather noisy,[29] and have hence been called "sitting ducks."[30] Significantly, China's naval buildup and operations appear defensive in nature.[31] Indeed, "China's navy rarely leaves its home waters and when it does patrol farther afield, it still does not cross the Pacific."[32]

Air Capabilities. Adversarians point out that China has by far the largest air force in East Asia, and one of the largest in the world, trailing only the United States and Russia. The PLA Air Force now boasts over 2,800 aircraft, of which 2,100 are combat aircraft. General Mark Welsh, the US Air Force chief of staff, warned in congressional testimony in 2016 that China could close the aircraft gap with the United States by 2030.[33]

Engagers once again note that while the quantity is impressive, the quality is less so. Although China has taken steps to modernize its aerial fleet, the majority of its aircraft are still older second- and third-generation fighters, and only 600 of its aircraft are what the Pentagon classifies as "modern aircraft." The RAND assessment concluded that the United States is able to meet the increased requirements, and the assessment did not find any scenario where the United States would "lose" a war with China in the air.

Engagers find a significant underlying vulnerability that threatens China's acquisition of military technology in general, and its procurement of aircraft in particular: the PLA is still reliant on foreign suppliers, primarily Russia and Ukraine, for military hardware.[34]

Continued reliance on Russian imports also poses a delicate challenge for China's air force modernization program: Russian officials have insisted that they do not want to upset the balances of military forces in the region, and both Chinese and Russian officials claim that Russia's arms sales to China do not include latest-generation equipment.[35] China may need to become more self-sufficient and develop a homegrown defense industry if it is to continue its technological progress, but this has proven difficult in other areas. For example, when Russia refused to sell China nuclear submarines, China attempted to build its own, which turned out to be noisier and easier to detect than even 1970s Soviet subs.[36]

Army Capabilities. PLA land forces have been marginalized in China's strategic military planning. Although the army remains the largest branch within the Chinese military, the army is expected to account for the majority of the 300,000 troop reduction announced by President Xi in 2015.[37] Nevertheless, Adversarians are troubled by several important shifts currently underway that signal the Chinese leadership's changing understanding of the role of its ground forces. Although it originally prepared forces for mass mobilization in "local wars under modern conditions," the PLA has now shifted to what it calls "local wars under informationized conditions,"[38] where technology and quality of forces play a greater role. This includes the development of Special Operations Forces (SOF), which are increasingly seen as an integral part of waging what the PLA calls "political warfare,"[39] which encompasses asymmetric, psychological warfare. Engagers are less concerned about these new forces: while China has grown and developed its SOF, actual deployment of these forces is limited by the PLA's lack of significant airlift capability.[40]

Moreover, Engagers point out that the PLA human capital remains underdeveloped. There are sufficient weaknesses in educational attainment and technical proficiency among PLA soldiers, and persistent concerns about corruption and professionalism pose challenges to operational security. Following a string of high-profile corruption probes into embezzlement and the sale of military positions, David Tsui, a PLA expert at Sun Yat-sen University in Guangzhou, found that corruption had become much more rampant in the PLA's ranks within the last decade.[41] Moreover, PLA publications note that there are still shortcomings in combat training; years of efforts to make trainings more "realistic" have still not adequately addressed the problem of combat readiness.[42] Dennis Blasko, a former senior military fellow at the National Defense University, has listed "ten reasons why China will have trouble fighting a modern war," which include the inexperience of commanders and staff and the PLA's army-dominated command structure, and he concludes that, based on these shortcomings, Chinese military leaders will prefer deterrent and nonmilitary measures to achieve their objectives.[43]

Nuclear Capabilities. China now has 260 nuclear weapons in its stockpile, while the United States has 4,670.[44] Adversarians claim that China is quantitatively increasing its nuclear arsenal[45] while the United States is gradually reducing its overall stock. However, one must take into account that, in this process, the United States is modernizing both its stockpile of warheads and its nuclear delivery systems.[46]

Engagers also point out that China has a "No first use" nuclear policy, and that the United States' nuclear triad would render any potential Chinese first strike nearly impossible.[47] In short, it is difficult to envisage a scenario where China's nuclear arsenal could threaten the United States.

Space. A significant concern raised by Adversarians is China's development of antisatellite (ASAT) weapons, which could be used to disrupt American reconnaissance, navigation, and communication satellites during a conflict. In addition to concerns about the vulnerabilities these ASAT weapons would create for the United States, Adversarians also criticize the destructive nature of ASAT test launches, pointing to a 2007 test that involved the deliberate destruction of a defunct Chinese weather satellite. A study by the Center for Space Standards & Innovation (CSSI) found that the test was the worst space debris–generating event on record, creating at least 2,087 pieces of space debris, far more than the previous record of 713; CSSI's study also predicted that 79 percent of this new debris would still be in orbit for another century.[48] The debris poses significant ongoing problems for satellites of all nations. Data from SOCRATES (Satellite Orbital Conjunction Reports Assessing Threatening Encounters in Space) found that this new debris increased the likelihood of conjunction (two objects passing within 5 km of each other, in the space context) between a space object and a payload by 37 percent, making collisions much more difficult to avoid.[49]

Engagers answer that China seems to have learned its lesson from the results of the 2007 ASAT launch. The Chinese government conducted further tests of missiles thought to be ASAT weaponry in 2010 and 2013[50] and most likely another in 2014,[51] but none have involved targeting or destruction of space objects. (A discussion of China's cyber-capabilities follows below in chapter 3.)

Military Capabilities—Summary. One may well point out that there is room for different, much more alarming, views of various Chinese military developments. One may also note that there are developments I did not cover. To be sure, it seems to me quite evident that China's program of military modernization has borne impressive fruits, and the country is now unrivaled in terms of both defensive and offensive capabilities among its East Asian neighbors. However, when measured against the United States' military capabilities, China lags far behind in a number of critical areas, related both to technology and human capital. China started from such a low baseline that increases that seem large when expressed in terms of percentages are actually much smaller in absolute terms. One should also note that China has very few allies that can augment its military force, whereas American allies in the Pacific include Japan, Australia, and South Korea. All this can change in the future, and one must take that into account, especially when developing arms that have a long lead time. However, for the foreseeable future, China's military seems to pose no credible threat to the United States in the region, let alone on a global scale. This conclusion is further supported by the observations of how and when China uses its clout—the subject of the next chapter.

Economic Assessments

A number of concerns have been raised by American and other Western observers about China's rising economic capabilities. These were raised particularly strongly during the first decade of the 2000s, a period in which China achieved very high economic growth rates, as high as 14.2 percent in 2007. These concerns can be grouped into five major categories:

(i) China's economy will grow much faster than that of the United States, with China's GDP projected to eclipse the United States' as early as 2021. Because of the assumed correlation between economic strength and military might, as well as associated prestige issues, the phenomenal growth of China's economy has engendered considerable concern. Many observers have pointed out, however, that the most relevant figure is not GDP but rather GDP per capita; China has to feed, clothe, house, educate, and provide medical services to four times as many people as the United States. Its GDP per capita in 2014 of $12,599 put it between the Dominican Republic and South Africa in the global rankings. A study by the Federal Reserve Bank of Minneapolis estimated that, by 2061, China's GDP per capita would still be only half that of the United States.

Furthermore, China's growth rates declined from their previous heights to only 6.9 percent in 2015. Moreover, analysts have become wary of these official growth figures; some estimate that China's GDP growth is closer to 4 or 5 percent. Unsurprisingly, talk of China overtaking the United States economically has largely subsided.

(ii) Another concern about China's economic capabilities is its currency manipulation, whereby the Chinese government prevents the yuan from appreciating, thus making it difficult for other nations to enter China's markets. China previously pegged the yuan to the dollar in order to keep its exports cheap and imports expensive. This led to the charge that China is a currency manipulator and should be subject to sanctions that would force it to let the yuan rise and fall in response to market forces. Former US representative Bill Owens claims: "These actions [currency manipulations] continue a decades-long attack on U.S. manufacturing, with China facing little or no negative consequences." The US Senate passed a bill in May of 2015 that would require the Department of Commerce to investigate suspected currency manipulators and to impose offsetting import tariffs.

In recent years China has, in fact, significantly reduced its manipulation of the yuan and allowed it to float close to levels that an open market would dictate. The economist Michael Klein points out that, in the decade from 2005 to 2015, the value of the yuan increased by 35 percent against the dollar, and the real relative price of Chinese exports rose by 50 percent during the same period.[52] Indeed, in May 2015, for the first time in more than a decade, the International Monetary Fund (IMF) declared the yuan to be fairly valued.

(iii) The erection of trade barriers—including unfavorable regulations, import restrictions, and unjustifiable customs requirements—is another reason why China's economic policies have come under scrutiny. The United States released a National Trade Estimate report in 2013 that documented "Chinese policies that favor domestic fertilizer products and set high thresholds for US bank and insurance companies to enter its markets," as well as problems with intellectual property rights, tariffs, import subsidies, "buy-national" policies, and corruption.[53] Such import restrictions on individual sectors must, however, be put in the context of growing US exports to China. The US-China Business Council reports that, from 2005 to 2014, US exports to China grew by an average rate of 13 percent per annum,[54] a rate significantly faster than for exports to any of the United States' other major trading partners. And while American exports may be disadvantaged in certain sectors, there are others where the United States enjoys a positive trade balance. For instance, according to USDA figures, the United States now exports five times as much food to China as it imports, and in 2012 China overtook Mexico as the largest importer of American food products. Even so, legitimate concerns persist about China's use of trade barriers, some of which could be addressed by engaging China in, rather than excluding it from, the Trans-Pacific Partnership (TPP) negotiations.

(iv) Economists argue that China's economy is unbalanced, and that its people need to be encouraged to consume more (and save less), thus increasing imports and making its economy less export oriented. A report by the Demand Institute documented the long decline in consumption as a percentage of GDP: from 1952 to 2011, consumption's share fell from 76 percent to 28 percent. The US-China Business Council argued in 2010 that "because external markets cannot absorb rapidly rising amounts of Chinese goods forever and may already be nearing saturation, growth in Chinese production will have to be absorbed by increases in Chinese demand."[55]

China's government has recognized the need to rebalance and has made increased domestic consumption an integral part of its twelfth five-year plan. It should also be noted that China continues to act as a major source of savings for the United States—by financing a significant portion of the American debt. As a sociologist, I cannot help noting that it is much easier to teach people to consume more than to save more. If Chinese people were to consume more and save less—and Americans did not start saving more—the United States might well find it difficult to finance its debt, and face rising interest rates, which would dampen its own economic prospects.

(v) One of the foremost concerns among American business leaders regarding China's capabilities is Chinese companies' acquisition of Western technologies through various illegal or illicit means, including reverse engineering, industrial espionage, and piracy. The result is that American corporations are disadvantaged in their competition with Chinese businesses. In 2011 the US Office of the National Counterintelligence Executive declared in a report to Congress: "Chinese actors are the world's most active and persistent perpetrators of economic espionage."[56] Estimates of the cost to the US economy of data stolen by China range in the tens of billions of dollars.[57] Cyberespionage remains a significant concern.

Economic Capabilities—Summary. The United States has legitimate reasons to be concerned about China's growing economic capabilities: its GDP continues to grow at much higher pace than that of the United States, the EU, Japan, and India. The main trend, though, has been on the positive side. China has allowed its currency to appreciate, its economic growth has returned to a reasonable level, and its domestic consumption is rising. The same cannot be said about China's economic espionage and violations of intellectual properties. To the extent that American businesses are supportive of countermeasures (many would rather the United States not act, out of fear of losing access to Chinese markets), the United States should use diplomatic and economic tools to encourage and pressure China to mend its ways. However, these challenges are hardly a reason to prepare for war with China.

Ideational Assessments

Adversarians warned that China's model of authoritarian capitalism has a growing appeal to nations who previously saw democratic capitalism as the model to follow. China's rapid economic growth and increasing wealth—almost twice that of India, the world's largest democracy—were expected to win the respect of other nations and encourage emulation. Observers argued that the "Washington Consensus," which held that countries all over the world were converging toward a Western model of political and economic governance—a consensus that was particularly strong after the collapse of the USSR in 1990—is increasingly being replaced by a Beijing Consensus that sees China as the model to emulate.[58] China's "soft power" was reported to have growing effects in developing countries. Lamedo Sanusi, the governor of the Central Bank of Nigeria and a skeptic of China's growing influence in Africa, said in 2013 that "a romantic view of China is quite common among African imaginations."[59]

While the politics of the United States and several other democracies seem to be gridlocked, China was viewed as being able to make strategic decisions expeditiously. Thomas Friedman favorably compared China's one-party autocracy to the United States' partisan paralysis in 2009 when he wrote: "One-party autocracy certainly has its drawbacks. But when it is led by a reasonably enlightened group of people, as China is today, it can also have great advantages."[60] Friedman predicted that China would overtake the United States in clean power and energy efficiency, because the former can impose politically difficult but necessary policies, while the latter is plagued by political deal making that produces watered-down compromises.

Critics responded by pointing out that those who praised China's authoritarian system have tended to focus only on its efficiency without carefully considering other characteristics. Stein Ringen, an emeritus professor of sociology and social policy at Oxford writes: "An advantage of democratic theory is that it offers a metric of successful governance. That starts with the individual and with his and her interests and rights. The purpose and responsibility of government is to give individuals protection and to improve their life chances. The only metric of success in The China Model is economic growth and the resulting reduction in poverty."[61]

Moreover, the party's tightening grip on communications and the

Internet—the so-called Great Firewall—is expected to stifle China's capacity for innovation and prevent a generation of would-be entrepreneurs from accessing cutting-edge technology and ideas that would allow China to become more competitive internationally.[62] And David Shambaugh argues that China has now entered the "middle income trap" where countries can no longer rely on industrialization for rapid economic growth and thus must reinvent their economies.[63]

In recent years, much of China's allure (seemingly never as potent as some in the West claimed) lost much of whatever appeal it had as China's economic growth declined.

Additionally, China faces growing environmental challenges, tensions from having a significant share of its population still living in poverty, ethnic conflict, and labor unrest. A much more engaged citizenry is also paying increased attention to rampant corruption in the government and party hierarchy.

Moreover, China's adoption of free-market policies has created the same inequality as in the United States; in fact, China's Gini coefficient in 2010 (the most recent year for which data are available at the time of writing) was slightly higher than that of the United States.[64]

The fear that many people in the third world will be keen to emulate China is being voiced with increasing rarity. The Cato Institute's Leon Hadar responds to concerns about the China model spreading in an article entitled "Don't Fear China." He writes that "very much like the Japanese, German, French, Scandinavian, Indian, or, for that matter, the Anglo-Saxon or American 'models' the Chinese 'model' cannot be 'exported' to, say, Somalia, Brazil, or Iran (which are developing their own 'models') or even to its neighbors in East Asia."[65] The best countermeasure the United States can take to whatever ideational appeal China has is to put its own political and economic house in order.[66]

Intentions

The threat that a foreign power poses to the United States must be assessed in terms not only of its capabilities but also of its intentions. In such assessments, one must take into account that the intentions of a nation can change much more quickly than its capabilities. Hence, intentions should be granted much less weight than capabilities in one's deliberations about how to relate to a given nation.

Before the reforms initiated by Deng Xiaoping beginning in 1979, under which China transitioned from "Marxist-Leninist-Mao Zedong" communism to "capitalism with Chinese characteristics," China was committed to exporting its communism to other countries, including through the use of force, if necessary. Together with the USSR, China's leaders aspired to a world remade by communism. These aspirations have largely faded since China moved, especially in the 1980s and onward, to focus on building up its economy.

Some Adversarians still see China as an expansionist power. Robert D. Kaplan warns: "China today is consolidating its land borders and beginning to turn outward. China's foreign policy ambitions are as aggressive as those of the United States a century ago."[67]

Engagers respond that, since the 1980s, China has focused on domestic economic development and rarely engaged in the use of force, and even when it does, it's at a very low level (for more details and discussion, see chapter 3). China continues to seek influence, especially in bordering countries, but largely through economic and diplomatic means. Kenneth Lieberthal of the Brookings Institution finds, "Both leaderships [of the United States and China] want the bilateral relationship to go smoothly. Neither is seeking to cause a major problem for the other as a key objective of national policy."[68]

Regional or Global?

Robert Kagan asks rhetorically if China seeks to become a global power: "Might not China, like all rising powers of the past, including the United States, want to reshape the international system to suit its own purposes, commensurate with its new power, and to make the world safe for its autocracy? Yes, the Chinese want the prosperity that comes from integration into the global economy, but might they believe, as the Japanese did a century ago, that the purpose of getting rich is not to join the international system but to change it?"[69]

Although there is little doubt that China's importance to both the global economy and international political order has increased in recent decades, there is disagreement over whether China aspires to become a global superpower, or merely a regional power. Many who believe that China has global ambitions point to its deepening ties and increasing investment in poorer, developing countries, specifically its One Belt, One Road initiative, which seeks to create a "New Silk Road." A *New York Times* report on China's "global ambitions" notes that "Chinese companies are at the center of a worldwide construction boom, mostly financed by Chinese banks. They are building power plants in Serbia, glass and cement factories in Ethiopia, low-income housing in Venezuela and natural gas pipelines in Uzbekistan." The article quotes Ecuador's former energy minister, who said, "The problem is we are trying to replace American imperialism with Chinese imperialism."[70] Kaplan suggests that China is just as ambitious as the United States was a century ago, writing, "China's emerging area of influence in Eurasia and Africa is growing, not in a nineteenth-century imperialistic sense but in a more subtle manner better suited to the era of globalization. Simply by securing its economic needs, China is shifting the balance of power in the Eastern Hemisphere, and that must mightily concern the United States."[71]

Some worry that China's growing ambitions will expand beyond trade and investment, pointing to its agreement with Djibouti in 2015 to build its first ever "overseas" military base in the Horn of Africa.[72] Elizabeth C. Economy adds that "as their economic might expands, they want not only to assume a greater stake in international organizations but also to remake the rules of the game."[73]

Others think that China's ambitions are much more limited. Even Andrew Nathan, who is critical of China's support for authoritarian regimes, concludes that "China's foreign policy remains essentially defensive." Noting the various challenges China confronts, he writes, "China's internal divisions and its geopolitical situation in the middle of Asia are, for the foreseeable future, likely to prevent it from establishing hegemony in its own region, which would be a necessary precondition for it to try to impose on the rest of the world an alternative vision of world order."[74]

Doug Bandow of the Cato Institute holds that "if Beijing poses a threat, it is to U.S. domination of East Asia, not the [United States] itself."[75] A special report on China from the London School of Economics argues that despite its growing military might, China lacks any grand strategic plan. Jonathan Fenby writes that "China knows its military limitations and increasingly recognises the economic benefits to be gained from softer diplomacy. . . . Beijing may not relish the prospect but its policymakers know that the US will remain the principal military power in East Asia and that any serious attempt to challenge it will only drive other countries further into its arms."[76] Looking specifically at the South China Sea, often cited as the primary theater for China's increasingly assertive ambitions, Katherine Morton argues that "maritime nationalism" rather than "maritime hegemony" is a better explanation for China's motivations.[77]

China is reported to have concluded from the experience of the USSR and from its own history that economic development, rather than military buildup, is the preferred route to follow. David Lampton points out that China took to heart what happened when the USSR engaged in an arms race with the United States, which it was unable to maintain owing to its comparatively smaller and weaker economy. Moreover, Henry Kissinger points out that the combination of militarily strong neighbors (India, Russia, Japan, etc.) and the need to ensure domestic harmony is leading to a more restrained foreign policy among China's leaders.[78]

Michael Swaine writes that China's leaders recognize that China is unlikely to be able to surpass the United States, and that an effort to establish predominance in East Asia would likely drive other countries in the region into the United States' corner. "Chinese leaders understand this and so are highly unlikely to seek predominance if they feel that they can achieve a decent amount of security in less confrontational ways."[79]

China's rise has indeed brought with it rising ambitions, but those ambitions seem to be limited to attaining regional power status. China has shown a willingness to settle disputes peacefully in many, albeit far from all, situations.

In 2003 China signed the Treaty of Amity and Cooperation with the ASEAN countries; the treaty's main tenet is to "settle such disputes amongst themselves through friendly negotiations," and not through "the threat or use of force."[80] That year, it also signed the Declaration of Conduct of Parties in the South China Sea, which resolved that future conflicts among the parties to the declaration would be worked out through dialogue and cooperation.

China used to describe its ambitions as "peaceful rise" but decided that the use of the word "rise" might seem too threatening and chose instead to employ the term "peaceful development." It calls for a "new kind of power relations," a long cry from Nikita Khrushchev's "we shall bury you." As long as such slogans and declarations about intentions do not conflict with the buildup and composition of capabilities, they can help to determine a nation's direction. China seems, for now, keen to develop its economy and establish itself as a regional power without resorting to war or using force.

I tend to agree with those who see China's ambitions as ensuring a secure flow of energy and raw material, securing its borders, and having its status as a rising power recognized after centuries of humiliation and foreign occupation. In private meetings, Chinese officials often marvel at the United States' willingness to risk the lives of its young and spend billions on protecting the freedom of the sea, keeping other nations within their borders, and otherwise serving the common good. They say they are happy to benefit from these arrangements and not to have to pay for them. And they oscillate between being proud of their recent rise (to a point of being arrogant) and seeing themselves as a weak, even declining nation.

Above all, intentions should be treated as less important than capabilities, as intentions can change much more quickly than assets. That said, there is little evidence of China having global or truly aggressive intentions. Furthermore, China's capabilities are no match for those of the United States and its allies. China's ambitions—whatever they are—should not lead anybody to lose sleep, or be used to call for a major military buildup.

Military and Geopolitical Responses

The analysis of China's military threat has shown that two cases can be made. First, that China is embarking on a course that would make it at least a powerful regional military force, and potentially a global one. Second, that China is not seeking to challenge the United States, is focused on domestic economic development, and is merely seeking to play a growing regional role. Complicating matters, whatever course China is set on now can change over time. Under most circumstances as ambiguous as this one, it would be best to prepare for the worst, lest a misjudgment result in serious consequences on the scale of Pearl Harbor, or Britain's poor preparedness on the eve of World War II.

However, it is also worthy of consideration that there are in fact grave costs for what might be called a war-hedging strategy.[81] This entails a major arms buildup, forward deployment of military assets, building up military alliances, and conducting military exercises—all steps the United States is taking. This strategy tends to invite responses in kind from the other side, thereby leading to an arms race.[82] It also commands funds that are direly needed to rebuild a deteriorating infrastructure, improve the education system, create jobs, and provide basic social services. Moreover, if the United States seeks to counter all potential threats worldwide through military superiority, it will become overstretched—

as some argue it already is. These are all side effects of a strategy that entails a massive buildup of arms that at best are never used, and at worst will lead to another major war.

Such a war-hedging strategy needs to be compared with a peace-hedging strategy, one that is slow to build up arms, bases, and other means of war and instead tests the limits of what might be gained by seeking to work out differences with China through peaceful means (see chapter 5). This approach is promising because there are many areas in which the core interests of the United States and China overlap and very few in which they are in conflict. Granted, such a strategy entails some risks if it turns out that China is the next Nazi Germany or Imperial Japan that is secretly engaged in a major arms buildup and will suddenly strike; or if China otherwise succeeds in rapidly developing its military capabilities—now far behind those of the United States—so that it could risk challenging the United States. However, it seems that in the Golden Age of Surveillance, such a buildup is very likely to be detected in a timely manner. Above all, the risks of a peace-hedging strategy seem small compared to those of a war-hedging one.

Moreover, if one examines the question at hand in a global context, one recalls that the United States and its allies are challenged by violent jihadists in scores of countries, as well in their respective homelands, and that the United States and its allies have not yet found the military or other means to cope with this current challenge. In contrast, one notes that even Adversarians see a possible confrontation with China as at least twenty years down the road. Indeed, Robert Kaplan in his alarmist 2005 essay "How We Would Fight China" concludes, "China has committed itself to significant military spending, but its navy and air force will not be able to match ours for some decades."[83] Robert Ross finds, "The transformation of the PLA into a region-wide strategic power will require many decades. . . . The transformation of the PLA into a global strategic power is an even more distant prospect."[84] And Kenneth Lieberthal contends, "There is no serious military man in China or in the United States who thinks that China has any prayer of dominating the U.S. militarily in the coming three or four decades."[85] Hence, the United States can safely continue to seek to turn China into a partner before concluding that a course of confrontation is unavoidable, which would also allow the United States to dedicate resources and attention to domestic problems, to violent branches of Islam, and to North Korea, Russia, and Iran—all much more pressing challenges.[86]

At the same time, there are changes in the American military that have a long lead time, and that recommend themselves anyhow, regardless of which course China follows. In opting to develop these technologies, one may refer to a "generic hedge" as distinguished from a "China hedge," which holds that the United States should develop capabilities specifically geared to a potential war with China. The main change of a generic hedge is the move away from "big platforms" (aircraft carriers, bomber wings, and armored divisions) that are costly and vulnerable to new technologies and toward investing in high-tech, low-cost weapons (such as drones and the tools of cyberwarfare), the building of highly mobile rapid deployment forces and tactics, and increasing the relative role of Special Forces.[87] The same holds for developing cyberarms and -defenses.

In short, the preceding analysis sees great benefit in a peace-hedging strategy that seeks to work out differences with China and treat it as a potential partner, while also scaling down the buildup and deployment of various military assets that reflect a strategy focused on containing China. At the same time (and as a sort of counterbalance to a peace-hedging strategy), investing in military elements that have a long lead time or can be applied to other regions is a course of action that seems to recommend itself.

Economic Responses

China's economic rise is considerable and has many consequences that require American responses, but none of these require adversarial approaches. Several keen analysts have pointed out that the best response for the West, particularly the United States, is to put its own house in order.[88] Nation building at home would gradually decrease the leverage China has over the United States as a major financier of its debt; it would also ensure funds are freed for economic innovations, educational reforms, and infrastructure maintenance, as well as other measures to ensure that the American economy will remain competitive in the world's markets.

There is ample evidence that China is acting as an unfair competitor. A simple response would be for the West to demand that China either allow other nations to compete in its markets on a near-equal basis ("near," taking into consideration that all nations favor their home industries to some extent) or face similar countermeasures by nations that import its products. However, for various reasons, both Western corporations and governments often choose to allow China to continue with its discriminatory policies. The reasons include the United States' dependence on Chinese financing; and American and other non-Chinese corporations' willingness to let China appropriate their trade secrets, violate their patents, require the hiring of local laborers, and siphon off much of their profits in order to not be excluded from the Chinese market, which the corporations see as likely to contribute greatly to their profit.[89] In other words, the West is acting as a major enabler of China's multifaceted discriminatory economic policies. But these findings hardly make China into an enemy.

The West will be ready to take effective economic countermeasures when it becomes clearer that the price the West pays for largely tolerating unfair Chinese practices is higher than often noted. Early signs of change on this front can be seen in the move away from idolizing free trade by both American political parties in the 2016 election campaign.

Ideational Responses

The best response to China's limited ideational appeal is to respond in kind. For instance, responding to China's opening of eighty-five Confucius Institutes around the world by increasing the budgets of America Houses in the same countries. China is providing scholarships for students and inviting leaders from around the world for training courses; leaving aside that the United States already provides many scholarships to international students, the ideational cause would be well served by even more scholarships and trainings. For each leader of a third world nation that visits China, the United States can invite two others.

In effect, on this front the United States is so far ahead of China that it can largely rest on its laurels. Moreover, even if China's authoritarian economic model appeals to one nation or another, military buildup is hardly a proper or effective response.

In short, the lessons of sectoral analysis reinforce the view that one must guard against the many forces that push a nation to seek for an adversary and declare one when it is far from clear that there is a true enemy. We also see that the United States can safely proceed by working toward a cooperative relationship with China and focusing on self-improvement, while making limited war-hedging preparations.

3

HOW AGGRESSIVE IS CHINA?

considerable number of elected officials, public intellectuals, and academics have stated that China is acting "aggressively." According to Andrew J. Nathan, "perceptions of China as an aggressive, expansionist power" are widespread.[1] In turn, these observations justify American policies that seek to contain China by increasing US military forces in the region, forming new military alliances (or extending old ones), conducting military exercises in the region, and dedicating a considerable portion of the military budget to weapons that are better suited for countering an aggressive China than for confronting diffuse jihadist networks like ISIS. Although both the United States and China often follow their actions with soothing statements about a desire to cooperate, both countries' populations seem to view the other as aggressive. Both states are already investing hundreds of billions of dollars in purchasing arms that can only be used in a major war between major powers, such as F-35 fighter jets and additional nuclear submarines, though both states clearly need those resources to address pressing domestic needs. For all these reasons it is important to determine how aggressive China actually is.

Aggression: A Suggested Definition

Observers point to different evidence, including speeches by public officials, statements by generals, expansive sovereignty claims, military buildups, and forceful occupations of other states' territory, as examples of "aggression." The validity of their observations is affected not so much by what China does, but rather by what they construe aggression to be. Because there is no registry for terms used to study international relations that would ensure that all who use key terms employ them the same way, none of these observers can be faulted. Much would be gained, though, if the use of the term "aggression" were limited to acts that involve the use of force, and if other acts that are often labeled aggressive were instead called "assertive" (or some other such term). This distinction recommends itself because it makes a great deal of difference whether a state merely makes assertive statements, legally builds up assets, and seeks to build alliances; or whether it uses military force, whether to enforce an exclusive zone, invade another country, occupy contested territories, or sink another state's ships.

This definition of aggression is preferable for three major reasons. First, a very extensive study has shown that there are substantial differences between the consequences of assertive and aggressive acts.[2] When people (or the state with which they identify) are forced to act counter to their own preferences, they tend to become highly resentful and alienated, and they often respond with more aggression or engage in other harmful behavior toward others or themselves. When someone persuades people to change, however, the opposite effect occurs. Millions will sacrifice their lives for their nation if they consider its causes to be legitimate. A third realm, which gives people material incentives to change course, falls somewhere between the coercive and the persuasive; it is called "soft power."[3] Thus, social science research undergirds the merit of the distinctions between aggressive and assertive power. One may say that by labeling as "assertive" acts that others consider aggressive, we are merely defining the problem away. However, there are very clear and significant differences between acts that use force and acts that do not.

The second reason to prefer this limited definition of aggression is that it keeps tensions between states in check by curbing tendencies toward escalating rhetoric. This definition seeks to dissuade those who conflate verbal actions such as speeches and declarations—which have few or no "real" consequences—with actual uses of force such as invasions by hostile forces. Without this distinction, it would be impossible to differentiate between planting a flag in the Arctic Circle (as Russia recently did) and annexing Crimea, or between flybys and acts of war. Painting developments such as building ports as aggressive acts because these fruits of those developments might be used for military purposes is a rhetorical trick of those who stand to benefit from increased tension. However, international tensions are worsened by labeling as aggressive both bombastic statements and bombings; land reclamation and terrorist attacks; demands that other states give prior notification of passage through a state's territorial waters and blocking that passage.

The third reason is that the definition of aggression here described has strong foundations in international law.

Aggression in International Law

Until modern times, what we would now term "aggression" was considered to be a right of states; the "norm of nonaggression" can be traced to the aftermath of World War I, when a set of states renounced aggression in the Covenant of the League of Nations and the Kellogg-Briand Pact alike.[4] The Nuremberg Charter of 1945 addresses aggression in Article 6(a), which defined crimes against the peace as including the "planning, preparation, or waging of a war of aggression."[5]

The UN General Assembly adopted A/RES/29/3314 in December 1974, chapter 1 of which defines an act of aggression as "the use of armed force by a State against the sovereignty, territorial integrity or political independence of another State, or in any other manner inconsistent with the Charter of the United Nations." The Charter assigns the jurisdiction to determine whether or not an act of aggression has occurred to the UN Security Council.[6] A/RES/29/3314, Article 3, lists state actions that prima facie constitute acts of aggression, including military invasion, military occupation, bombardment, blockade, attack on another state's armed forces, and the use of private actors or mercenaries to carry out acts of armed force against another state.[7]

Until 2010, the question of how to define the "crime of aggression" remained unresolved.[8] However, according to the Congressional Research Service, a consensus now exists among the International Criminal Court member states following the Kampala Review Conference of the Rome Statute in 2010. The ICC thus defines an act of aggression (based on the applicable UN resolution) as "the use of armed force by a State against the sovereignty, territorial integrity, or political independence of another State, or in any manner inconsistent with the Charter of the United Nations."[9] That is, "at least eighty-four delegations of legal advisors and experts from States Parties to the Rome Statute" agree that this definition of aggression is clear. The uniformity with which law journal chapters on the subject define "aggression" and outline the concept's pedigree, as well as the substantial similarities between codified definitions of "aggression,"[10] suggests that the definition supplied in the UN A/RES/29/3314 is the generally accepted, baseline definition of aggression.[11] Stahn[12] makes reference to A/RES/29/3314, as do Mancini,[13]

Koh and Buchwald,[14] and many more. The ICC adheres to the same concept of aggression, although it differentiates between "crimes of aggression" attributed to individuals (over which the court exercises jurisdiction), and "acts of aggression" that are attributed to entire states.

Of course, disagreements exist. For example, there is disagreement among international legal scholars about whether the provision of arms to rebel forces constitutes an act of aggression. Moreover, any force that falls within the scope of self-defense or is carried out with the consent of the state in whose territory military force is used does not constitute an act of aggression. And there is some disagreement about how specific the UN definition of aggression really is.

The Evidence

There is little question that until 1980 China was an aggressive state. Its troops played a significant role in the Korean War, which took place from 1950 to 1953; it played a key role in the Vietnam War by supplying Vietnam with supplies and support troops; in the 1960s it engaged in a brief war with India over territory; and from the 1950s to the 1970s it supported several revolutionary movements and coup d'états. To quote Thomas Robinson and David Shambaugh: "China supported the Thai and Malayan Communist parties because they opposed governments closely aligned with the West; it supported the PLO because it opposed Israel; it endorsed national liberation movements in Southern Africa directed against colonies of Western countries that did not recognize Beijing; and it aided insurgencies in Afghanistan and Cambodia because they were aimed against governments supported by the Soviets and the Vietnamese."[15] In 1979 China even invaded Vietnam (the Sino-Vietnamese War) to punish Vietnam for invading Cambodia and occupying parts of the Spratly Islands. This invasion was also meant to antagonize the USSR, with which China had recently had a diplomatic falling-out. However, from 1990 to 2005 China settled twenty out of twenty-three territorial disputes without the use of force and seventeen of them through substantial compromise, according to M. Taylor Fravel of MIT.[16]

Because China's approach to international relations has shifted before, some observers worry that it is shifting again and that China is once again becoming more assertive in its dealings with its neighbors and with respect to the international order. Specifically, they point to the global financial crisis and the drawdown of United States forces in Iraq and Afghanistan as signaling to China's leaders that the international balance of power was shifting in Beijing's favor and "allowing it to challenge aspects of its international environment that it previously had been forced to tolerate."[17] While China has indeed become more assertive in its backyard—particularly in the East and South China Seas—none of these assertions constitute acts of aggression, as we shall see. Moreover, although China may initially have viewed the United States' withdrawal from Iraq and Afghanistan as a sign of declining military power, the "pivot" to Asia presents a significant obstacle to any expansionist ambitions China may have.

This chapter examines more recent events. It first lists the incidents that various observers have categorized as Chinese "aggression" and then turns to evaluating these claims.

Defense Secretary Robert Gates stated in May 2014 that China had become "significantly more aggressive" in the preceding two years; as evidence he pointed to China's new air defense identification zone (ADIZ) in the East China Sea, its use of planes and ships to support its claims to the Senkaku/Diaoyu Islands, and its installation of an oil rig in Vietnamese maritime territory.[18] Keith Johnson, in *Foreign Policy* in April 2015, referenced "China's maritime aggression," or more specifically, "an aggressive interpretation of its rights in the South China Sea" through land reclamation and the building of military installations on the resulting islands.[19] On March 18, 2015, Admiral Samuel J. Locklear, the commander of US Pacific Command, referred to "aggressive Chinese air intercepts of Japanese reconnaissance flights, inflammatory strategic messaging, and the no-notice declaration of a Chinese Air Defense Identification Zone in the East China Sea" as well as to China's land reclamation program and its shipbuilding program.[20] Similarly, Bonnie S. Glaser described some of China's interceptions of US reconnaissance flights as "aggressive."[21] On June 1, 2015, President Obama condemned "aggressive actions" in the South China Sea in reference to land reclamation projects.[22] In February 2015, Director of National Intelligence James Clapper called China's expansion in the South China Sea, which would give China new capabilities to use anti-air and other weapons, "aggressive."[23] Moreover, China has of late been labeled aggressive on a new front: "cyber-aggression."[24] James Lewis of the Center for Strategic and International Studies considers "state-sponsored cyber-aggression" to be a "well-established part of China's strategy for global influence."[25]

The legal issues involved are complex, and the details of what actually occurred are often murky or classified. One could readily dedicate a whole chapter to each of the incidents. However, it is possible to determine fairly conclusively whether aggressions occurred in most of the oft-cited cases.

Reconnaissance Interceptions

The United States routinely conducts aerial surveillance and naval patrols along China's coastline.[26] On a few occasions, China is reported to have sent its fighter jets within thirty feet of American reconnaissance planes; Pentagon press secretary John Kirby called one such maneuver "aggressive."[27] These maneuvers echo the Hainan Island incident of 2001, in which a Chinese military plane flew too close to and collided with an American EP-3 reconnaissance plane.[28] China also seems to regularly fly dangerously close to Japanese reconnaissance planes in the East China Sea.[29] Likewise, in December 2013 a Chinese aircraft navigated dangerously close to a US plane.[30] These and several other similar incidents do not quite qualify as aggression by the UN definition, but they do come close. They are best viewed as acts of "mini-aggression."

ADIZ

On November 23, 2013, China declared an air defense identification zone (ADIZ) in the East China Sea, an area that encompasses the Senkaku/Diaoyu Islands[31] and overlaps with Japan's ADIZ.[32] China claimed that it had a right to be informed when other states' aircraft (and commercial aircraft) entered an extension of its territorial airspace; China implied that it would use force ("defensive emergency measures") against states that did not comply with the notification requirements.[33] However, when the United States sent two B-52 bomber fighter craft through the ADIZ without first announcing their flight pattern, China did not react with force to enforce its ADIZ. And when the United States sent the USS *Lassen* within the twelve-nautical-mile area surrounding Subi Reef in 2015, China protested but did not use force to enforce its ADIZ. One may say that China's lack of follow through reflects the fact that it is not ready to confront the United States; this is likely the case, but it does not change the fact that China did not act aggressively.

One should note that similar ADIZ declarations have been made by many states in the area, including Japan and Vietnam. The matter would change greatly if China were to use force to enforce these zones by shooting down planes without prior notification or sinking ships that enter the claimed territory. Otherwise, these declarations—made only of words—are akin to lawyers' opening statements and do not constitute acts of aggression. This does not mean that they should be ignored, but that the best path to preventing undue escalations is for the United States and its allies to respond in kind.

Cyberaggression?

There are no established norms and few international laws that directly apply to this new practice. There are three overarching realms of cyberactivity within which actions could be potentially deemed "aggressive." The first concerns spying and counterintelligence; the second concerns the interconnected domains of intellectual property and industrial espionage; the third is the use of kinetic cyberwarfare.

Regarding the first, spying and other forms of illicit information gathering are part and parcel of normal counterintelligence activity. And while it can be assumed that Chinese hackers are engaged in spying and counterintel operations against the United States, it is not at all clear that China has an advantage. Jon Lindsay writes, "For every type of purported Chinese cyberthreat, there are also serious Chinese vulnerabilities and Western strengths that reinforce the political status quo."[34] Nevertheless, China has successfully carried out "hundreds" of successful network warfare operations against targets in the United States since 2006, according to one cybersecurity firm.[35] Most notably, in June 2015 operatives linked to China hacked a server at the US Office of Personnel Management, compromising the personal information of 22 million federal employees.[36] Yet while such unprecedented breaches raise serious concerns about the state of the US government's cybersecurity and about the sophistication of China's hackers, it would still seem a stretch to apply the term "aggression" to such activities, using the UN definition.

Regarding espionage and intellectual property theft, it is almost indisputable that the Chinese government and state-owned enterprises engage in various forms of cyberespionage. It seems useful, though, to note that the United States and China have both agreed that using cybertools for espionage cannot be completely halted, since espionage has existed since the beginning of history, and both sides engage in it. Even so, the United States protests China's use of cybertools to violate property rights and to steal trade secrets, and President Obama went so far as to describe cyberespionage as "an act of aggression that has to stop."[37]

But there are reasons to believe that the benefit to Chinese companies (and the corresponding loss to American businesses) is much less than the hype suggests. Lindsay points to the cautionary tale of the Soviet Union, which relied on imitation rather than innovation, writing: "Chinese espionage can potentially narrow the gap with the West, but only at the price of creating dependency through investment in a large-scale absorption effort."[38] It is also worth noting that China is as likely to be a victim as a culprit of cyberattacks: there has been such a considerable proliferation of "freelance" hackers in China that they are causing significant damage to the Chinese economy—as much as $873 million in 2011 alone.[39] The characterization of China's cyberespionage as "aggressive" also seems disingenuous when one notes that, for various reasons, American corporations have resisted improving the security of their computers and servers, as paradoxical as this may seem.[40]

Other troublesome aspects of China's military include its development of advanced cyberwarfare capabilities, which could be used to sabotage infrastructure dependent on information systems (including power grids) and steal sensitive military information.[41] The use of cybertools to cause damage to power grids, financial systems, or any other physical infrastructure—as Russia did to Ukraine in 2015—would qualify as aggression, as the outcome would be equivalent to that of a major use of force. However, so far there is no evidence that China has engaged in this sort of "kinetic" cyberattack against the United States or its allies. In short, it seems erroneous to label China's cyberacts "aggression," at least according to the definition here followed, which is aligned with that of the United Nations and international law.

The Senkaku/Diaoyu Islands

On September 7, 2010, a Chinese fishing vessel collided with two Japanese coast guard ships operating off the coast of the Senkaku/Diaoyu Islands after Japan instructed the vessel to leave the area.[42] In July 2012 China conducted a series of military drills in the East China Sea, including one that involved PLAN troops simulating "an amphibious assault on the Diaoyus";[43] and a few years later, China repeated these maneuvers.[44]

In October 2012 China sent four surveillance ships within a twelve-nautical-mile radius of the Senkaku/Diaoyu Islands.[45] In the year following Japan's nationalization of the Senkaku/Diaoyu Islands, China sent its official government vessels into the disputed territory 216 times.[46]

In April 2013 China identified the Senkaku/Diaoyu Islands as one of its "core interests" and sent more than forty aircraft and eight maritime surveillance vessels to the area of the disputed islands in a single day.[47] Of these actions, only the fishing vessel's ramming of two Japanese ships constitutes an act of "mini-aggression."

Critics argue that although China has not used force, its use of what the West has called "salami tactics" cannot be ignored because it has a cumulative effect similar to an outright occupation. However, a close examination of the details shows that so far China has achieved surprisingly little through these means. The Senkaku/Diaoyu Islands remain fully under Japanese control. China should be expected to learn from such ill-advised maneuvers, which have raised considerable opposition and mobilized other nations while gaining little for China.

One must also consider the dynamics of Chinese nationalism and the tightrope that the Chinese government must walk as it balances nationalist sentiment at home with its foreign policy, especially as it pertains to any conflict or potential conflict with Japan. Resentment toward Japan's historical aggression is such a potent force in stoking Chinese nationalism that the Chinese government cannot easily suppress anti-Japanese protests—as it has done on occasion when dealing with anti-American or anti-Philippine sentiments—nor can it risk ignoring them. But paradoxically, the depth of anti-Japanese sentiment among Chinese nationalists has what Allen Carlson describes as "an ossifying effect on Beijing's approach to the East China Sea." In effect, China seems to have calculated that the domestic reaction to any actual "battlefield death" in a confrontation with Japan would provoke such a toxic reaction domestically that it could be impossible to manage. Thus, according to Carlson, "Such a collective identity makes the prospects for peace over the Diaoyu/Senkaku Islands exceedingly remote, but it also has a calcifying effect on the conflict itself. It leaves it frozen in place, unlikely to be resolved, but equally unlikely to devolve into an armed confrontation."[48]

While arguing that China's foreign policy toward Japan has ossified seems to me an overstatement, there is no question that nationalism sets limits on the policy options of the Chinese leadership. Indeed, China is playing with fire every time it stokes public sentiments toward foreign powers. A mobilized Chinese public could easily turn against its government were it not to prevail in conflict, or were it to settle conflict in a peaceful manner, which tends to involve compromise. True, so far China has largely succeeded in—to mix metaphors—negotiating this tightrope. However, world peace (as well as China's domestic needs) would be better served if China followed a course less fraught with risks.

South China Sea Islands

In 2009 China published its "nine-dash line," which makes a legal claim to sovereignty over islands and territorial waters amounting to roughly 80 percent of the South China Sea. This claim was submitted to the Commission on the Limits of the Continental Shelf in response to two submissions made by Vietnam (one jointly with Malaysia) claiming areas of the continental shelf in the South China Sea beyond two hundred nautical miles, as per the UN Convention on the Law of the Sea (UNCLOS). After these competing submissions, China took various steps to challenge or change the legal status of several islands in the South China Sea. These developments led to considerable criticism and pushback from several countries in the region, supported by the United States and its allies. Consequently, these islands and their surrounding waters have become a major focus of the evolving US-China relationship. Our discussion next turns to an overview of the particular issues involved, focusing on the Spratly Islands and Scarborough Shoal.

Chinese fishermen have frequented the Spratly Islands and surrounding waters for centuries. However, the Chinese government did not publish maps including the islands in the country's territorial waters until 1948, after the islands had been returned to China by Japan following World War II.[49]

In fact, there are at least three separate geographical areas (with their accompanying disputes) that are often conflated when discussing China's actions in the region.

1. The Spratly Islands, an archipelago of largely uninhabited islands claimed (to varying degrees) by China, Taiwan, Vietnam, Malaysia, and the Philippines. This island chain has seen the most contested activity, both historically and in recent years. The islands are spread out over a large area of more than 160,000 square miles, far from the Asian mainland.
2. The Paracel Islands are a separate group of islands in the South China Sea that are approximately equidistant from the coastlines of Vietnam and China. These two countries and Taiwan are the claimants to the Paracels. China, however, has maintained control of the entire archipelago since 1974.

3. Scarborough Shoal, a small, isolated group of rocks and reefs that are located 500 miles from mainland China, but only 150 miles from the Philippines. Both countries claim the area, but China has effectively controlled it since a standoff between the two countries in 2012.

Most attention has been focused on the Spratlys and Scarborough Shoal, since these were the subject of a case brought against China by the Philippines before the Permanent Court of Arbitration in 2013.

SCARBOROUGH SHOAL

The confrontation between China and the Philippines over Scarborough Shoal began in April 2012. The details about what happened are complex, and the events unfolded over several months. On April 8, 2012, Philippine Navy aerial surveillance identified a group of eight Chinese fishing vessels poaching corals and other wildlife at Scarborough Shoal. The Philippines sent a warship, the 378-foot BRP *Gregorio del Pilar,* to investigate on April 10. In response, China sent two unarmed China Maritime Surveillance (CMS) ships to sail between the Philippines warship and the Chinese fishing vessels, to prevent the arrest of the Chinese fishermen.[50] Over the course of the ensuing standoff, the Philippines replaced its ship with two coast guard vessels, while China increased its number of ships at the shoal.[51] By May 2012, there were five Chinese government ships, sixteen Chinese fishing vessels, and seventy Chinese "utility boats" at the shoal. China then violated a June agreement that both sides would vacate the shoal, and instead became the sole presence at the disputed area,[52] where it has since maintained a permanent presence.[53] By August 2012 China had fully restricted access to Scarborough Shoal by stringing a rope across its entrance to prevent boats from entering.[54] In January 2015 the Philippines stated that Chinese coast guard ships rammed three Philippine fishing boats that were operating in the vicinity of the shoal.[55]

THE SPRATLY ISLANDS

Observers of international relations have accorded considerable attention to China's dredging and artificial island-building activities in the Spratly Islands (and to a lesser extent, the Paracel Islands). Some have noted that other states in the region are also pursuing island-building activities, albeit less extensively.[56] According to official US estimates,

China reclaimed a total of three thousand acres of land between December 2013 and October 2015. Some of the new islands have already been built up, including a runway on Fiery Cross Reef and the possible construction of smaller airstrips on other islands, according to satellite imagery.[57]

Dredging and land reclamation around reefs is significant for two reasons: (1) expanding the surface area of these features allows for more equipment and infrastructure to be built, and (2) the size and elevation of these "islands" determine the territorial rights they confer. Maritime law recognizes three different types of marine landforms: "low-tide elevations" (which are not entitled to any territorial seas), "rocks" (entitled to 12 miles of territorial seas) and "naturally occurring islands" (entitled to an EEZ of 200 miles). Thus, China's land-building activities seem to serve in part to change the legal status of the reefs under consideration so that China can gain territorial rights over the surrounding seas.

The United States and its allies have objected to these unilateral changes to the legal status of the islands.[58] Director of National Intelligence James Clapper has also called China's expansion in the South China Sea (which would give China new capabilities to use antiaircraft weaponry) "aggressive." In response, the United States has sent both ships and aircraft to conduct freedom of navigation exercises within twelve miles of the disputed islands (for details and discussion, see chapter 9, on freedom of navigation operations).

PHILIPPINES V. CHINA

In 2003 the government of the Philippines filed a case against China, under UNCLOS. A tribunal convened by the Permanent Court of Arbitration (PCA) agreed to consider the case, which challenged China's territorial claims in the Spratly Islands. (Because the Philippines issued its claim in accordance with UNCLOS, the PCA could not rule on the ownership status of the islands themselves, but merely on the extent of territorial waters that China can claim.) The Philippines initially brought fifteen claims against China, but the PCA only agreed to arbitrate seven of them.[59] Specifically, the court was asked to determine which features are reefs, which are low-tide elevations, which are rocks, and which are naturally occurring islands. The court also agreed to arbitrate the Philippines' claims that China had failed to protect and preserve the environment around Scarborough Shoal and Second Thomas Shoal, that

China had violated the Convention on the International Regulations for the Prevention of Collisions at Sea, and that China had unlawfully prevented Philippine fishermen from carrying out traditional fishing activities within the territorial waters of Scarborough Shoal.

China unwisely refused to participate in the PCA's arbitration and sought bilateral negotiations rather than an "internationalization" of the dispute.[60] China pointed to the Declaration on the Conduct of Parties in the South China Sea (DOC), which was signed in 2002 by China and the Association of Southeast Asian Nations (ASEAN), of which the Philippines is a member. The DOC commits signatories to bilateral negotiation of disputes; on this basis, China argued that seeking international arbitration is a violation of previous commitments.[61] Per UNCLOS, if a party in a dispute does not select its preferred binding means of resolving the dispute, it is deemed to have chosen arbitration by default; thus the PCA did hear the case even though China did not participate. The result of China not being involved was that four out of the five judges on the tribunal were selected by then president of the International Tribunal for the Law of the Sea Shunji Yanai, a former Japanese diplomat.[62] Normally in such arbitration cases, each side selects one judge and the two sides must agree on the other three, but China forfeited its rights to participate in the selection process.

In July 2016 the court ruled against China on every significant point. China announced that it does not recognize the rulings. Its Foreign Ministry stated that the court's ruling "is invalid and has no binding force. China does not accept or recognize it."[63]

In June 2016 Rodrigo Duterte—who had promised better relations with China—became president of the Philippines. During a visit to China in October 2016, he announced that "America has lost now. I've realigned myself in your ideological flow." The following month, however, he expressed a desire for better relations with the United States, saying, "I don't want to quarrel anymore, because Trump has won." By some accounts, Duterte is tilting toward China; by others, he is trying to play the two sides against each other to maximum advantage for the Philippines. As of November 2016, China and the Philippines had reached an agreement to allow Philippine fishing boats to operate around the Scarborough Shoal. One must anticipate further developments in the US-Philippines relationship.

The Main Issues

The ongoing dispute over islands in the South China Sea has prompted debate among Adversarians and Engagers. The main points of contention can be summarized thusly:

1. Whether China is engaging in salami tactics—incremental acts of aggression that are too minor to merit a response but which, cumulatively, will give it total control over the South China Sea
2. What China's refusal to recognize the PCA's ruling reveals about its respect for the global order, and its belief in aggression versus the rule of law
3. Whether China is responsible for militarizing the South China Sea dispute through its construction of artificial islands and placement of military equipment on them

Salami Tactics

China has been accused of using "salami tactics." Nobel Prize–winning economist Thomas Schelling describes these tactics as "a continuous gradation of activity, one can begin his intrusion on a scale too small to provoke a reaction, and increase it by imperceptible degrees, never quite presenting a sudden dramatic challenge that would invoke the committed response."[64]

Robert Haddick writes, "For China, that would mean simply ignoring America's Pacific fleet and carrying on with its slicing, under the reasonable assumption that it will be unthinkable for the United States to threaten major-power war over a trivial incident in a distant sea."[65]

The United States, by encouraging the Philippines to bring the case, and through its FON assertions, is in effect sending a message to China that the salami tactics will not work, and that the United States will respond even to low-level incursions and to limited attempts to change the status quo. This message is valuable in urging China to stop trying to change the status quo unilaterally rather than through negotiations. However, it raises several questions: for one, is the United States willing to allow a new rising regional power an opportunity to increase its position in the region—if this power uses the preferred means? One notes that the United States sought and succeeded in blocking bilateral China-Philippine negotiations and has been encouraging ASEAN to negotiate with China only as a bloc.

Moreover, the same kinds of unilateral attempts to create facts on the ground—or on the sea—are often ignored by the United States and its allies. For example, Russia has in recent years claimed a large swath of Arctic territory (nearly 500,000 square miles) that includes the North Pole. The United States largely ignored Russia's territorial ambitions in the Arctic, even though rival claimants are NATO allies (Canada, Denmark, and Norway). Also in recent years, a longstanding border dispute between Guyana and Venezuela has flared up over rights to the territorial waters in the Esequibo region that could hold $40 billion worth of oil.[66] In May 2015 the Venezuelan president Nicolas Maduro issued a decree claiming sovereignty over the territorial waters of Guyana,[67] later deploying marine and ground forces to its eastern border with Guyana. US officials have basically ignored these moves.

True, just as the fact that other cars are speeding and have not been ticketed cannot be used as a defense by the driver who is ticketed, the fact that unilateral acts that seek to control territory—or otherwise change the status quo—are quite common does not justify any particular incursion. However, treating them as major acts of aggression seems to ignore that such incursions are quite common and often tolerated.

Finally, the danger of minor conflict sparking a major war (akin to the start of World War I) should not be dismissed. Doug Bandow of the Cato Institute argues, "None of the claims generating so much controversy is worth war. China is carefully using 'salami-slicing tactics,' successively grabbing small pieces of a larger whole to avoid a conflict. But who is prepared to fight even for the larger whole?"[68] One may argue that the United States has to draw the line somewhere; that the United States has to discourage salami tactics. The question is whether such maintenance of order and attempts at stabilization can be achieved by means other than military maneuvers. (For discussion on such "other means," see chapter 5 on mutually assured restraint.)

Rule of Law

China has been criticized by Western observers for refusing to participate in the arbitration process and for its announcement that it would not recognize the court's ruling. David Kilgour, a former Canadian secretary of state, Asia-Pacific, wrote, "No one appears to agree with Beijing that the tribunal is illegitimate. The party-state ignores the rule of law at home, but would harm itself even more severely by indicating that it considers itself above international law."[69] China watcher Gordon

Chang wrote just before the ruling was released, "Beijing, with its declarations that it will ignore the court's findings, looks set to put itself outside the international community. That community now needs to think about what it will do to defend the systems of laws, resolutions, pacts and treaties that make up the world's rules-based order. Nations, in general, should begin imposing costs on China for its renegade stance."[70]

While China is a signatory to UNCLOS, the United States is not (although it regularly states that it will operate consistently with customary maritime law[71] and in effect respect UNCLOS). Thus the United States is seeking to enforce a treaty it refuses to sign. This concerns not only some liberal critics of the United States but also military officials like the chairman of the Joints Chiefs of Staff, General Joseph F. Dunford. He warned that "by remaining outside the Convention, the United States remains in scarce company with Iran, Venezuela, North Korea, and Syria," and "by failing to join the Convention, some countries may come to doubt our commitment to act in accordance with international law."[72]

Moreover, Graham Allison, director of the Belfer Center for Science and International Affairs at Harvard, observes that "no permanent member of the UN Security Council has ever complied with a ruling by the PCA on an issue involving the Law of the Sea. In fact, none of the five permanent members of the UN Security Council have ever accepted any international court's ruling when (in their view) it infringed their sovereignty or national security interests."[73]

Indeed, as Allison points out, China's conduct in the South China Sea echoes American conduct in the 1980s when it was sued by Nicaragua for mining its harbors. The United States not only refused to recognize the PCA's jurisdiction or to participate in the proceedings but also denied the court jurisdiction on any future case involving the United States. True, one may argue that the answer is not for China to be encouraged to ignore the PCA, but for other nations to begin heeding the PCA's rulings. In any case, these considerations seem to suggest that China's disrespect for the court's ruling needs to be kept in proper perspective.

Militarization of the South China Sea

China is said to be militarizing the South China Sea by placing military equipment on the disputed islands. China has indeed stationed some military equipment on several of the islands, including surface-to-air missiles on Woody Island in the Paracel chain,[74] and radar facilities on the Spratly Islands.[75] China has also landed military aircraft on Fiery Cross Reef, a man-made island in the Spratly Islands.[76] Clapper warned in early 2016 that "based on the pace and scope of construction at these outposts, China will be able to deploy a range of offensive and defensive military capabilities and support increased PLAN [PLA Navy] and CCG [Chinese Coast Guard] presence beginning in 2016. Once these facilities are completed by the end of 2016 or early 2017, China will have significant capacity to quickly project substantial offensive military power to the region."[77]

China claims that its military buildup on the disputed islands is in response to the United States' military acts. In July 2015 China's Defense Ministry spokesman Yang Yujun said, "China is extremely concerned at the United States' pushing of the militarization of the South China Sea region. . . . Recently, they have further increased military alliances and their military presence, frequently holding joint drills."[78]

After Admiral Harry Harris, commander of the US Pacific Command, testified before Congress that China was seeking regional "hegemony" and proposed more freedom of navigation operations, the Communist Party–affiliated *Global Times* published a front-page report accusing Harris of "China-bashing" and warned that "Harris' words and deeds keep reminding us that we have to put more efforts into the building of islands in the South China Sea and deploying more weaponry."[79]

Regardless of who is responding to whom, the strategic value of the islands is very limited. Retired US rear admiral Mike McDevitt noted, "Putting garrisons on Woody Island or elsewhere in the Paracels would effectively maroon these guys, so the only advantage would be just showing the flag—to say, 'We are serious.'"[80] Tetsuo Kotani, who specializes in maritime security at the Japan Institute of International Affairs, notes that, even with antiship defenses, military installations on disputed islands would merely duplicate capabilities that China already has in Hainan: "They're basically just sending a political message. I'm not sure what other role those troops could play."[81] The islands are comparable to broken-down aircraft carriers; they are sitting ducks.

Adversaries worry that if China gains effective control over the South China Sea, it could disrupt commercial shipping in the region. This threat would be significant, as some $5 trillion worth of trade passes through the South China Sea every year.[82] General Dunford warned that "in the South China Sea, Chinese activity is destabilizing and could pose a threat to commercial trade routes."[83] Peter Lee of the *Asia Pacific Jour-*

nal notes, "Admiral Harris invoked the $5 trillion dollar figure in his recent testimony before the Senate Armed Services Committee. Western media reports reproduce it almost as a mandatory piece of journalistic boilerplate when covering the South China Sea."[84]

In contrast, the shipping industry seems much less bothered. Reuters quoted Captain Bjorn Hojgaard, chief executive officer at Anglo-Eastern Univan Group, one of the world's biggest ship management companies as saying, "From our point of view, it's just another military base. It's only politics, commercially it makes no difference."[85]

Moreover, China would be the most heavily affected if the South China Sea shipping lanes were disrupted. Greg Austin, a professorial fellow with the EastWest Institute in New York and a professor at the Australia Defence Force Academy, points out that China would have little incentive to disrupt shipping lanes, since it is highly dependent on this route for its own oil imports and raw materials, as well as for shipping its exports, which still constitute a significant portion of its GDP.[86]

In Conclusion

Whether one is alarmed by China's island building and sees it as part of its drive to bolster its territorial claims in the South China Sea—or whether one views such maneuvers as of limited import and insufficient grounds for a major escalation of tensions and possible conflict with China—there can be no doubt that these assertive acts do not qualify as acts of aggression. To be sure, in the process of China's island building there were some very minor acts of aggression, such as ramming a few fishing boats and roping off the waters around a shoal. But not a single shot was fired and no one was killed, making this area one of the most peaceful in the world.

We have seen that by most legal interpretations, China is clearly in the wrong, but that this same kind of "infraction" is rather common and usually accepted as a fact of life in international relations (in the same way that smoking a joint is accepted in much of the United States).

The reason for the US reaction seems to lie partially in the fact that these Chinese activities are the most visible expression of China's attempt to change the status quo, and to establish itself as a regional power. The United States and its allies sometimes seem to act as if they have decided that no changes to the status quo will be tolerated. True, one can argue that the United States does not oppose changes achieved through the consent of the parties involved. This point would be enhanced if the United States stopped promoting negotiations through channels unfavorable to China, such as urging the nations of the region to bind together and deal with China as a group and not bilaterally. One may hold that this is done in order to protect small nations from undue pressure from China, and to prevent China from "bullying" these nations. The issue, then, is how one can ensure fair deals while also allowing a rising regional power, one that has long been humiliated, to gain more clout in its region.

Two major avenues suggest themselves:

1. Codevelopment of the resources in the South China Sea between China and other littoral states. This is not without precedent: from 2005 to 2008, the national oil companies of China, the Philippines, and Vietnam conducted a joint seismic study in the South China Sea.[87] Indeed, as Chunjuan Nancy Wei points out, China initially developed the concept of joint development of South China Sea resources under Deng Xiaoping in the 1980s.[88]

2. A trade-off, in which it is agreed that China will be free to develop this or that island and the region around it in exchange for some concessions, perhaps regarding other land disputes.

These two avenues presume that China continues not to act aggressively, not to use its military to advance its territorial claims, and that the United States and its allies accept that China will play a greater regional role, rather than try to contain it and oppose any changes to the status quo.

China's salami tactics in the South China Sea have become a symbol of its ambitions of territorial expansion. What start as small steps escalate, not necessarily by turning local skirmishes into larger conflicts, but by amplifying the issue in the American media and public imagination. In any case, China would be better served if it found ways to reassert itself that are less escalatory, even in merely psychological terms (for more on this, see chapter 5).

Furthermore, any of the acts that various commentators label "aggressive" and that this chapter treats as "assertive" might well be considered to be "provocative." To properly examine them, one must consider the context. Were China's actions made in response to provocative acts taken by other states—for instance, the United States' almost-daily reconnaissance flights off of China's coastline, which are legal but which

China views as highly provocative? Moreover, one ought to note that, to a significant extent, an act's degree of provocation is in the eye of the beholder. When China sent its ships within twelve nautical miles of the Aleutian Islands in Alaska in 2015, the United States responded calmly by acknowledging that China had conducted "a legal transit of U.S. territorial seas in accordance with the Law of the Sea Convention."[89] By contrast, when the United States sent USS *Lassen* within a twelve-nautical-mile radius of Subi Reef, China viewed the act as provocative and protested vocally. The question of whether or not force has been used provides a clearer set of guidelines about what acts should be considered aggressive.

The observation that provocation is largely a subjective matter (unlike aggression, which others can readily observe and recognize as such) is not to deny that provocative acts contribute to tensions. How one responds to provocations and other assertive but nonaggressive acts depends to a significant extent on the more encompassing strategies employed by the United States. If the United States seeks to avoid the Thucydides trap and to accommodate a rising China without sacrificing core US interests, then American policymakers need to understate their interpretations of Chinese actions that are merely assertive and underreact so as to defuse tensions while still drawing clear red lines. For instance, the United States should not tolerate China's use of force to integrate Taiwan into the Chinese mainland, or China's attempt to prevent the United States or other states from freely traveling in China's EEZ or ADIZ. By contrast, habitually interpreting Chinese acts of assertion as aggressive ones is symptomatic of a strategy that holds that China cannot be accommodated and that it must be contained by any means necessary.

4

IS CHINA A RESPONSIBLE STAKEHOLDER?

China recently has been criticized for not being a "responsible stake-holder," for not being a good citizen of the international community, and for not contributing to global public goods. China "is refusing to be a responsible stakeholder in the international political system, cultivating, as it has been, good relations with some of the world's most odious regimes," according to Robert Kaplan, writing in the *Atlantic*.[1] An editorial in the *Wall Street Journal* asserts that "China won't be a responsible stakeholder" and acts as a "free rider."[2] Observing China's growing assertiveness in foreign policy and purported attempts to undermine the current liberal world order, Elizabeth Economy writes in *Foreign Affairs,* "China is transforming the world as it transforms itself. Never mind notions of a responsible stakeholder; China has become a revolutionary power."[3] This viewpoint was reinforced in the wake of its attempts to claim large portions of the South and East China Seas as its own territory.

This chapter explores the application of the concept of stakeholding and how it pertains to China's international conduct. It proceeds by applying sets of criteria to evaluate whether China is acting as a "responsible stakeholder" in the international system. In the process, the chapter raises questions about frequently employed criteria on the subject. The chapter first utilizes a communitarian set of standards of international responsibility that distinguish between the status of a member of a community and that of a citizen of a state. The chapter then briefly studies China's conduct from a less demanding standard, one that considers whether China has fulfilled its duties as a partner in projects in which it has shared or complementary interests with other nations. The chapter's last section examines China's conduct from a third set of criteria that involves conceptions of power, rather than value- or interest-based considerations.

Within History

The first major break in the American view that China was part of the Soviet-run global communist threat came with the well-known "opening to China" during the Nixon administration. In a 1967 essay in *Foreign Affairs*, Richard Nixon wrote that China should be drawn into the community of nations, because a globally engaged China would act in a more "civilized" and less dogmatic manner.[4] However, many Americans and others in the West continued to see China as an aggressive, expansionist, communist nation until the end of the Cold War. During the Clinton administration, Secretary of Defense William Perry argued that engagement was a strategy for getting China to act like a "responsible world power," and Secretary of State Madeleine Albright called on China to become a "constructive participant in the international arena." The George W. Bush administration's view of China was less optimistic; Secretary of State Condoleezza Rice declared that China was not a status quo power.[5] However, it was during this administration, in 2005, that Deputy Secretary of State Robert Zoellick called on China to become a "responsible stakeholder" in the international community—a phrase that echoed widely.

The "stakeholder" concept is a highly communitarian one, since it holds that while the members of a given community are entitled to various rights, these go hand in hand with assuming responsibilities for the common good. The term stakeholder has been used in recent decades mainly in reference to corporatism and societies. Communitarian economists argue that the corporation should be viewed as belonging not to the shareholders but to all those who have a stake in it and are "invested" in it, including the workers, creditors, and the community in which the plants are located. Tony Blair championed a stakeholder society in the year leading up to his election as prime minister and during his first years in office; he spoke of an economy "run for the many, not for the few . . . in which opportunity is available to all, advancement is through merit, and from which no group or class is set apart or excluded."[6]

In Zoellick's speech urging China to become a "responsible stakeholder" in the international system, he listed an extensive number of changes that China would need to undertake in order to qualify, including major changes in its domestic policies as well as in foreign policy in major areas, from North Korea and Iran to trade. A critic might argue that he basically asked China to become like the United States and to do its bidding, all in the name of service to the common good of the world. (A similar idea is often expressed in the argument that after World War II the United States erected a set of "liberal" global rules and institutions that, while tying its own hands to some extent, helped promote world peace, order, human rights, and democracy, and that China should now buy into these arrangements.) Several other authors have also employed this term, seeking to determine whether or not China is becoming a responsible stakeholder based on more universally applicable criteria. This chapter joins this examination from the viewpoint of a global community.

In the same years during which American policymakers urged China to become a more "responsible" or more "status quo" international power, academics set out to analyze China's conduct in similar terms. Robert Ross argued in a 1997 essay in *Foreign Affairs* that China was acting as a "conservative power" even though it may also be considered "revisionist" in the sense that it is dissatisfied with aspects of the status quo in Asia, especially with regard to Taiwan and Japan.[7] Alastair Johnston in a 2003 article in *International Security* concluded that China is a status quo power and criticized the notion that it is a revisionist power, one currently outside the international community that must be brought in. He held that there is no well-defined global community with well-defined norms. Nonetheless, Johnston defined criteria of what would make a status quo power and said that, despite some problem areas, China meets them. For example, China's participation in international institutions and organizations increased dramatically in the post-Mao era. He criticized those who describe grandiose Chinese goals of regional hegemony. For example, while some of China's actions with regard to the Spratly Islands raised red flags, "China is like the Spratlys' other claimants. Indeed none of the claimants has sound legal basis."[8] And when it comes to potential for conflict with the United States, Johnston argued that China seeks to constrain the United States' behavior, not violently push against American power.

Chinese policymakers themselves have sought over the past few decades to show that China intends to act responsibly. President Jiang Zemin stated, "China needs a long-lasting peaceful international environment for its development." And in 1997, he initiated China's "New Security Concept," which stresses "mutual respect" and "peaceful coexistence." Since then, Chinese leaders, such as Hu Jintao and Wen Jiabao, have declared that they are seeking a "peaceful rise" and that they want to focus on domestic development, not international expansion. The concept was furthered by the Chinese scholar Zheng Bijian in a *Foreign Affairs* article entitled "China's Peaceful Rise to Great-Power Status," in which he wrote, "Beijing remains committed to a 'peaceful rise': bringing its people out of poverty by embracing economic globalization and improving relations with the rest of the world. As it emerges as a great power, China knows that its continued development depends on world peace—a peace that its development will in turn reinforce."[9] President Xi Jinping has likewise emphasized that China's rise and "great national renewal" will positively impact the international community and that "as its strength increases, it will assume more international responsibilities."[10] In his first speech before the UN General Assembly in September 2015, President Xi pledged $1 billion over the next decade to create a peace and development fund, eight thousand Chinese troops for the creation of a peacekeeping force, and $100 million for peacekeeping in the African Union over the next five years.[11] Also, the concept of a China that is a "responsible great power" has been widely discussed by Chinese intellectuals.

Critics argue that China is merely trying to "pull the wool over Western eyes," that is, to generate the impression that it has peaceful inclinations, while it is preparing to emerge as an aggressor once it gains the capabilities to carry out its true intentions.[12] In the current context, one cannot avoid asking: "By what criteria is one to judge the extent to which a nation is acting responsibly?" The chapter turns next to grapple with this key question from the viewpoint of key values, interests, and power relations.

Membership and Citizenship

From a communitarian viewpoint, the term "stakeholder" requires unpacking, because the assessments that employ it often conflate two distinct concepts by blurring the differences between being a member in good standing of a community and an upstanding citizen of a state. The expectations of members are significantly higher than those of citizens. Moreover, contributions to the common good are voluntary and undergirded by informal norms and informal social controls (such as appreciation for those who contribute and criticism of those who fail to do so). Citizens' duties, meanwhile, are set by law, and serious violations are punished by financial penalties (or sanctions) and coercive means (e.g., armed interventions). By conflating membership with citizenship, Adversarians tend to be unduly condemning, and may rush to call for penalties and coercive measures when only stronger moral appeals are justified.

To highlight the distinction between these concepts, it is fruitful to first examine how they apply to individuals. An upstanding citizen pays the taxes owed, serves as a juror when called, and abides by the laws of the land. (I deliberately avoid the term "good citizen," because good implies a moral standing, which is appropriate for community membership, but not for a purely civic role). Such citizens may also keep up with public affairs and vote regularly; however, these requirements already move the analysis from the notion of a mere citizen toward the status of a member. A good member—aside from being an upstanding citizen— also contributes to the common good of the community by volunteering, making donations, heeding the informal norms of the community, and helping to enforce those norms by exerting informal social controls over those who do not heed them. One reason citizenship and membership are often conflated is that a given societal entity can be both a state and a community. Indeed, this is a widely used definition of a nation.

When these concepts are applied to international affairs, one must take into account that the international community is a very nascent one. At the same time, although there is no global state of which one can be a loyal citizen, there is a nontrivial and growing body of established international law, as well as decisions made by international institutions, that nations are expected to heed. Hence, in the international realm, too, it is important to distinguish between a "bad" member (e.g., a nation that makes few or no donations to countries devastated by earthquakes or does not contribute troops to peacekeeping operations) and a nation that acts like a poor citizen (e.g., a nation that violates the rulings, for example, of the World Trade Organization or the United Nations). Acts of poor citizenship include engaging in hostile activities such as supporting terrorism, invading other countries without due cause, and failing to live up to agreed treaties.

The discussion next turns to examine several areas of China's conduct with this dual perspective in mind. The analysis is deliberately limited in two major ways. Firstly, it does not seek to encompass all or even most areas of international conduct, but merely to examine a sufficient number to highlight the difference between membership and citizenship, and to gain a preliminary assessment of China's conduct in both capacities. Second, the discussion focuses almost exclusively on conduct rather than on declarations and statements. One can readily find belligerent statements by both Chinese and American military officials, politicians, and observers. Behavior speaks more clearly, although it too is open to different interpretations.

China Is Neither a Good Member nor a Good Citizen

China is reported to have contributed very little to whatever is considered the common good (or "public goods") of the global community. It was roundly criticized for providing very little help when nations donated relief aid to those struck by the 2010 earthquake in Haiti and the 2004 Indian Ocean tsunami. For example, according to *Foreign Policy*, the low levels of China's pledged relief aid at the UN donors' conference following the earthquake in Haiti were pitiful. "More than 50 countries kicked in $5.3 billion in all, at least a billion dollars over their initial goals. But the world's fastest-growing economy ponied up a miserly $1.5 million, comparable to the donations made by Gambia and Monaco—hardly top-three economies—and less than the cost of a house in some of the tonier suburbs of Shanghai."[13]

After the tsunami struck in 2004, China's initial emergency aid amounted to less than $3 million. It was raised to about $60 million in the following week, arguably so as not to be outdone by Taiwan, which pledged $50 million.[14] This sum, plus its decision to dispatch medical teams, marked China's largest relief operation.[15] In comparison, Australia granted the equivalent of $810 million American dollars in grants and loans to the tsunami-affected countries; Germany, about $700 million; Japan, $500 million; and the United States, $350 million.[16]

One should note, though, that while such donations are expected from good members, declining to give generously—unlike avoiding paying taxes—does not make a nation a bad global citizen. The same holds for China's failure to support interventions to stop genocides. China opposed humanitarian intervention in Kosovo, continued to sell arms to Sudan while it was committing genocide, and made a concerted effort to block UN Security Council authorization to send peacekeeping troops to Darfur.[17] In short, China is indeed a rather deleterious member, but not necessarily a bad citizen.

Turning to examine China as a citizen, one ought to consider that although international law is subject to different and changing interpretations, there is a widely recognized body of law that China does not abide by. That said, as far as aggression is concerned, we have seen that China has become much less aggressive as of the 1980s. Even so, China still clearly pays little mind to the Universal Declaration of Human Rights.

The Chinese government "has been a major beneficiary of technology acquired through industrial espionage," concluded the US-China Economic and Security Review Commission.[18] Also according to the commission's 2010 report, China is placing requirements on firms operating in China that are designed to force these firms to expose "their security measures or even their intellectual property to Chinese competitors" as the price of doing business in China.[19] According to the cybersecurity firm CrowdStrike, Chinese hacking attempts to gain industrial secrets have continued with regularity in contravention of the cybersecurity pact signed by both the United States and China in September 2015.[20]

Moreover, China's inadequate enforcement of intellectual property rights laws has led to rampant piracy and counterfeiting. Chinese trade in illegal copies of software, films, records, books, pharmaceuticals, and a variety of other goods—ranging from luxury items to shampoo—is reported to cost American companies billions of dollars a year.[21] The Motion Picture Association of America estimates that the entertainment industry lost $2.7 billion in one year alone.[22]

According to the report of the House of Representatives Select Committee on US National Security and Military/Commercial Concerns with the People's Republic of China (the Cox Commission report), China "has stolen classified information on all of the United States' most advanced thermonuclear warheads, and several of the associated reentry vehicles."[23] In April 2010 a state-owned Chinese telecom firm "re-routed traffic sent to about 15% of the Internet's destinations, including branches of the U.S. armed services."[24] In 2007 hackers, believed to potentially be Chinese agents,[25] stole several terabytes of information—nearly equal to the amount of information in the Library of Congress—from, among others, the Departments of State and Defense.[26] And in 2015 Chinese hackers gained access to a server at the US Office of Personnel Management, compromising the personal information of 22 million federal employees.[27]

In short, both those who rate China as being a far from good member of the global community, and those who see China as failing to meet the standards of an upstanding citizen, have considerable bases for their judgments—at least as long as one accepts the precept that nations ought to be good members of the international community and good global citizens.

Aspirational Standards

So far, the evaluations of China have been based on the concept of a stakeholder and the normative assumptions that constitute it. However, in evaluating China's conduct, one should take into account that the standards involved are aspirational standards, especially regarding community membership but also regarding citizenship. Aspirational standards are the expressions of norms and even laws employed by those who argue that nations ought to abide by said norms and laws, and who argue that the world would be a better place if these standards were more widely honored. These aspirational standards are far from mere lip service. The global community, despite being very weak, does recognize and reward those who abide by these standards, while chastising and sometimes punishing those who do not. It uses approbations and censures, which have an effect. Nations do care whether their acts and regimes are considered legitimate and respected by others, and how a government is viewed by the world affects its domestic politics. Thus, the ways in which many nations reacted to the 2003 American invasion of Iraq had considerable and adverse consequences that were, in fact, "real." These sorts of consequences are an element of what is considered soft or persuasive power. However, one must assume that various actors will often not fully heed norms, try to circumvent norms, or even change them altogether.

At the same time, one must take into account that even in the most closely knit communities, in families and villages, members vary in the extent to which they adhere to norms and contribute to the common good. The same holds true for members of a national community. The situation is amplified many times over when one deals with the international community, which is in a very preliminary state; its norms are still young and being formed. It follows then that although it is productive to have such norms and to promote them, before one condemns—let alone seeks to punish—those who do not live up to them, one ought to take into account their aspirational nature. For example, China is properly criticized for doing little to stop genocides in other nations. However, while the United States and its allies are credited for stopping the ethnic cleansing in Kosovo, they failed to do so in Cambodia, Rwanda, the Congo, and Sudan.[28] In a class in which many get a C or lower grade, those with a D should not be treated as if the class is full of A students. All should be expected to improve their conduct. The same arguments apply to global governance.

Contextual Factors

So far, this chapter has assumed that all nations can be expected to abide by the same standards as far as their international roles are concerned. However, in making such judgments, it is common to take into account differences in capabilities such as stages of development and magnitude of assets. How do these particularistic adjustments affect the applications of universal normative standards in an evaluation of China, given its recent, current, and expected capabilities?

Relative Affluence

Even in well-formed communities, contributions expected from community members are scaled according to their affluence and, thus, their abilities. Among the nations that did make substantial contributions to the tsunami and Haiti relief are the more affluent countries, such as the United States, Germany, and Japan. Although China is the world's second largest economy, it does not see itself—and by many measures is not—an affluent nation. It points to its income per capita as well below that of the main donor nations, a point that is confirmed by the most recent (2014) data from the World Bank, which shows that the average per capita GNI in the Organisation for Economic Co-operation and Development countries is above $44,000, compared to about $12,600 in China.[29] At the same time, given China's rapid economic growth, one would expect it to become more generous in the future.

China's Improvement

Bates Gill, director of the Stockholm International Peace Research Institute, carefully reviewed China's conduct in a number of areas, including regional and international security, energy security, economic development and assistance, peacekeeping, trade and economic affairs, and human rights. He concluded in a 2007 memo that "looking back over the past 15 years and looking ahead to the next 10 or 15, the trend is clear that China is becoming a more responsible stakeholder."[30]

Turning first to membership, China has decided to increase the number of troops it sends to peacekeeping operations.[31] China has also increasingly participated in counterpiracy operations in Somalia, sending its naval fleets to help in the endeavor,[32] as well as committing to share intelligence and conduct humanitarian rescue operations in coordination with other countries involved in antipiracy efforts.[33]

In terms of becoming a better global citizen, China has somewhat improved with regard to its protection of intellectual property rights. Although piracy and counterfeiting remain widespread in China, the government has taken some steps to curb the practice since it joined the WTO in 2001.[34] Changes in China's conduct are reflected in its rise in the annual rankings of countries according to their level of intellectual property rights protection.

Moreover, China is exhibiting a more positive attitude toward international organizations and laws. A review by two leading scholars concluded that China accepts international law, actively participates in the UN, and represents itself ably in a variety of multilateral institutions—an improvement from past decades when it "rejected what it called the 'bourgeois' rules and institutions that dominated the world community" and silenced its international law experts. They point out that China participated in the drafting of the UN Convention of the Law of the Sea (UNCLOS) and ratified it in 1996 (in contrast to the United States, which has yet to do so), and that China joined regional organizations protecting maritime environments in East Asia.[35] Furthermore, until Iran signed the nuclear deal in 2015, China imposed sanctions on Iran in line with UN resolutions, despite China's keen interest in purchasing oil from Iran. China also played a key role in bringing about the 2015 Paris agreement on climate change. Additionally, China is the first country to buy newly issued bonds from the IMF to help countries worldwide weather the global financial crisis, spending $50 billion.[36]

Different Interpretation of Norms and Duties

China by and large has ceased to claim that human rights are bourgeois, Western ideas. China now tends to argue that it is observing human rights, or that it is first advancing socioeconomic rights with legal and political rights to follow, once development is more advanced. Nor can one ignore that many other nations violate human rights on a similar or greater scale than China, and that Western nations—quick to chastise China for violations of human rights—are often willing to turn a blind eye to such violations by other nations, for instance, Saudi Arabia.[37] One should not ignore either that the UDHR includes several socioeconomic rights that the United States does not recognize as such.

Finally, one ought to take into account the lens through which nations perceive themselves, albeit as a mitigating factor and not one that absolves them from the responsibilities of good members and the duties of upstanding citizens. China views itself as a nation that has been humiliated, exploited, and occupied for generations by Western powers and Japan,[38] a view that has significant historical grounding. It considers many of the demands now laid on it as an attempt to keep it in a weakened state. Gradually, with a developing economy and growing international respect, China will likely liberate itself from these sensibilities. However, in the meantime, they continue to affect its international conduct.

China, on some occasions, identifies itself with the South and sees itself as part of the global struggle to move away from an uneven distribution of resources and assets that disproportionately favors the North. Thus for instance, its $50 billion bond purchase from the IMF was dedicated to a program that focuses on the developing and emerging market countries of the South.

In short, it is rather simplistic to measure China against an idealized image of a community in which common goals and values are clearly established and each member contributes its share. China seems to be increasingly abiding by the rules in many areas while remaining noncompliant in a few others—but many other nations do not conduct themselves any better, in terms of both membership and citizenship.

China as a Power: Challenge or Transformation?

Up to now, China's international conduct has been examined against relatively high aspirational standards, which ask whether China meets the expectations of a good member of the global community, and those of an upstanding citizen of global governance. However, China's conduct (and that of other nations) must also be assessed by much more realpolitik standards that concern the actual and changing power relations among the nations of the world.

Some who apply such standards see the United States as the de facto world government, as Michael Mandelbaum explicitly does.[39] From this vantage point, rising new powers and their assertive demands are seen as upsetting the global order, and hence must be contained. In contrast, to the extent that one views the global architecture as moving from unipolar to multipolar, in which various powers become the focus of one region or another (e.g., France and Germany as the main drivers of the EU), or as moving toward a number of new power centers that share the task of remaking the global order (e.g., the G-20 or some other such number), then the actions of rising powers can seem much more acceptable, indeed transformative. Thus, if one views the United States as the hegemon that needs to contain and balance China, it would be logical for it to push its armed forces to the border of China if the North Korean regime collapses and the two Koreas are unified. In contrast, if one views the world as moving toward a multipolar order, and sees China as a legitimate regional power (albeit not as a regional hegemon), one would favor the United States committing itself to keeping its troops at the Demilitarized Zone or even beginning a gradual withdrawal from Korea.

Conclusion

China is not a responsible stakeholder, but few nations are. Urging China to become a better member of the global community and a better global citizen is quite legitimate, as long as one recognizes the aspirational nature of these expectations. And one ought to take into account China's history, low income per capita, and improving conduct. Finally, if one views the United States as a hegemon, there are good reasons to seek to contain China. These reasons are much less evident if one accepts that the world is becoming more multipolar, that China is a legitimate regional power, and that China has an important role to play in transforming the international order by peaceful means rather than merely signing up—or being "integrated"—into an order the United States and its allies formed shortly after World War II.

5

ACCOMMODATING CHINA

A central concern of this book is the increasing indication that the United States and China are on a collision course. Political scientists argue that since the days of the ancient Greeks, history demonstrates that when a new power arises and an old power does not yield ground, wars ensue.[1] However, the record also shows there are no ironclad laws of history, no trends that inevitably unfold. As we already noted, Harvard's Graham Allison points to four cases out of sixteen since the sixteenth century in which the emergence of a new power was *not* followed by war.[2] Thus, to those who hold that the United States and China are fated to clash, I say it is not written in the stars. War—to paraphrase the UNESCO Constitution—starts in the minds of men, and there it can be ended. The United States can accommodate China without compromising its core interests or values. To do so, both nations would be well served by further collaborating on shared or complementary interests and embracing a strategy of mutually assured restraint (MAR), here outlined.

Shared and Complementary Interests

At the outset one should note that accommodations should not be misconstrued as appeasement, as unilateral concession making, or as evidence of weakness. They aim to serve the interests of both sides and of global stability. They assume that relations between international powers need not be a zero-sum game (in which power gained by one nation comes at another's expense), but that nations exist in a system in which they can find significantly shared and complementary interests, despite having occasional conflict. Among the shared or complementary interests that can serve as the basis for US-China cooperation are preventing the spread of terrorism (obviously a major concern for the United States and its allies but also for China, where Uighur separatists—allegedly linked to al-Qaeda and trained in Pakistan—have launched terrorist attacks on the government since the 1990s);[3] nonproliferation of nuclear arms (in 2016 China voted with the US at the UN to board all ships on their way to or from North Korea to ensure that they are not carrying nuclear materials); financial stability; preventing the spread of pandemics; and environmental protection, in particular, climate change. Michael Swaine notes that effective action on climate change will "require far higher levels of mutual assistance and cooperation between Beijing and Washington if the potentially disastrous consequences of global warming are to be avoided."[4] Indeed, even Mike Pillsbury, an advisor to the Trump transition team, said in an interview after the 2016 election, "If I were writing a list of things to think about for China for the next president, I would make a list of areas of conflict, friction, tough negotiations. I would also make an area of cooperation, and climate change obviously would be on the area of cooperation."[5]

Growing Tensions

China and the United States mistrust each other greatly. This distrust has increased in recent years, despite a tightening interdependence between the two countries' economic well-being and an increase in trade between the two nations. The United States is a key market for China's goods, and China is a leading foreign holder of US Treasury securities. However, this relationship is a source of mistrust rather than mutual trust. A study by Kenneth Lieberthal and Wang Jisi held that China accused the United States of attempting to "sabotage the Communist Party's leadership" and that the United States alleged that the PRC's "mercantilist policies harm the chances of America's economic recovery."[6]

Military developments add to the existing tension. China is energetically building up its military, although it started from a relatively low base. If current trends continue, with escalating tensions and growing militaries, the prophets of a war between a rising power and an established one may yet be proven correct. For this reason, curbing tensions and capping military buildups are both vital objectives.

Moreover, nations in effect have a sort of collective psyche; they can feel humiliated, insulted, cornered, and so on. Nations often become ensnared in a vicious cycle in which gestures considered hostile by one nation (even if these gestures are not made by official leaders) trigger similar gestures by another nation, which are then viewed as validation of the first nation's ill feelings, leading to further such gestures and responses.[7] Lieberthal and Wang show that such a positive feedback loop of strategic distrust has deep roots in the history of US-China relations and has been reinforced since 2008 by the fear in the United States that the Chinese are "catching up," while concurrently there is a fear in China that the United States is attempting to obstruct China's rise.[8] Giving such feelings, it becomes "very difficult to accept an outcome to any contest, however minor, that can be portrayed as a defeat for one side or a win for the other," and thus "it becomes almost impossible for either side to step off the escalator and start compromising."[9] "The worst outcome for Asia's long-term stability as well as for the American-Chinese relationship would be a drift into escalating reciprocal demonization," according to Zbigniew Brzezinski.[10]

Tension Reduction Measures

Various measures have been suggested to reverse this spiral and reduce the tension between the two countries (in popular parlance, to engage in "psychological disarmament"). The value and effect of such measures can be judged from events that took place in 1963. At that time, merely a year after the Cuban missile crisis, when tensions between the United States and the USSR were much higher than the current ones between the United States and China, and the USSR had clear ambitions to become a global hegemon, President Kennedy unveiled the Strategy of Peace. His transformative speech was followed by a series of minor accommodative moves by the United States that were quickly and fully reciprocated by the USSR.[11] These moves led to a major change in the US-Soviet relationship known as the détente. It was left to President Reagan to build on this foundation of basic trust with a major treaty that led to a reduction of nuclear arms by both nations. Since a new administration is taking over the White House in 2017, it is a particularly opportune time to reexamine the pivot to Asia that President Obama launched in 2011 and determine whether it is a quest for regional accommodation, or a step down a slippery slope at the bottom of which lurks military confrontation.

Mutually Assured Restraint

A group of American and Chinese scholars proposed reducing tensions and increasing trust between the two powers by following a new concept, called "mutually assured restraint" (MAR).[12] MAR seeks to inject substance into the vague phrases mouthed by both powers: China ought to have a "new model of major-country relations"[13] with the United States, and the United States seeks to build a "cooperative partnership" with China.[14] MAR is a foreign policy based on mutual respect, a quest for confidence building, and a set of new institutionalized arrangements that would move both powers away from situations that could escalate into major conflicts. Accordingly, each side would limit its military buildup and coercive diplomacy as long as the other side limits its own. Furthermore, these self-restraint measures would be vetted in ways spelled out below. Thus, China would be free to take the steps it deems necessary for its self-defense and the maintenance of its relations with allies without extending them to the point where they threaten other nations or the international commons. At the same time, the United States would be free to take the steps it believes are necessary to preserve its self-defense, fulfill its obligations to allies in the region, and otherwise maintain the existing international order. The United States and China can take seven steps as part of a policy of mutually assured restraint; these are as follows.

First, the two states could establish a neutral buffer zone. Instead of further shoring up partnerships with regional states (which gives the impression of encirclement and expanding influence), both states should treat nations that share land borders with China similarly to the way Austria was treated during the Cold War: as a buffer zone. (One additional model is that of East Germany following reunification; a 1990 agreement between Germany and the USSR stipulated that although the former East Germany would be given the status of NATO territory, neither NATO troops nor nuclear weapons would be stationed in these areas.)[15] Both powers would be free to continue engaging these nations economically by investing, trading with them, providing foreign aid, sharing information, and promoting educational programs. However, neither the United States nor China would be permitted to extend any new military commitments to countries in the buffer zone, and both would be required to gradually phase out existing military commitments. MAR would also stipulate that the two countries limit joint military exercises and the placement of military assets in this zone. Above all, both powers would make it clear to their allies that they should not assume the automatic, guaranteed involvement of the United States or

China if they engage in armed conflict or war with either of these two powers.

The second component of this approach involves scaling back each side's investment in the outcomes of territorial disputes in the South and East China Seas. As outlined in chapter 3, tensions between China and Japan have escalated over the Senkaku/Diaoyu Islands, a tiny chain of uninhabited islands in the East China Sea. Notably, China criticized the United States' attempts to intervene in the dispute, insisting that bilateral negotiations be the mechanism for reaching a resolution.[16] At the same time, both China and Japan have taken steps that show a measure of self-restraint of the kind called for by MAR. The Japanese coast guard prevented Japanese nationalists from landing on the contested islands, and China relied on its maritime law enforcement agencies and coast guard rather than involving its military in the area.[17]

To further diffuse the tension, all countries involved should not merely curb the means by which Japan and China carry out their conflict over the Senkaku/Diaoyu Islands but also find a resolution for the conflict itself. Experts have suggested several ways of doing so. Japan and China could submit the dispute to the International Court of Justice or the International Tribunal for the Law of the Sea.[18] Alternately, the two countries could jointly administer and develop the resources in and around the islands. Sovereignty over the territory could be awarded to one state, while resource-related rights could be assigned to all claimants.[19] Although some may adjudge the probability as small that the United States and China could be drawn into a war over these small and uninhabited islands, wars have been known to begin over less important matters when other factors already predispose the parties to conflict, and when national pride and credibility are evoked. The principles of MAR should therefore be extended to conclusively settling the dispute over the Senkaku/Diaoyu Islands, one way or another.

Third, the two powers can make some accommodations through military repositioning, which is likely to be more consequential than diplomatic and even economic moves. For example, Bonnie Glaser of the Center for Strategic and International Studies has suggested that American planes and trawlers stop their near daily surveillance patrols of Chinese coastlines.[20] One realizes just how provocative these patrols are if one imagines how the United States would react if Chinese planes and boats regularly patrolled the East and West Coasts of the United

States. Such patrols add little to intelligence gathered by technological means (such as satellites and cyberagents) or by human agents (which have much more access now to China than a generation ago). Indeed, these patrols appear primarily to be of service for planning an attack on short notice. That is, they are mainly of tactical and not strategic value. At best, these patrols reflect the notion that the United States has been ordained to keep a world order in the seven seas; at worst, they reflect the macho, confrontational attitude articulated in off-the-record meetings with US naval representatives. These patrols have already led to at least one troubling incident, namely, the accidental collision of an American EP-3 reconnaissance plane and a Chinese F-8 fighter jet in April 2001, which left the PRC pilot dead and resulted in the eleven-day detention of twenty-four US crew members by the Chinese.[21] In short, stopping these patrols would serve as a major tension-reduction measure that would entail little or no loss to the United States.

Of greater importance is stopping the forward positioning of military assets in the region, the formation of military alliances with China's neighbors, and the joint military exercises with these nations, which include Japan, South Korea, Vietnam, Thailand, Taiwan, Australia, Singapore, Indonesia, and India. These military ties and commitments have been extended since 2011 when the United States pronounced the Asia-Pacific to be its first priority as it "pivoted" from the Near to the Far East.[22] It moved marines to Australia, adding to the already sizable military forces in the area, and announced an increase in warships stationed in the Pacific, which will rise to 60 percent of the navy's total fleet by 2020.[23] Singapore agreed to open its naval facilities to four of America's newest littoral combat ships.[24] The United States views these arrangements as agreements between sovereign nations, a way of burden sharing, and part of a drive to contain or "counterbalance" China; China, however, perceives these moves as an attempt at Cold War–era encirclement. Combined, they send the unmistakable message, in China's estimation, that the United States and its allies are ringing China with military forces and making preparations that only make sense if one concludes that the United States must prepare for a war with China. Chas Freeman, a former US diplomat with extensive experience in China and across Asia, warns, "The 'rebalance' will not work. Far from avoiding the 'Thucydides trap,' it walks right into it. It is likely to be seen in retrospect as an historic blunder."[25]

Moreover, the various treaties and understandings between countries in East and Southeast Asia and either China or the United States have given several states in the region "a finger on the trigger" of a gun belonging to their superpower sponsor by stipulating that if the nation in question enters a war with one superpower, the other superpower will come to its aid. Some treaties explicitly entail such a commitment (e.g., the Treaty of Mutual Cooperation and Security between the United States and Japan, which is said to cover the Senkaku Islands). Others are ambiguous and easily misconstrued by the countries involved (e.g., the Mutual Defense Treaty between the United States and the Philippines, as well as the overall relationship between China and North Korea).

It is therefore particularly troubling that some of these smaller states have engaged in provocative behavior. Such provocative behavior could not only lead to war between them and other states in the region but also drag both superpowers into a confrontation with each other. This is most obvious in the case of the two Koreas. For example, some analysts have acknowledged a possible connection between the construction of a South Korean naval base on Jeju Island and the United States' "strategic interests in Asia." Opponents of the base hold that giving the United States access to the base—as is likely to occur—will "provoke China" and "trigger a naval arms race."[26] Other examples—like the conflict between China and the Philippines over Scarborough Shoal, as described in chapter 3—are much less dramatic and conflict prone, but are worrying nonetheless.

Fourth, the United States should make explicit what is viewed by many as an implicit understanding between China and the United States regarding the status of Taiwan. The American and Chinese governments have already demonstrated considerable self-restraint in the matter of Taiwan. Beijing has not yielded to demands from those who call for employing force as a means of "reclaiming" Taiwan as part of the mainland; meanwhile, Washington has not yielded to Americans who urge the recognition of Taiwan as an independent country. These measures of self-restraint should be made more explicit by letting it be known that so long as China does not use force to coerce Taiwan to become part of China, the United States will continue to refrain from treating Taiwan as an independent state. The prevailing understanding between the United States and China is opaque; although some experts in international relations say an understanding exists, some suggest the substance of such an understanding is unclear, and still others hold no such understanding has ever existed.

I recently asked eight experts on Taiwan whether there was an implicit understanding between China and the United States about the ways Taiwan should be treated. Five responded that there was no such understanding; two said that the answer to my question was not clear; and one held that indeed there was such an understanding. The range of their responses serves to verify that the issue could benefit from clarification. Indeed, it turns out that the matter is far more complex than it may at first seem. One scholar wrote, "You are correct that there is an implicit agreement between U.S. and China that China will not use military force to "reclaim" Taiwan. . . . There is an implicit understanding between U.S. and Taiwan that should China invade Taiwan, the U.S. may intervene, partly to honor the fact that Taiwan has been an important ally in the Pacific Rim and partly to protect U.S. interests in the region." Another scholar, however, wrote, "I am not aware of any such implicit understanding. That is why the Taiwan issue remains such a sensitive issue in U.S.-China relations. Many assume that the U.S. would defend Taiwan if China attacked without provocation, but that it would not if Taiwan declared independence unilaterally. The U.S. [government] has never made clear what its policy actually is, if it indeed has a policy other than encouraging neither side to upset the status quo." Note that after indicating that he is unaware of such an understanding, this expert outlines a key element of such an understanding. The fact that it is not "clear" and merely "many assume" sounds like what others might view as an implicit understanding. A third scholar's response was different still. He held, "No, there is NO such implicit understanding on this between [China] and [the United States]. One wishes so, but it's not the case. China has NEVER renounced the option of using force, if necessary, but in the 1982 Joint Communique did use language to the effect that it seeks 'peaceful unification.'" A fourth expert captured the ambiguities well, writing, "It is hard to say there is an implicit agreement because an agreement implies is it is more than just implicit! I think China would never acknowledge that there is such an agreement. They have not given up the right to use force to resolve the Taiwan problem. But since they have not used force to this end, you can argue that there is an implicit agreement. [It gets] rather circular. . . . The position of the [United States] has always been that the Taiwan problem should be resolved peacefully with the consent of the people on both sides of the Taiwan Strait." This scholar proceeded to note that "the United States 'acknowledges that all Chinese on either side of the Taiwan Strait maintain there is but one China and that Taiwan is a part of China. The United States Government does not challenge that position' [according to the Shanghai Communiqué]. This [is the] one China 'principle' in contrast to China's one China 'policy' (more simply that Taiwan IS in fact part of 'one China'). Implicit in this, though, is the understanding, expressed by various administrations[,] that the [United States] will not support a Taiwan declaration of independence." He closed with the pregnant lines, "So this might be seen as a basis for an implicit agreement. We oppose a declaration of independence; China forgoes the use of force." Evidently, the treatments of the status of Taiwan could benefit from clarification.

One may ask whether it is not best to let sleeping dogs lie. This notion has already been rejected by then-president-elect Donald Trump, who called into question the One China Policy.[27] One reason to clarify both sides' policies is that hawks in both nations use the cause of Taiwan to justify building up the United States' and China's respective military forces. Indeed, a 2013 report to Congress from the Department of Defense states: "Preparing for potential conflict in the Taiwan Strait appears to remain the principal focus and primary driver of China's military investment."[28] Moreover, China carried out a military exercise in which the PLA simulated "a Normandy-style invasion" of Taiwan.[29] In the United States, a 2003 report from the Council on Foreign Relations examined China's growing military power and held that "minimizing the chances that a cross-strait crisis will occur means maintaining the clear ability and willingness to counter any application of military force against Taiwan."[30] Making an explicit commitment to maintain the status quo standing of Taiwan—unless the people of Taiwan freely and peacefully choose otherwise—would reduce tensions between the United States and China and would highlight the effectiveness of MAR as an overarching strategy for US-China relations.

Fifth, the United States and China should establish mechanisms for collaborating on space and cybersecurity, the dangers of which demonstrate the merits of avoiding a collision course. Indeed, several highly regarded military analysts warn that space and cyberarms are rapidly becoming as dangerous as nuclear weapons. Secretary of Defense Leon Panetta warned that the "next Pearl Harbor we confront could very well be a cyber-attack that cripples our power systems, our grid, our security systems, our financial systems."[31] Cyberwarfare's lower cost (in terms of resources and human life) as compared to conventional fighting makes it an attractive option—but it is also unfamiliar and hazardous territory. Cyberworms have the potential not only to wreak havoc on stock markets and the banking sector but also to compromise key infrastructure and unleash biological and chemical toxins. These arms allow the nation that strikes first to wreak tremendous devastation on the other and hence incentivize powers to strike first—a dangerous and destabilizing condition.

This is all the more unsettling because tensions and mistrust between the United States and China are escalating in cyber- and outer space. Many of China's anti-access/area denial military developments involve these kinds of weapons and are seen in the United States as threats to its military dominance of the global commons.[32] Still, the United States maintains a strong advantage in these technologies, and that unsettles China. According to Li Yan, a Chinese scholar at the China Institutes of Contemporary International Relations, "The U.S. is suspicious of Chinese intentions to invest. At the same time, China feels more and more pressure from U.S. aggressive actions. With this sense of insecurity, any potential investment by one side is probably viewed as a new threat by the other side."[33]

The need for some cooperative framework has been acknowledged on both sides. In May 2012, during a visit by a Chinese defense minister to the Pentagon, Panetta stated that "because the United States and China have developed technological capabilities in [cyberspace], it's extremely important that we work together to develop ways to avoid any miscalculation or misperception that could lead to crisis."[34] China and three other countries proposed an International Code of Conduct for Information Security to the UN.[35] The United States rejected the code because of provisions that would hinder the free flow of information on the web and benefit authoritarian regimes seeking to stamp out dissent.[36] This remains a critical security concern that requires cooperation among the big powers. Because US-China outer space and cyberdisarmament is both "impractical and unverifiable," the way forward is augmenting deterrence "by mutual restraint in the use of strategic offensive capabilities."[37] Each country should pledge not to be the first to deny the other the use of outer space nor to launch the first attack on cybernetworks vital to general welfare.[38] A first step in this direction could be the agreement announced in September 2015 during President Xi's visit to the United States that the two countries would not conduct or support cybertheft of intellectual property, and would cooperate with investigations of malicious cyberactivity originating from within their respective territories.[39] It goes without saying that this and all such declarations are counterproductive if they are not followed by implementation.

As mentioned above, a draft code that seeks to forestall cyberconflicts has already been proposed. In September 2011 four countries—China, Russia, Tajikistan, and Uzbekistan—submitted an International Code of Conduct for Information Security to UN Secretary-General Ban Ki-moon. The draft calls for a "consensus on the international norms and rules standardizing the behavior of countries concerning information and cyberspace at an early date." The document further asks states to pledge "not to use [information and communication technologies] including networks to carry out hostile activities or acts of aggression and pose threats to international peace and security."[40] Critics have found fault with this draft, suggesting it may lead to increased state censorship and control of the Internet; however, these critics have failed to propose an alternate text. It seems more constructive to amend and modify the suggested text than to dismiss it out of hand.

Technical experts have yet to determine whether countries seeking to deploy kinetic cyberweapons in the case of war would benefit if they planted malware in another country's cyberspace before carrying out such attacks. If planting malware in advance is of much benefit, both the United States and China should be able to establish an understanding that neither side will plan to use cybertools for kinetic cyberattacks by verifying whether or not malware has been planted by the other in their respective networks. True, an attacker might proceed without engaging in such preparations, just as a country might deploy a nuclear weapon without pretesting it; however, the absence of malware in a country's networks indicates some welcome level of restraint.

Sixth, the United States and China should develop a tangible plan for their behavior in the event of collapse of the North Korean government. As a RAND report describes: "As chaos develops in North Korea, the ROK [Republic of Korea], the United States, and China would all likely send special operations forces (SOF) into the North for special reconnaissance, focused in particular on North Korean WMD facilities. Somewhere, the Chinese SOF would make contact with ROK and U.S. SOF, and unintended or accidental conflict could develop . . . if conflict were to begin between the ROK-U.S. forces and the Chinese forces, that conflict could escalate significantly in ways that neither side would want."[41]

The RAND report thus recommends that both the United States and China minimize the risk of confrontation by defining a "separation line for Chinese forces versus ROK and United States forces," according to which Chinese forces would stay north of the line and both American and ROK. forces would remain south of the demarcation.[42] Policymakers implementing MAR should draw on these RAND suggestions and other similar ideas to advance an understanding between the United States and China that if North Korea's regime were to collapse, neither American nor Chinese troops would move into the country. Countries in the region would be much better off if American troops were not based next to the Yalu River and if Chinese forces were not massed next to the DMZ; such a step would reduce the danger of the United States and China clashing as a result of misunderstandings or local provocations. The demilitarization of such a buffer zone would be easy to verify using contemporary surveillance technology. Consideration should also be given to the possibility of positioning UN peacekeeping forces in the area to supervise the removal of nuclear weapons, facilitate the destruction of chemical weapons, and provide humanitarian aid to avoid a massive flood of refugees from North Korea into China or South Korea. Such understandings would encourage China to more forcefully encourage North Korea to stop developing its nuclear arsenal, consider returning to the Treaty on the Nonproliferation of Nuclear Weapons, and refrain from provocative behavior.

The seventh and last step is for both sides to do more to guarantee the flow of raw materials and transportation in the region—upon which both states depend. China is highly dependent on the import of raw materials and energy, a great deal of which arrives in China via the sea. China sees itself as highly vulnerable because the United States, which has a strong naval presence in the region, could readily block these imports.[43] Some American commentators openly discuss the option of such a blockade, which is considered a moderate way of confronting China relative to the AirSea Battle concept.[44]

In order to secure its access to the energy and raw materials on which it depends, China has been pursuing the development of an initiative called "One Belt, One Road" which seeks to develop two trade routes that thrived during earlier epochs. The first is a land-based pathway (the "One Road") through Central Asia and on to Europe, with road, rail, and pipeline projects roughly retracing the fabled Silk Road. The second is a maritime Silk Road (the "One Belt") that will see the expansion of port infrastructure and trade routes from China to South and Southeast Asia, and eventually to Africa.[45]

Both the maritime and land-based Silk Road routes are legitimate strategies for promoting trade and for allowing China to secure access to necessary resources. Nevertheless, the sea route is likely to cause more anxieties for a couple of reasons. First, the increase of China's naval presence in the South and East China Seas (discussed in chapter 3) has created considerable controversy, and in order to secure new shipping routes, China might feel that it needs to increase its presence in the disputed islands, provoking further tensions. Second, China's investments in port infrastructure in other countries has been regarded with suspicion by some who see it as an attempt to create a "string of pearls" across the Indian and Pacific Ocean, namely by investing in commercial ports that can later be used for military purposes,[46] thereby allowing China to project power well beyond its own region. In contrast, China's pursuit of land-based pathways is less conflict prone than the sea-lanes. Unfortunately, some Americans view these pathways as a sign of China's expansionist tendencies and interest in asserting global dominance.[47] In turn, some Chinese view American opposition to select pathways—for instance, a pipeline from Iran to China—as an attempt to contain China's rise. Under MAR the United States would assume, unless clear evidence is presented to the contrary, that extending land-based pathways for the flow of energy resources and raw materials will make China less inclined to build up its military, particularly the naval forces needed to secure ocean pathways—which would be a win-win for both powers.

Two of the best minds deliberating on this subject are James Steinberg and Michael O'Hanlon, whose book *Strategic Reassurance and Resolve: U.S.-China Relations in the Twenty-first Century* deserves much more attention than it has received so far.[48] Steinberg, who served as the deputy secretary of state to Hillary Clinton, is known in academic and think tank circles for his tough mind—but constructive approach—when it comes to China. O'Hanlon is a major voice in all matters concerning national security in Washington, though he is far from a dove.

The restrained approach that they outline relies much more on tit-for-tat measures of self-restraint and de-escalation (of the kind previously discussed) than on negotiated agreements. By "tit-for-tat" I mean measures that each side takes unilaterally but for which each side expects the other side to reciprocate with similar measures. The merit of a tit-for-tat approach is that it does not entail lawyerly haggling over texts, layers of approval by various departments and authorities in both nations, and above all the ratification of the US Senate (or the similar approval of a Chinese legislature), which is often unobtainable.

President John F. Kennedy's Strategy of Peace provides a powerful example of how a tit-for-tat approach can effectively reduce tensions. It was launched with a speech at American University on June 10, 1963, at the height of Cold War tensions. The president announced the first unilateral initiative: the United States was stopping all atmospheric nuclear tests and would not resume them unless another country did. The Soviet response was to publish Kennedy's speech in full in the Soviet government newspapers *Izvestia* and *Pravda,* with a combined circulation of 10 million readers—a degree of attention rarely accorded a Western leader in those days. Radio jammers in Moscow were turned off to allow Russians to listen to Voice of America's recording of the speech. This was reported in the United States and had some tension-reduction effects of its own. Soviet premier Nikita Khrushchev followed by matching the Kennedy initiative.

On June 11, the Soviet Union removed its objection to a US-favored initiative to send UN observers to war-torn Yemen. The United States reciprocated by removing its objection to the restoration of full status to the Hungarian delegation to the United Nations.

The implementation of a direct US-Russia communications link, proposed by the United States in 1962, was suddenly agreed to by the Soviet Union on June 20, 1963. True, many of these were minor steps whose value was largely symbolic, but they reduced tensions between the major powers of the day and opened the way to bilateral negotiations.

Steinberg and O'Hanlon now suggest applying a similar strategy to US-China relations (although they do not explicitly refer to it as a unilateral reciprocal approach and do include a few bilateral negotiated items in their list of twenty-two special recommendations). Thus, for example, they call for:

- "For China, level off military budget growth as military budget approaches 50 percent of the U.S. level."
- "For the United States, adapt Air-Sea Battle to Air-Sea Operations, and for China, limit development and deployment of anti-ship ballistic missiles and similar prompt attack capabilities to reduce the risk of preemption and quick escalation in crisis."

- "For China, commit to exclusively peaceful means toward Taiwan in response to U.S. commitment not to support unilateral Taiwanese declaration of independence."
- "For the United States and China, provide advance notice of military exercises and deployments in the South China Sea and East China Sea."

The authors themselves acknowledge that each of these recommendations is modest compared to the importance of the challenge of preventing the United States and China from slipping from a fairly cooperative relationship into one that leads to an arms race and confrontation. However, they correctly point out that the suggested measures point to an approach that can avoid an escalation of tensions and conflicts—and thus open the way to much bigger deals.

Above all, Steinberg and O'Hanlon stress that the United States and China are at a crossroads. Unless both nations embrace a strategy of the kind they outline (similar to one outlined in a position paper endorsed by thirty plus American and Chinese public intellectuals and former officials),[49] the two nations may well fall into Thucydides' trap.

While MAR can improve the conditions for give and take and reduce tensions, major issues must be dealt with through negotiations. The most important of these is a threat to US security that the new president will have to confront, that of North Korea. North Korea may well, in the near future, possess intercontinental missiles tipped with nuclear warheads. The development of these weapons—whose maximum range may be up to six thousand miles, and thus may be capable of targeting Los Angeles—is being pursued by a country whose leader, Kim Jong-un, is notoriously bellicose and erratic.

The United States and its allies have not found a way to rein in North Korea's accelerating nuclear program. Instead, we get political theater. Each news item about more advancements of the North Korean program is followed by statements from US officials that call on Pyongyang to behave better and on the United Nations to pass resolutions, with requests that China help rein in Pyongyang. These hollow gestures supposedly demonstrate that our leaders did not ignore the news and are doing something, but have no discernible effect. Thus, we read that the Security Council condemned the latest missile launches as a "grave violation" of North Korea's international obligations, which showed "flagrant disregard" for previous Council resolutions and statements and called for other member countries to "redouble their efforts."[50] But the United Nations left open the question of how to get tougher. David Ignatius observes that "the U.N. sanctions seem to have had no effect in curbing these provocative actions."[51] North Korea views efforts to tighten sanctions as "laughable," and "it has proven adept at skirting them, thanks largely to China, its ally and biggest trading partner, which has enforced them only laxly."[52]

China is the only power that has the capacity to force North Korea to change course. It is North Korea's only ally, as well as its biggest trading partner and its largest supplier of food, weapons, and energy. Hence, a common response to news that North Korea is moving more quickly than expected toward developing long-range missiles and miniaturized nuclear warheads is to "urge" China, or otherwise try to shame China into acting. Shortly before he left his office as secretary of defense, Ashton Carter stated, "China shares important responsibility for this development and has an important responsibility to reverse it."[53]

Governments can be shamed and are willing to make some concessions to shore up their reputations and soft power. However, there are severe limits on the extent to which one can motivate governments, in particular authoritarian regimes and rising powers such as China, to absorb the kinds of costs and challenges involved in this case solely on the basis of Western exhortations. The costs to China if it were to move to rein in North Korea are considerable. China views living with a Communist-ruled nuclear-armed state on its border as preferable to the chaos of its collapse. Shi Yinhong, a professor of international relations at Renmin University of China in Beijing, explained that the "Chinese leadership is confident that North Korea will not turn its weapons on China, and that China can control its neighbor by providing enough oil to keep its economy afloat. The alternative is a strategic nightmare for Beijing: a collapsed North Korean regime, millions of refugees piling into China and a unified Korean Peninsula under an American defense treaty."[54]

Instead, China needs to be offered a deal based on differential salience—an idea that requires some elaboration. Nations tend to differ in the weight they accord to various national interests. This makes a deal possible when Nation A makes concessions in matters that matter little to it but that matter a great deal to Nation B in exchange for concessions on matters that rank low in Nation B's priorities but that matter a great deal to Nation A.

How can the salience-based bargaining method be applied to Sino-US relations? First, the United States needs to rank its interests (not necessarily publicly). As I see it, stopping additional development of the North Korean missile and nuclear program—or, better yet, rolling it back—is very high on this list for obvious reasons. The question then is: what interest is salient enough for China to assume the high costs of pressuring North Korea to cap or cut back its program? And can the United States accommodate these interests at a low cost to itself? The best approach is to ask China what it would take to ensure its cooperation. (Its initial response may well be treated as an opening bid in a negotiation, and not the final offer.) However, for the sake of this exercise, let me try to figure out what China might seek and what the United States could quite readily afford to grant.

First of all, China might well have a high interest in gaining assurances that if the North Korean regime collapses and the two Koreas are unified, the United States will not move its troops to the border with China. (It may well prefer for the entire Korean Peninsula to become a neutral buffer zone.) This is a no- or low-cost proposition for the United States, because once the North Korean nuclear program folds or the regime collapses, the United States should be quite content not to move its troops north.

Second, China might well be very interested in the United States' committing itself not to install the Terminal High-Altitude Area Defense (THAAD) missile defense system, which is currently due to be installed in 2017 in South Korea. THAAD, the United States says, is intended to defend South Korea against North Korean missiles, and is not aimed at China. The system "does not change the strategic balance between the United States and China," President Obama said after meeting with Xi Jinping in Hangzhou recently.[55] But China is not persuaded. Chinese officials argue that the THAAD radar can detect Chinese missiles on the mainland, undermining its nuclear deterrent. Once North Korea's nuclear missile program is no longer an acute threat, the United States should be quite willing not to place THAAD in South Korea.

China may well ask for more. The United States may find that it can agree to stop the almost daily reconnaissance flights up and down China's coastlines, which China finds very troubling and which are of little value to the United States. Most of the intelligence collected in this way is of value only if one plans to attack the mainland within weeks or months. It reveals which Chinese military units are in place, who their commanders are, how they communicate, and so on. However, most of these details change over time and thus are of limited value if one believes—as most military analysts agree—that China is at least a decade away from being ready to confront the United States. China may also ask for US planes to comply with the Air Defense Identification Zone (within which all planes are required to identify themselves), which China has declared it seeks to enforce over most of the South China Sea. China may have other items it considers salient that the United States does not. These are best revealed through bargaining. My purpose here is not to guess what such a bargain will look like in the end, but merely to illustrate what I mean by a bargain based on salience differentials.

Moreover, both sides may wish to add other items to the negotiations. For instance, as I see it, the second greatest concern to the United States in the region is the risk that terrorists will get their hands on nuclear weapons in Pakistan. There have already been six such attempts, and Pakistan's nuclear arms are not well protected. China has much more leverage over Pakistan than does the United States because it is a major supplier of arms to Pakistan; in fact, over half of Pakistan's weapons imports come from China.[56] China also has much more substantial investments in Pakistan, possibly twenty times higher than those of the United States. What China will seek in return one can only guess, although it may well include the United States ceasing to arm countries that border China.

Granted, there is no guarantee that the United States and China can strike a salience-based deal. However, it seems worth trying, and it is a lot more promising than trying to cajole China, lecture it, or shame it into absorbing the kinds of costs and risks it would incur in order to rein in North Korea's nuclear program.

Liberal International Rules and the South China Sea

Most significantly, none of these trust-building exercises or mutual accommodations would threaten the United States' core interests or force it to ignore egregious violations of international law. At the same time, any use of force to change borders or gain control of seas or islands or integrate other nations into China should be considered a gross violation of the international order and not be "accommodated"; on the contrary, such moves should face a full measure of pushback. It is too late to apply this rule to Tibet and, many believe, to Taiwan, which the United States already recognizes as part of mainland China.[57] But this is not so for the South China Sea. The fact that China made very expansive claims to this sea should by itself not be considered a violation of the international order; such posturing is comparable to the kind of overreaching claims lawyers commonly make at the opening of a court case, or the demands made by labor and management during the first round of negotiations. Moreover, such positioning is far from unprecedented.[58] Canada, Russia, Denmark, and Norway have made overlapping claims to the North Pole and the Arctic Ocean, and have conducted exploratory expeditions and military exercises in the region to strengthen their positions. Ultimately, the claims will be settled before the United Nations in accordance with the UN Convention on the Law of the Sea.[59]

In contrast, given that avoiding the use of force across borders is the major foundation of the global order,[60] whether or not China is taking that fact into account should be considered the litmus test of China's conduct (and of other nations). Honoring agreements and treaties, including those at the WTO, is also essential. However, adding ever more such demands—for instance, denying a nation the status of a responsible stakeholder if it does not contribute enough to peacekeeping forces or humanitarian relief, or if it seeks to secure favorable terms of trade—is unwarranted. One should distinguish between law-abiding citizens of the international community and good citizens that voluntarily do more than is required. A nation that follows the law should be free from coercion at the hands of other nations; nations doing good should win accolades. If China is simply a law-abiding nation but neglects to go above and beyond what international law requires, that is not sufficient reason to abandon a policy of accommodation with what is, after all, a nascent and primarily regional power.

Power Sharing

Many more far reaching steps to accommodate China have been suggested by highly regarded international mavens. An informal "G2" was proposed by Zbigniew Brzezinski, who envisions a partnership comparable to what the United States already has with Japan and its close European allies. American and Chinese leaders would meet regularly for extensive discussions not only on matters pertaining to US-China relations but also on other issues of global import.[61] Another concept put forward as a nonconfrontational trajectory for the United States and China is that of "coevolution," defined by Henry Kissinger as a relationship in which each country pursues its vital domestic interests, cooperates where interests are shared, and adjusts their policies to avoid conflict.[62]

Accommodating the rise of China as a regional power by forming an Asian "concert of powers," comparable to the power-sharing arrangement that emerged in post-Napoleonic Europe, is put forth by the Australian security and foreign affairs strategist Hugh White. He suggests the great powers in the region—the United States, China, India, and Japan—negotiate "a new order in which China's authority and influence grow enough to satisfy the Chinese, and America's role remains large enough to ensure that China's power is not misused."[63] This would mean China acknowledges the legitimacy of continued American presence in the Western Pacific, and the United States allows China a sphere of influence and a redistribution of power that reflects regional realities. White acknowledges that reaching such a compromise would be politically difficult for leaders on both sides, but he believes it might be possible given that the alternative—war between nuclear-armed nations—is so catastrophic. Whether or not one holds that the United States should partner with China in governing the world (or that China has an interest in assuming such a burden) may not matter in the near future, as there are no signs that even much less demanding accommodations are under consideration by those in power. Even allowing China more influence in its region is a contentious issue. It seems that tensions between these two powers will need to be reduced before one can consider significant accommodations.

In Conclusion

There is a considerable array of steps the United States and its allies can take to move China and the West off a collision course. MAR is a strategy, outlined above, that seeks to reduce tensions between the United States and China as the two powers learn to accommodate limited, gradual changes in their relative power and roles in the region. It draws on elements already in place; while these elements were not instituted as components of MAR, they nevertheless—especially if further strengthened and extended—could serve as building blocks for such a strategy. Other elements must be added de novo.

Critics might argue that MAR deals merely with the symptoms rather than the underlying causes of friction between the United States and China or that MAR fails to recognize that the strategic goals of the two countries are inherently in conflict.[64] Regarding the first point, there are situations in which reducing a rising fever is of value while searching for more profound cures. As for the second point, MAR holds that the differences between the United States and China do not concern significant national or "core" interests and that there are few signs that China seeks to become a global power, let alone a hegemonic one. On the contrary, China seems content to allow the United States to absorb the financial and other costs of ensuring the global flow of oil, free passage on the Seven Seas, and stabilization of Middle Eastern governments.

As for regional differences, once one scrapes away any symbolic importance that can be attached to even a pile of rocks, and once one ceases to view every conciliatory move as a sign of weakness, it becomes clear that these problems can be worked out quite smoothly. This is a thesis worth testing, as both powers have a major shared interest in avoiding an arms race, let alone a war. Both sides also face pressing needs that demand they invest whatever uncommitted resources and available attention they have in nation building at home.

6

IS THE UNITED STATES TRYING TO INTEGRATE CHINA INTO THE INTERNATIONAL ORDER?

The United States often calls on China to join the prevailing international order and play by its rules. American president Barack Obama, in an interview in November 2014, "absolutely" rejected the notion that the United States seeks to contain China, and instead stated that a principal goal of his administration's China policy was to "integrate China into the global economy." Various American international experts, especially John Ikenberry, strongly favor this approach.[1]

Such a call would be best combined with recognition that these rules were mainly set shortly after World War II, when the United States was the only major power. (Germany and Japan had severely wounded the United Kingdom, Russia, and China—and the United States had devastated Germany and Japan.) Revising the rules to reflect current realities seems worth considering even if only to make the existing institutions more inviting to rising major powers. But in fact, the United States has systematically acted to make it more difficult for China to be integrated into the existing international order.

I turn first to present a brief case study which demonstrates how the United States in effect stood in the way of China's responses to demands that it contribute more to the development of developing nations (part 1). Then, I consider how the United States worked to hinder the integration of China into key international institutions, and the implications of these efforts (part 2). Finally, I draw on these findings to differentiate between what might be considered two rather different kinds of containment (part 3).

I. US Efforts to Block China's New Development Bank

The United States has repeatedly called on China to shoulder part of the burden of international duties such as peacekeeping and humanitarian aid. In 2013 China launched a new multilateral development bank called the Asian Infrastructure Investment Bank (AIIB). In the following pages we shall see that the United States refused to join the bank and pressured its allies and other states to do the same; nevertheless, many states applied to be founding members of the new international institution. We will also see that the United States offered a variety of explanations for its position, but these rationales do not stand up well to close examination.

The launching of the AIIB and the United States' response are by themselves of limited importance and likely to be soon forgotten as a minor diplomatic brouhaha. However, the formation of the bank and the US response cast light on two issues of much greater importance: the difficulties the United States faces when seeking to "integrate" China into existing international institutions (part 2), and the difference between multifaceted containment and aggression containment (part 3).

China Launches the AIIB

In late 2013 China proposed the creation of the Asian Infrastructure Investment Bank, a new development bank that would specifically cater to Asia and to the development of regional infrastructure.[2] From the onset, the AIIB was intended as a multilateral institution. States were invited to participate by providing funds for the new bank and participating in its management. By late October 2014, twenty-one Asian states had signed a memorandum of understanding to establish the bank,[3] indicating their intentions to serve as founding members.[4] China furnished most of the bank's initial $50 billion in capital,[5] but its voting stake is estimated to be about 28.5 percent of the total.[6] Like other such banks, the AIIB is very likely to raise considerably more funds by issuing bonds.

Despite the United States' opposition to the AIIB and its calls on its allies and other states to steer clear of the new bank,[7] China released a list of fifty-seven prospective founding members of the bank on April 16, 2015. The list includes nearly all Asian and many Western European countries, such as the United Kingdom, France, Germany, and Italy, as well as all of the BRICS countries.[8] Several states that initially did not seek to join, owing to US pressure, are reconsidering their position, including Japan.[9] These founding members turned to negotiate the AIIB charter in May 2015.[10] In response, the United States has suggested collaboration between the AIIB and existing institutions like the World Bank or the Asian Development Bank.[11]

Experts have nearly universally concluded that the United States' attempts to block the establishment of the AIIB were embarrassing and misguided. The *Economist* characterized the AIIB's story as one of "a victorious campaign against American-led scepticism. American attempts to persuade its friends to shun the AIIB seemed merely churlish."[12] Robert Zoellick wrote in June 2015 that the Obama administration's treatment of the AIIB had been an "embarrassing experience."[13] Hugh White, the Australian strategist, called US attempts to block the AIIB "a massive diplomatic failure."[14] Lawrence Summers, the former US Treasury secretary, called it a "failure of strategy and tactics,"[15] and Robert Keatley, a career journalist with extensive experience in China, said the effort "failed miserably."[16] Other experts chimed in to call it "a major strategic blunder," "a new and embarrassing low," "ironic," "hypocritical," and a "folly."[17] Madeleine Albright simply said, "We screwed it up."[18]

Rationales for the United States' Position

The United States advanced several arguments to justify its position vis-à-vis the AIIB; however, none of these stand up to close scrutiny. Most notably, the United States expressed concerns that the AIIB would fail to follow proper accounting procedures or what management experts call "best practices."[19] The National Security Council maintained, "We believe any new multilateral institution should incorporate the high standards of the World Bank and the regional development banks. Based on many discussions, we have concerns about whether the AIIB will meet these high standards, particularly related to governance, and environmental and social safeguards."[20] The United States also expressed concern about "unhealthy debt buildups, human-rights abuses, and environmental risks"[21] as well as about China's ability to model or enforce transparency, good governance, anticorruption mechanisms, protections for the poor and vulnerable, and intellectual property rights within the AIIB and in AIIB-funded projects.[22] Many of these concerns, especially about standards of governance and transparency in lending, have been advanced directly by Obama administration officials.[23] These arguments ignore that by joining the AIIB, the United States and other Western states could work to ensure that it follows proper practices.[24]

Moreover, the United States participates in and supports numerous international organizations that themselves do not fully embrace best practices, to put it mildly; the United Nations is one rather major example. Claims that the AIIB will not promote human rights are well founded, but to demand that China—or any other state—change its basic regime and ethos and embrace values championed by the West in order for its economic development assistance to be welcomed seems, in effect, to rule out any participation in international enterprises and institutions.

In addition, the United States has justified its opposition on the grounds that the AIIB will compete with other multilateral financial organizations, most notably the World Bank and the Asian Development Bank. However, the AIIB specializes in infrastructure; the other organizations do not. Moreover, the Asia-Pacific's need for infrastructure funding is huge and unmet—by some estimates, as high as $800 billion a year.[25] Another estimate puts the number at $8 trillion between 2010 and 2020. As Matthew Goodman of the Center for Strategic and International Studies put it, "There's a big infrastructure gap in Asia, [and] existing institutions are not filling it."[26] There is ample room for all of the development banks to invest. Indeed, World Bank President Jim Yong Kim stated, "From the perspective simply of the need for more infrastructure spending, there's no doubt that from our perspective, we welcome the entry of the Asian Infrastructure Investment Bank."[27]

Also, having a development bank besides the World Bank is far from unprecedented. In addition to the already mentioned Asian Development Bank, other such banks include the Development Bank of Latin America, the African Development Bank, and the Inter-American Development Bank. If there is some competition among these banks, it seems odd for Western policymakers to oppose or to seek to curb competition, which is considered the essence of sound free market economics and capitalism.

Finally, the United States worries that the AIIB will funnel infrastructure projects to Chinese contractors and serve as a way to twist the arm of Asian states that need infrastructure funding in such a way as to suit "Chinese political objectives."[28] However, the AIIB's multilateral governance should greatly alleviate this problem. Notably, China announced that it will not exercise veto power at the AIIB.[29] In any case, using investment, credits, or humanitarian aid to secure political objectives is far from unknown in other such international organizations. For example, the International Monetary Fund granted Ukraine a $17.5 billion loan in 2015, to be disbursed over four years, as part of a broader $40 billion program.[30] This grant sought to support the struggling regime, and was not granted solely on standards of merit.[31]

Indeed, the United States has little cause to hold that granting an emerging state economic assistance will induce it to favor the granting state; it turns out that such granting states often gain rather little leverage over the beneficiaries of their support and that whatever leverage they gain is often temporary. In fact, recipient states often are rather hostile to their benefactors. This is the United States' experience in much of South America, Central America, and elsewhere; now China is experiencing similar reactions from states in Africa.[32]

2. Integrating China into the Liberal International Order

Some supporters of the United States' rejection of the AIIB argue that China should not form its own international institutions but rather should increase its contributions to existing ones. They hold that the AIIB and similar institutions are designed to compete with the liberal international order as it currently exists and will cause "a fraying of global governance"[33] by "asking countries to choose between the existing arrangements or the new ones," thereby "[helping] to undermine and destroy the current international world order."[34] They argue that China should learn to abide by the prevailing international rules and should join and contribute to the already existing international institutions formed by the West. G. John Ikenberry and Robert B. Zoellick, among others, have articulated this position, although they recognize that the liberal international order may require some limited modifications to accommodate China.[35] As will be seen presently, the United States has been reluctant to offer such accommodations to China in existing international institutions.

The WTO

The United States made it difficult for China to join and exercise influence commensurate with its status in the WTO. Some argued that the United States should entirely block China's participation in the WTO.[36] Instead, the United States engaged in fifteen years of negotiations that ended only in 2001—one of the "longest accession negotiations in the history of the GATT/WTO."[37] The resulting terms of the accession were particularly exacting; in all, China had to make 685 commitments leading to 7,000 reductions in trade barriers.[38] These terms were notably more stringent than those applied to other countries that sought membership.[39] Observers called these "the most complex and ambitious commitment made to GATT/WTO over the years,"[40] and "the most onerous requirements placed on any member to join the organization."[41] Another observer noted, "Never in the history of the world has a country committed so much, on a voluntary basis, to change as China has done to adhere to the rules of the World Trade Organization."[42] Indeed, China viewed these concessions as deeply embarrassing.[43]

The World Bank

The World Bank was created after World War II as one of the Bretton Woods Institutions. China only joined the World Bank in 1980, and has since expressed growing discontent with its voting share in the organization. The United States, which traditionally nominates the bank's leader, usually nominates an American.

In 2001 the voting structure of the bank was "determined by each country's shares and capital contribution to the Bank's coffers," such that the United States held 16.96 percent of the Bank's shares and 16.49 percent of the votes on the bank's executive board.[44] In practice, the world's five richest countries controlled roughly 40 percent of the votes on the executive board, compared to a mere 4 percent controlled by forty-four countries in Africa.[45] The United States exercised "de facto veto power" over attempts to amend the bank's charter, and the bank president was, "by gentlemen's agreement, always American and traditionally the exclusive choice of the US president."[46]

After years of calls for reform of the World Bank's voting structure, some reform was undertaken in 2010, which afforded a slightly greater voice to some of the most important emerging economies, including China.[47] Nevertheless, the current voting structure of the World Bank remains a weighted system in which each member state has an equal number of "basic votes" as well as further votes determined by the amount of funds the state is committed to contributing to the bank's pool of lending capital (i.e., a state's "quota").[48] In practice, the shift amounted to a 3.13 percent change in the balance of voting power between developed and emerging economies, and the United States did not lose any of its voting share. The change has been called "primarily symbolic."[49] Even under the new voting structure, China only has a voting share of 4.42 percent, compared to the United States' 16.4 percent and Japan's 7.9 percent,[50] which is at odds with China's economic size and global role.

The voting structure thus remains "overwhelmingly dominated by rich countries" and "illegitimate and outdated."[51] China's move to establish the AIIB is reported to reflect "China's open dissatisfaction" with the influence the United States wields at the World Bank and other existing international financial institutions.[52] Many analysts agree that China's establishment of the AIIB was in part caused by "the U.S. Congress' refusal to approve legislation giving China greater voting rights at the IMF and World Bank following the global financial crisis."[53]

The IMF

When the IMF was first conceptualized, the member states that planned to contribute most to its funding reserves rejected a one-country-one-vote system on the grounds that their contributions warranted greater control over the ways their money was disbursed to developing countries.[54] Thus, the IMF's voting system was formed in such a way that the number of each member state's votes correlates to the amount of funding they provide, which in turn correlates to the size of their economy. As of 2006, this meant that each member state received "250 'basic' votes, plus one additional vote for every 100,000 SDR [an IMF reserve currency] of its quota."[55] Thus, the voting share of any given member state is based on a complex and, some say, obscure set of formulas to determine the amount of funding a member state is obliged to contribute to the collective pool of reserve funds. These formulas incorporate select metrics of economic size, and member states negotiate quotas every five years based on the results of the formulas.

There is much criticism of the IMF's voting system and of the quotas accorded to each member state; in particular, some hold that the system shortchanges states such as China. Although a bias exists that favors developing and emerging economies, which are technically overrepresented in voting share compared to their economic size, many smaller member states still "[lacked a] meaningful, equitable, or effective voice" in the IMF insofar as even this overrepresentation paled in comparison to the disproportionate voting share wielded by the United States.[56] Proposed reforms included changing the number of basic votes allocated to member states in order to dilute the impact of quota share on voting share, consensually negotiating quota redistributions without amending the charter, implementing consensus-based decision making, changing the structure of the executive board to increase the representation of developing and emerging economies, divorcing voting shares from quota share and instead pegging them to economic importance, or adding or revising variables to the formulas used to determine quotas.[57]

Although the Obama administration negotiated alterations to the IMF's voting structure that would have accorded China and other "emerging economies" more influence, Congress has blocked these alterations from being ratified,[58] even though the United States' own voting share would not decrease.[59] As of April 2015, out of the fund's 188 members, 147 had accepted an amendment that would restructure the executive board, representing 77.24 percent of the votes—just shy of the 85 percent needed to adopt the amendment. China has ratified the agreement; the United States, however, has so far failed to ratify it.[60] The same is true of changes to quota allocations that would "shift voting power to emerging economies."[61] The Obama administration has called on Congress to ratify these reforms, but Republicans in the House blocked them, including the capital increase the Obama administration agreed to in 2010. The finance ministers of other members of the G20 presented the United States with "an ultimatum" that threatened that "if the 2010 reforms are not ratified by year-end, we will call on the IMF to build on its existing work and develop options for next steps" for bypassing the United States.[62] As of 2015, the basic format of the IMF's voting system has not changed; each member state retains equal "basic" votes, and further votes still are based on each state's "allocation of 'special drawing rights' (SDRs)."[63]

The TPP

The United States excluded China from the negotiations that could have led to its participation in the Trans-Pacific Partnership (TPP), a large-scale trade agreement that was agreed upon in October 2015, but later abandoned, following Donald Trump's election. The TPP originated from the 2005 Trans-Pacific Strategic Economic Partnership (TPSEP) among Brunei, Chile, New Zealand, and Singapore. The United States became involved informally in the expansion of the TPSEP in 2008–9[64] and later led the negotiations to form the TPP,[65] negotiations that included twelve countries (Australia, Brunei, Canada, Chile, Japan, Malaysia, Mexico, New Zealand, Peru, Singapore, the United States, and Vietnam). Although American officials stated that China was welcome to join the TPP, the United States effectively set prerequisites for inclusion that China would be unable to meet without profound regime changes, prerequisites that were not used to exclude Singapore or Vietnam from the negotiations. There would have been many benefits to joining the TPP, given that the proposed trade agreement covered 40 percent of the world's GDP and 26 percent of global trade.[66]

It would have been in China's economic interest to join the TPP.[67]

The benefits of joining would hypothetically include a 4.7 percent boost to its national income over ten years.[68] The chief economist of China's central banks has stated that China's joining the TPP would "increase the size of its economy by about 2 percent."[69] It would also have conferred a degree of legitimacy on China, offered China the opportunity to help to shape the formation of an important multilateral trade agreement, and helped China reform its economy. Accordingly, China has expressed that it is "open" to joining the TPP.[70] In February 2015 Deputy Secretary of State Antony Blinken stated that China's attitude toward the TPP had shifted from one of "rejecting" the TPP to becoming "quite interested" in participation in the negotiations and eventual partnership."

The United States claimed that excluding China from the TPP negotiations did not signal that the TPP was a means of containing, isolating, or otherwise negatively impacting China, contrary to China's complaints.[71] Indeed, American officials indicated that China could participate in the negotiations. National Security Advisor Susan Rice stated in November 2013, "We welcome any nation that is willing to live up to the high standards of this agreement to join and share in the benefits of the TPP, and that includes China."[72] Her statement echoed almost verbatim the statement made by then secretary of state Hillary Clinton in 2012: "We welcome the interest of any nation willing to meet the 21st century standards of the TPP, including China."[73] The problem was that the standards the United States set for China to qualify to participate in the TPP were so high as to have effectively precluded its participation. These include respect for human rights, transparency, crackdowns on hacking and cyber industrial espionage,[74] and meeting demanding definitions of free trade and open markets,[75] including reductions to trade barriers (which one Chinese official said were "an American trap for China, a threshold we can't possibly reach").[76]

Several commentators and officials with access to the negotiations hold that the Obama administration viewed the issue in terms of curbing China's influence in the Asia-Pacific.[77] They suggested that the efforts to form the TPP were intended in part to exclude and isolate China.[78] Thus, according to Senator Charles E. Schumer, the Obama administration had privately emphasized the TPP's centrality to the project of preventing China from developing a sphere of influence in the Asia-Pacific: "When the administration sells me on this, it's all geopolitics, not economics: We want to keep these countries in our orbit, not China's."[79] Indeed, the United States included Vietnam as part of the TPP despite its poor human rights record, according to the US State Department itself, as part of a broader coordinated response to the rise of China.[80]

Ashley Tellis, from the Carnegie Endowment for International Peace, advocates using economic arrangements to "consolidate the economic and technological power of the West" and "mitigat[e]" the "dangers of China's rise . . . through an economic strategy," namely, "keeping China out of these regional FTAs [free trade agreements, including the TPP] for as long as possible."[81] Other parties to the TPP perceived the partnership largely as a means of countering Chinese influence, and the TPP was central to the United States' continued influence and credibility among these states.

Chas Freeman noted in 2015 that "no country in Asia wants to choose between political allegiance to the United States and economic alignment with China. Nor can any country in the region be forced into such a choice. Efforts by Washington to do so create a zero-sum game with zero appeal."[82]

Although the United States will not be pursuing the TPP any further, it serves as a particularly poignant example of the United States' not only attempting to put hurdles in China's way but actively working to exclude China.

Major Implications

Calls to "integrate" China into the prevailing liberal international order (an order that was formed largely by the United States in line with the values it cherishes and out of its newfound status as a dominant power after World War II) often suggest that China should abide by the existing rules because they are inherently good (i.e., reflect liberal, "Wilsonian" values),[83] because they serve the world community by maintaining peace and stability, or because other states abide by them. However, as the preceding discussion suggests, the United States is seeking to integrate China only as long as the United States can maintain its dominant position in international institutions and in the world order. It is not enough for China to play by the rules; it must not gain a significant share of the power to run these institutions. To argue that the United States is out to have its cake (by asking states to make concessions in order to qualify as members of the liberal international order) and eat it too (by dominating the system) may be to put the thesis too strongly.

Indeed, the United States seems to share power within these institutions to some limited extent, especially with its close allies such as the United Kingdom and Japan. However, the United States is clearly unwilling to accord influence to China in these institutions that would be commensurate with China's size, contributions, or growing power.

Moreover, as power transition theorists point out, when a new power rises, the established power must make some concessions in order to avoid war.[84] In the area under discussion, this suggests that the United States should agree to some modifications to the rules, and not just as they pertain to the distribution of power within institutions as they currently exist.

For example, Ikenberry states that China should be permitted to influence the international order to some extent, in accordance with its own values. "The challenges of reforming and renegotiating [the] liberal world order are, if anything, welcome ones," Ikenberry writes. These modifications will be relatively minor, he holds, in part because "all the great powers have alignments of interests that will continue to bring them together to negotiate and cooperate over the management of the system. All the great powers—old and new—are status-quo powers. All are beneficiaries of an open world economy and the various services that the liberal international order provides for capitalist trading states."[85]

And Michael Swaine points out that the viability of an effort to turn China into a "responsible stakeholder," as proposed by Robert Zoellick (see chapter 4), is contingent upon the degree to which the United States is able to accommodate Chinese interests, particularly in the political and security arena.[86]

However, the record so far suggests that the United States and its allies have shown great reluctance to make such changes. Freud famously held that there are no accidents, and that behaviors that seem random or irrational can be shown to serve "subterranean" needs.[87] The same holds for societies and states. The formation of the AIIB and above all the United States' reaction to the bank's launch are not accidental; they reflect a basic underlying power structure and the established power's strong reluctance to accommodate a rising one. Moreover, as the next part of this discussion indicates, the United States' reaction to China's rise has taken a particularly tension-engendering form, one that could be avoided without undermining the United States' role as the super power.

3. Multifaceted versus Aggression-Limiting Containment

The United States often states that it does not seek to contain China.[88] Thus, in April 2014 President Barack Obama stated, "Our goal is not to counter China. Our goal is not to contain China."[89] Secretary of State John Kerry repeated the sentiment a month later, saying that the "U.S. does not seek to contain China."[90] However, there are often great discrepancies between the statements made by top officials and the conduct of the states they speak for. The actions of the United States reflect a containment strategy that seems to have evolved—rather than developed—through complex interactions among various agencies, with the Pentagon being particularly influential (see chapter 1).

The strategy's main element involves positioning military forces or allied forces along China's borders and in the regional areas into which it might seek to extend. Thus, the United States has announced that it views the contested Senkaku Islands to be covered by the Treaty of Mutual Cooperation and Security between the United States and Japan, while also encouraging Japan to build up its military. The United States has also developed military ties with Vietnam; reopened its military bases in the Philippines; provided India with nuclear know-how and access to uranium, in violation of the Nonproliferation Treaty, as a means of inciting India to "balance" China; and moved troops and naval vessels to the area, among many other such actions. In sum, these moves all draw a red line that, if crossed by China, could lead to war. The Asia pivot thus appears to be "a thinly veiled China containment strategy."[91]

John Mearsheimer has pointed out that involving regional states in various military alliances raises the risk that the United States and China will engage in war owing to reckless actions taken by one of the allies.[92] Barry Posen concurs, and points out that an alliance with the United States gives allies a false sense of security and encourages them "to challenge more powerful states, confident that Washington will save them in the end,"[93] a point that also applies to China–North Korea relations.

At the same time, one may argue that the most basic foundation of the international order is that states may not use force to change the status quo and must not invade other states; this tenet is even accepted by many of those who do not necessarily accept the liberal elements of the existing order. Thus, one might argue that for the United States to position its military forces or allied forces in places into which China could consider expanding would help stabilize the international order. However, the same conclusion cannot be reached for other elements of American policy toward China, as highlighted by the United States' response to the AIIB's launch, which itself was of limited import.

One Kind of Containment Is Worse than the Other

To proceed, I suggest a distinction between a strategy of all-encompassing containment and a strategy that combines containment in some sectors (especially the military sector) with competition in others (especially the economic and ideational sectors) and with integration in still other sectors (especially the governance of international institutions). To distinguish between these two kinds of containment, I refer to the first as *multifaceted containment* and the second as *aggression-limiting containment*. Multifaceted containment seeks to block practically any and all gains of another state, whether territorially, economically, or in status, in voting rights, or through some other form of advancement. By contrast, aggression-limiting containment seeks to block only those advances that are made through the use of force, while granting room for competition in other sectors as well as cooperation in still other sectors. It is useful to think about aggression-limiting containment as a flashing red light in some lanes and a green one in others, as opposed to multifaceted containment as a barrier that blocks all lanes. Or, aggression-limited containment is the strategy preferred by Engagers, whereas Adversarians may be drawn to multifaceted containment.

In a previous book, I examined how the United States sought to contain the USSR during the Cold War, and showed that the United States sought multifaceted containment.[94] Thus, if the USSR sought landing rights for its civilian aviation in Bolivia, the United States sought to block them. If the USSR granted foreign aid to Ghana, the United States pressured Ghana to reject it. The United States sought to suppress USSR ideological and cultural outreach. The USSR treated the United States in the same manner, and the result was high levels of tension that led several times to the brink of nuclear war. When President John F. Kennedy unveiled his "Strategy of Peace," he scaled back these nonmilitary forms of containment, which resulted in considerably diminished tensions— a détente.[95]

US efforts to contain China have not been limited to countering Chinese aggression—to positioning military forces, building military alliances, conducting more military exercises, and ordering major weapons systems to respond to a possible attack from China, all of which it has done. Instead, the United States has also sought to block China in other, nonmilitary sectors. For example, the United States pressured states on China's borders to resist China's economic overtures; blocked Chinese efforts to begin negotiations on a free-trade zone spanning the Pacific;[96] cautioned regional states against depending too strongly on China for humanitarian aid and pledged $187 million to Cambodia, Laos, Thailand, and Vietnam in an effort to decrease China's influence over those states;[97] and seems to be diplomatically and economically working to halt the expansion of Chinese influence in Africa[98] and Latin America.[99] The United States also notably encouraged states in the Western Pacific region to handle China multilaterally. For example, without involving its military, the United States has quietly favored ASEAN's involvement in solving territorial disputes in the South China Sea;[100] China, meanwhile, would prefer bilateral negotiations because they increase the likelihood that the dispute would be resolved more favorably for China.[101] US actions regarding the AIIB fit this pattern. They seem to indicate that the United States is leaning toward multifaceted containment in its drive to contain China.

There are strong reasons for the United States and the international community not only to oppose changes to the status quo brought about by the use of force but also to provide institutional channels through which differences can be worked out in an equitable and peaceful way. The United States and its allies should facilitate Chinese membership in existing international institutions and modify them to accommodate the legitimate considerations of China and other new members. Established powers should also grant countries like China a proper voice in managing these institutions. These steps—part of an aggression-limiting containment strategy—would help minimize the risk of major conflict with China. This is because containment that is limited to curbing aggression (i.e., aggression that uses force, not the "aggressive" articulation of claims or "aggressive" speech) is much less conflict prone than multifaceted containment. Such aggression-limiting containment provides outlets for the energy generated by the rising power, rather than bottling it up everywhere it turns.

Aggression-limiting containment also enables the rising power to find legitimate ways to attend to its core interests. This generalization applies in particular to the AIIB. China has a strong interest in ensuring a secure flow of raw materials and energy, because its economy depends on massive imports of these goods. Also, China specifically favors the development of land-based pathways across Central Asia to secure the flow of raw materials and energy, as discussed in chapter 5. The AIIB serves as one building block in such a construction. The United States does not claim that it is charged with controlling the roads, railways, pipelines, and other elements of the infrastructure of Central Asia in the same way that it maintains it is obligated to uphold the freedom of navigation in the South and East China Seas and the rest of the world.

The United States and China have a variety of "track 1" channels for cooperating on and discussing issues important to the two states. For example, in September 2015 the two states held joint meetings to address cybersecurity concerns and are reported to have arrived at an "important consensus" about how best to fight cyberattacks.[102] And the United States and China in June 2015 signed an agreement to "deepen" military cooperation between the two states,[103] and for the first time, China was invited in June 2014 to join naval drills held by the United States.[104] Before then, in 2009, the two states initiated a new annual meeting known as the US-China Strategic and Economic Dialogue, of which there have now been seven rounds.[105] However, this track of diplomacy does not seem to be leading to much change regarding the main substantive points of contention between the two states. As James Clad and Ron Wahid point out, the veneer of positivity that follows these meetings "evaporate[s]" quickly.[106]

Neither the United States nor China seems to have moved toward supporting extensive development of unofficial or "track 2" channels for resolving conflict between the two states. Clusters of track 2 diplomatic initiatives and organizations to which both American and Chinese experts and scholarly institutions are parties include the Northeast Asia Cooperation Dialogue and the Council for Security Cooperation in the Asia Pacific,[107] and track 2 diplomacy between the two has arguably helped ease tensions in the past,[108] but little scholarship seems to exist on the extent or effectiveness of track 2 diplomacy between experts from both countries. Indeed, participants in track 2 diplomatic meetings between American and Chinese experts have noted that a serious disconnect exists between the meetings that do take place and resulting policy or government action.[109] David M. Lampton of the Johns Hopkins School of Advanced International Studies points out, "One of the problems we have in US-China relations now is that we basically don't know these people" or the unofficial proxies that existed between Chinese and

American leaders during periods of past tension.[110] The underdevelopment of Sino-American track 2 diplomatic channels contrasts starkly with the relative wealth of unofficial, track 2 channels for resolving tensions that exist between the United States and Russia, many of which were begun during the Cold War and are now well established.[111] Indeed, scientific and other unofficial cooperation between experts from both the United States and Russia dates back more than fifty years.[112]

In short, we have seen that the United States has not adequately accommodated China in these international institutions, and that an aggression-limiting containment strategy is preferable to the multifaceted containment strategy currently in place.

7

TO CONTAIN OR NOT?
WHEN AND WHERE IS THE QUESTION

The United States often says that it seeks a constructive, cooperative, and comprehensive relationship with China. To provide but one example, President Obama stated in March 2016 that "the United States welcomes the rise of a peaceful, stable, and prosperous China, working with us to address global challenges."[1] However, American actions often reveal moves toward containment. These actions include reopening American military bases in the Philippines, forming military alliances with Vietnam, stationing more naval vessels in the Pacific, positioning marines in Australia, building a missile defense shield in South Korea, conducting military exercises that practice invading a country like China, and above all, encouraging the military buildup of Japan.

These are all legal acts as far as international law is concerned, and have been carried out with the consent of the nations involved. However, to China they give the appearance of the United States and its allies marshaling military forces along its borders, with the United States giving these nations a finger on the trigger that could start a major US-China confrontation.

I am not arguing that China's feelings should decide American foreign policy. If the United States has concluded that it cannot or is unlikely to work out its differences with China in a peaceful manner, containment might well be warranted. However, it seems that since China is, at the very least, a decade away from posing any kind of military threat to the United States and its allies, containment is premature, and it has considerable costs. It undermines the credibility of America's statements that it seeks diplomacy and negotiated solutions to differences with China, it costs billions of dollars that are direly needed for nation building at home, and it leads to some very unwise moves, to put it mildly. The most troubling of these moves is discussed next. It concerns the acceleration of the nuclear arms race between India and Pakistan, and the increasing probability that terrorists will get their hands on nuclear weapons—all in order to push India to play a role in containing China. This effort, as we will see, has cost the world a great deal in terms of safety, but achieved rather little in terms of containment.

The Threat (Background)

It is widely agreed that a major threat to the security of the United States and its allies is the combination of terrorism and nuclear arms. Currently, the most likely place for terrorists to acquire such a weapon is in Pakistan. Although various measures have been undertaken to improve the security of Pakistan's weapons, the West is concerned about its safety, given that Pakistan, suspicious of the United States, has rejected America's offers to help further secure these arms. Western powers realize that they are unaware of the location of all these weapons. And attacks on Pakistani military bases raise concerns that one day nuclear weapons may get into the wrong hands.

This is not a hypothetical scenario; there have already been several attacks by terrorist groups at Pakistani nuclear facilities. In November 2007, a nuclear missile storage facility in Sargodha was attacked; the following month, a suicide bomber attacked a nuclear airbase at Kamra.[2] In August 2008, suicide bombers affiliated with the Pakistani Taliban blew up several entry points at one of Pakistan's main nuclear weapons assembly plants in Wah.[3] A 2011 attack, on a highly secured naval base in Karachi, is reported to have been aided by al-Qaeda infiltration of the Pakistani army.[4] And in 2012 a base thought to house some of Pakistan's nuclear weapons in Kamra was attacked.[5]

The West is also concerned that even if terrorists cannot acquire nuclear arms by usurping them or gaining them from supporters within the Pakistani armed forces, insurgents may topple the government. The government is weak and unstable, and anti-American sentiments in Pakistan are widespread and intense.

The Deal: Feeding the Devil to Exorcise a Ghost

During much of the Cold War, the West viewed India as leaning toward the Soviet bloc and Pakistan as a staunch anticommunist ally. Pakistan played a major role in helping the United States drive the USSR out of Afghanistan, and over the decades of the Cold War, Pakistan received considerable amounts of foreign aid, military aid, equipment, and training from the United States, while India was largely spurned.

By 2000, however, the United States was increasingly concerned about the rise of China as a superpower and was looking for ways to "balance" it. Washington believed that India could play a key role in this new geopolitical landscape. Additionally, India, as a democratic and economically successful nation, was held up as a countermodel to the Chinese model of state capitalism, which had a growing appeal among developing countries. As a result, the United States "tilted" toward India by expanding bilateral cooperation and investment in a number of areas. These overtures were capped by the signing of a nuclear cooperation deal in 2008.

Up to this point, India and Pakistan had been barred for decades from nuclear trade with the West because the two countries had not signed the Non-Proliferation Treaty.[6] Such a ban is a core element of both the treaty's letter and spirit, aimed at discouraging states from building nuclear arms. The Bush administration ignored this long-standing ban, providing American aid to India's civilian nuclear energy program and expanding US-India cooperation in nuclear technology. True, this assistance was to be used only for nonmilitary purposes. However, by allowing the sale of uranium to India for its civilian reactors, the United States enabled India to reallocate the limited amount of uranium it had to military use. (Before then, to make more nuclear bombs, Indian power plants were operating at reduced capacity.)

The Bush administration justified these steps by claiming they would help improve American relations with India, which the United States considered the West's best hope to "balance" China.[7] The deal was highly controversial in India;[8] indeed, it took years of wrangling before it was finally approved by India in August 2010.

In response to the Bush administration's deal with India, Pakistan increased its nuclear program on its own by rapidly expanding its plutonium production, and China granted Pakistan two more reactors as part of an agreement parallel to the US-India one. (Some might argue that the China-Pakistan deal was underway before the US-India one. Although this is true, the China-Pakistan deal was not implemented until after the US-India one.)

Pakistan expanded its nuclear arsenal from sixty warheads in 2007 to more than one hundred in early 2011.[9] As of April 2016, Pakistan was estimated to have between 110 and 130 nuclear weapons, although it could have more.[10] Its fourth nuclear reactor became operational in 2015.[11] Pakistan has also introduced short-range tactical nuclear weapons, carried by mobile Nasr missiles, in response to India's "Cold Start" doctrine (which calls for limited conventional attacks against Pakistan that are designed to stay below Pakistan's strategic nuclear threshold).[12] Such mobile tactical nuclear weapons are particularly difficult to secure.

The nuclear arms race between Pakistan and India appears to be moving underwater as well. In February 2016, India's first ballistic missile submarine completed sea trials, including weapons release tests.[13] Pakistan is currently working to modify its nuclear-capable cruise missile for launch from its current submarines.[14] India's naval nuclear ambitions are being driven by a desire to have an effective sea-based deterrent; Pakistan is in turn stepping up its naval nuclear ambitions to avoid any imbalance with India.[15] Both India and Pakistan are reported to be delegating responsibility for launch control to field officers aboard the submarines (as opposed to the command–and-control hierarchies for land-based nuclear weapons), significantly increasing the risk of incidental firing.[16]

As far as containment is concerned, India continues to be a very reluctant container. As Ted Galen Carpenter of the Cato Institute notes, Delhi never had much enthusiasm for a "crude, anti-China partnership with the United States." Although India has been quite content to improve its relations with Washington, and remained uneasy about China's growing influence, it "had no desire to become Washington's geopolitical cat's paw."[17] Nuclear assistance notwithstanding, India is much more dependent on China than on the United States. The $4 billion of American investments in India that President Obama announced in January 2015 is dwarfed by the $20 billion pledged by President Xi several months earlier.[18] In short, Indian "containment" of China, such as it is, was purchased at a heavy price, at a time when it seems hardly needed. Moreover, it is pushing Pakistan closer to China.

Daniel Markey at the Council on Foreign Relations has noted that Pakistani officials talk openly about China as a "strategic alternative to the United States."[19] The government has described China as an "all weather friend" (a pointed contrast to the United States, which is often characterized as only a fair-weather friend). China benefits from an alliance with Pakistan by gaining an alternate route for its energy and raw material supplies.[20] In 2011 China announced the sale of fifty fighter jets to Islamabad. The fighter, known as the JF-17, was developed jointly between Pakistan and China.[21] In 2013 the two countries reached a deal to build two new nuclear power plants in Karachi with Chinese financing.[22] In 2015 Pakistan announced that it had agreed to purchase eight Yuan-class submarines from China, which are meant to give it anti-access/area denial capabilities against India.[23] In 2015 Pakistan produced sixteen JF-17 fighters and plans to produce twenty-four in 2016.[24] Seventy percent of its tanks are Chinese. China allowed Pakistan to test its first nuclear device on Chinese soil and aided in its transportation of missiles purchased from North Korea.[25] The two nations also conducted five joint military exercises.[26]

Furthermore, China has made investments in Pakistan's infrastructure, including construction of the deep-sea port of Gwadar and the Karakoram Highway, a roadway that connects China to Pakistan.[27] China's investments in Pakistan constitute Beijing's biggest commitment to any one country, with other announced projects including a high-speed railway and an oil pipeline from the Arabian Sea to the province of Xinjiang, on the other side of the Himalayas.[28]

In Conclusion

The United States might well need to contain China by military means if China uses its military forces to invade other nations and annex them as it did with Tibet in 1950, or if China uses "volunteers" similar to Putin's strategy in Ukraine. Containment might be necessary even earlier, if there are signs that China is moving in such an aggressive direction. However, given China's current military weaknesses, decelerating economic growth, and pressing domestic needs, a containment strategy seems premature. Moving to help India and Pakistan settle their differences and decelerating the nuclear arms race will make a great deal of sense for the next American administration if it assumes that, while China may need to be contained in the future, hedging for peace is the preferred course for now.

8

ARMED HUMANITARIAN INTERVENTIONS VERSUS REGIME CHANGES

Many of the issues raised with regard to the US-China relationship concern sovereignty. In particular, China claims sovereignty over much of the South China Sea, as do several other nations in the region. As we have seen previously, there are questions and concerns about whether China's claims on contested reefs or islands grant China territorial rights over the waters surrounding them. These questions and concerns reflect the broader question of what grants sovereignty. Indeed, few issues are more likely to inflame public opinion and international relations than violations of sovereignty. In effect, though, we shall see next that there has been a fairly strong movement to downgrade sovereignty, one in which China has participated. This movement has expressed specifically the right of nations to use their armed forces to interfere in the internal affairs of other states, especially to prevent genocide, a right often referred to as the Responsibility to Protect (RtoP). China has voted for this major change in international law and norms. However, the movement runs into trouble when the United States and its allies use RtoP as one way to legitimate interventions that seek to change regimes rather than merely prevent genocide. China, Russia, and many other nations have opposed this conduct. To protect RtoP, I suggest clearer criteria for when armed interventions are legitimate and when they are not. There are signs that China would support such a tighter set of criteria for interventions. The chapter closes with a suggestion that involves an alternative way by which sovereignty might be downgraded, one that China may well find it can support.

Defining Down Sovereignty

"Defining down sovereignty" refers to the normative thesis that sovereignty should not grant a state absolute protection against armed intervention in their internal affairs by other states, and that instead the international community should condition such immunity on states living up to particular standards. This principle constitutes a major modification to what many hold to be the most profound foundation of the international order,[1] the concept of state sovereignty, which in contemporary thought and practice has been largely understood in association with the Westphalian principle that forbids armed interference by one state in the internal affairs of another.[2] Respect for international borders is a crucial part of this order. They are the markers that separate that which is fully legitimate and that which most assuredly is not. If the troops of a given state are positioned within its boundaries, the international community considers them to be a legitimate part of an orderly world composed of states. The international community holds that the same troops crossing a border with hostile intentions is a severe violation of the agreed-upon world order; the international order and the invaded state are inclined to respond violently. The news regularly reports that people in very different parts of the world feel personally aggrieved, insulted, and humiliated when they learn that their state's sovereignty has been violated, even if another state's troops merely crossed a minor, vague line in the shifting sands.[3] That millions of people have shown their willingness to die to protect their state's sovereignty is an indication of the depth of their commitment to this precept.

The respect for sovereignty[4] is ensconced in a slew of international laws and institutions, such as the International Criminal Court (ICC) and most notably the Charter of the United Nations.[5] For example, the Preamble as well as Articles 17 and 53 of the Rome Statute, which established the ICC, identifies the court's jurisdiction as complementary to the jurisdiction of its member states, which means that the ICC may only pursue cases that states are unable or unwilling to prosecute themselves.[6] Article 2 of the United Nations Charter, meanwhile, states that the United Nations is based "on the principle of the sovereign equality of all its Members."[7]

The Westphalian sovereignty paradigm has faced criticism, both from those who considered claims of sovereignty to be a form of idolatry and from those who saw the paradigm as a shield for tyrants' abuses.[8] For example, the political philosopher Jacques Maritain contends that the concept of sovereignty is intrinsically faulty, since it both separates the will of the nation from that of the body politic and creates insurmountable complications for international law.[9] Others, such as Stephen Krasner, have characterized sovereignty as "organized hypocrisy," criticizing it on the grounds that it is universally recognized but, at the same time, widely violated.[10] Other scholars insist that sovereignty has never been considered absolute. Bertrand de Jouvenel, for example, argues that people often understand the sovereign will as being an absolute authority, but that it is itself subject to constraints of morality that are independent of it.[11] According to this view, sovereignty rests upon a further moral framework that serves to justify the paradigm—but that can also justify deviations from and exceptions to the paradigm.

Proponents of sovereignty as responsibility (RtoP) sought to fundamentally shift the role played by the international community in the internal affairs of states by establishing an a priori category of conditions that, if met, would cause states to forfeit their sovereignty. As such, states that called for armed humanitarian intervention would not need to justify interventions in principle, but rather would merely need to show that a state had not fulfilled its responsibilities. States that manifestly neglect their responsibilities to prevent mass atrocity crimes forfeit their sovereignty, and the international community has the responsibility to intervene with coercive measures, including military intervention.

Contemporary international theory and practice is departing from the view that sovereignty is absolute and is instead adopting the idea of conditional sovereignty—that is, that sovereignty is contingent upon states fulfilling certain domestic and international obligations. This is largely a communitarian approach, and it is one built on a communitarian notion of citizenship. In other words, it recognizes that states (like individuals) have not only rights but also responsibilities; they are entitled to self-determination and self-government, but must also demonstrate their commitment to the common good by protecting the environment, promoting peace, and refraining from harming their population.[12] Recent humanitarian crises have further called into question the inviolability of sovereignty. The international community widely accepts that states have a responsibility to refrain from committing (or allowing) mass atrocities against their citizens (for example, genocide), and that in failing to uphold such responsibilities they forfeit their sovereignty. This understanding is manifested in RtoP.[13]

Francis Deng and his associates, in a 1996 book entitled *Sovereignty as Responsibility*,[14] argued that when states do not conduct their domestic affairs in ways that meet internationally recognized standards, other states have not only a right but also a duty to intervene. Deng forcefully stated this modification of the Westphalian norm and, at great length, defended his thesis that "the sovereign state's responsibility and accountability to both domestic and external constituencies must be affirmed as interconnected principles of the national and international order. Such a normative code is anchored in the assumption that in order to be legitimate sovereignty must demonstrate responsibility. At the very least that means providing for the basic needs of its people."[15]

The International Commission on Intervention and State Sovereignty (or the Evans-Sahnoun Commission) further developed the idea in its 2001 report *The Responsibility to Protect,* and centered its proposals on sovereignty as responsibility. It held: "There is no transfer or dilution of state sovereignty. But there is a necessary re-characterization involved: from sovereignty as control to sovereignty as responsibility in both internal functions and external duties."[16] In 2004 the UN Secretary General's High-Level Panel on Threats, Challenges, and Change (the High-Level Panel) advanced this view in its report, *A More Secure World—Our Shared Responsibility,* which argues, "Whatever perceptions may have prevailed when the Westphalian system first gave rise to the notion of State sovereignty, today it clearly carries with it the obligation of a State to protect the welfare of its own peoples and meet its obligations to the wider international community."[17]

RtoP not only holds that states must fulfill their obligations to protect their citizens from mass atrocity crimes in order to maintain their sovereignty—but also holds that *other states* have the *obligation to intervene* if a state fails to uphold its responsibility to protect.[18]

The UN Security Council previously authorized interventions in states such as Somalia and Haiti rarely and on an ad hoc basis; before the advent of RtoP, it had not developed a general case for downgrading state sovereignty. The UN General Assembly endorsed RtoP unanimously in 2006.[19] Since then, "numerous resolutions by the Security Council and General Assembly" have referenced RtoP, which has ascended to a place of prominence in the international debate and has been invoked by a wide range of state and nonstate actors.[20] China has voted for and endorsed RtoP throughout its gestation.

Since 2003 RtoP has also suffered setbacks. The employment of RtoP as the rationale for the 2003 invasion of Iraq and the 2011 NATO intervention in Libya caused the concept to lose support.[21] Accordingly, some of RtoP's normative grounding—namely, conditional sovereignty—has been eroded, as will be seen presently.

How Far Is "Down"?

While considerable international consensus exists about RtoP, the United States and China (as well as the United States and Russia) differ greatly about the point at which a state's neglect of its responsibilities justifies armed intervention by other states, and about which authority should determine that this point has been reached. Deng, who is credited with coining the concept of sovereignty as responsibility, holds that in order to avoid being stripped of its sovereignty a state must maintain good governance and provide for the "general welfare of its citizens and those under its jurisdiction."[22] This formula sets the bar very low; very few states would be safe from armed intervention if the international community were to adopt Deng's guidelines. Deng does not spell out which authority should judge whether intervention is justified. The tenor of his writing suggests he intends the UN Security Council to fill the role, or possibly the General Assembly—not each nation or superpower on its own.

In 1995 the Commission on Global Governance recommended that the United Nations craft legal opportunities for armed humanitarian intervention under specific circumstances. In the commission's holding, the "acceptable basis for humanitarian action"—which it grounded in the fundamental principle that "all states have an obligation to protect [the right of all people to a secure existence]"—is vague: "The line separating a domestic affair from a global one [that is, one validating intervention] cannot be drawn in the sand, but all will be known when it has been crossed."[23] The document proposed "restricting [the scope of a new Charter amendment] to cases that constitute a violation of the security of the people so gross and extreme that it requires an international response."

Another approach is to hold that armed humanitarian intervention, as authorized by the Security Council, should be undertaken whenever a humanitarian crisis escalates to the point that it poses a "threat to international peace and security."[24] This is the justification that supported the intervention in Libya in 2011 (e.g., the establishment of a no-fly zone). This approach focuses more on determining which agency has the authority to rule on the necessity of an intervention than on determining the degree of harm done to a population that justifies an intervention.[25]

The International Commission on Intervention and State Sovereignty, chaired by Gareth Evans and Mohamed Sahnoun, spells out where to "draw the line in determining when military intervention is, prima facie, defensible." It offers two "threshold criteria" that constitute just cause for humanitarian intervention: "large scale loss of life, actual or apprehended, with genocidal intent or not, which is the product either of deliberate state action, or state neglect or inability to act, or a failed state situation; or large scale 'ethnic cleansing,' actual or apprehended, whether carried out by killing, forced expulsion, acts of terror or rape."[26] This is by far the clearest set of criteria and does not set the bar so low that any state can claim justification for humanitarian intervention. China did not, and seems to have no reason, to oppose this or similar approaches.

No Coercive Regime Change

By contrast, intervention for the purpose of regime change and nation building should be limited to noncoercive means and should exclude the use of force. Neither adding to the set of responsibilities a state must fulfill to guarantee its sovereignty nor demanding a certain form of government at the threat of armed intervention is justified; these matters should be the purview of the people of the states involved, and intervention over these issues often results not in a free regime but rather in new forms of authoritarianism, anarchy, or civil war.[27] Pushing beyond RtoP toward regime change threatens the possibility of a new international consensus regarding changes to the international paradigm. China and Russia—both states that have, in the past, strongly endorsed the Westphalian norm[28]—have in part come to accept armed interventions for humanitarian purposes provided that those interventions do not advance other causes.[29] China first endorsed RtoP in 2005 at the UN World Summit, and again in 2006 in UN Security Council (UNSC) Resolution 1674.[30] In 2006 China's then ambassador to the United Nations Liu Zhenmin stressed that, per the World Summit, RtoP pertains to "genocide, war crimes, ethnic cleansing and crimes against humanity," and that "it is not appropriate to expand, willfully to interpret or even abuse this concept."[31] In 2009 Liu echoed these sentiments and further outlined limitations in the interpretation of RtoP according to China's views, noting the importance of strict adherence to the UN Charter. He stated, "The Security Council must view the responsibility to protect in the broader context of maintaining international peace and security" and "there must be no wavering with regard to the principles of respect for state sovereignty." However, he did acknowledge the "divergent views" on RtoP and expressed that China was "prepared to communicate with others in the interest of forging a universal consensus."[32]

Despite significant reservations, China abstained rather than vetoed UNSC Resolution 1973 authorizing military intervention in Libya in 2011. However, the subsequent overthrow of Gaddafi reinforced China's concerns that RtoP can be used as a means to carry out other objectives, notably regime change.[33] At a Security Council meeting in 2011, Chinese Ambassador Li Baodong stated, "There must be no attempt at regime change or involvement in civil war by any party under the guise of protecting civilians."[34] China has since blocked several UNSC draft resolutions on Syria, although as Andrew Garwood-Gowers writes, "Beijing *has* been willing to support several [other] UNSC resolutions on Syria, including those mandating the UN Observer Mission, the destruction of Syria's chemical weapons, and most recently a humanitarian aid access plan" (emphasis in original). Although a few of these resolutions lacked approval by the Syrian government, Garwood-Gowers reiterates China's aversion to "non-consensual measures under R2P's third pillar."[35]

Pushing for too expansive a challenge to sovereignty might, thus, sour China on the more limited responsibilities outlined above. However, China appears interested in shaping norms surrounding RtoP, especially with regard to the permissibility of intervention; this is seen particularly in the concept of "Responsible Protection" developed by the Chinese scholar Ruan Zongze at the official think tank of China's Ministry of Foreign Affairs, which augments RtoP criteria.[36]

The issue of regime change has also arisen in Syria. The United States has long demanded as a precondition for any peace deal that President Bashar al-Assad may not play any role in a transitional government.[37] This position not only extends the very massive atrocities but ignores the observation that Syria is very likely to remain under authoritarian rule regardless of whether he maintains power.[38] The United States should long ago have abandoned its stipulation that Assad be removed from office as a precondition for negotiations and allowed the various groups to negotiate whatever settlement can be achieved. China, on the other hand, maintains its opposition to coercive regime change and notably vetoed a draft Security Council resolution in 2012 that would have called for President Assad to step down.[39]

The preceding analysis suggests that China and other nations would continue to support RtoP if it were firmly decoupled from coercive regime changes; this decoupling can be realized both by defining accordingly the conditions under which interventions are justified, and by requiring a UN authorization for any such intervention. The United States and its allies have good reasons to accept these clarifications of RtoP given that coercive regime changes very often have disastrous effects for all concerned.[40] Early indications suggest that Trump's administration will prefer stability over regime change, saying in December 2016, "We will stop looking to topple regimes and overthrow governments."[41]

The Duty to Prevent Transnational Terrorism

The discussion next turns to a new idea, for another ground on which to downgrade sovereignty. Neither the United States nor China nor any other nation has embraced this novel normative principle. However, both the United States and its allies and China have objective, self-serving reasons to favor it.

It may seem obvious that if terrorists based in one nation attack the people of another nation, the forces of the attacked nation should have the right to use force against these terrorists. However, many scholars and members of the general public view such acts—like the use of unmanned aerial vehicles (UAVs), or Special Forces strikes against transnational terrorists (i.e., terrorists based in one nation attacking people in another)—as violations of state sovereignty. Hence, when the United States conducted UAV strikes in Pakistan or Yemen, it typically notified the Pakistani and Yemeni governments (albeit "concurrently")[42] or stressed that the United States' actions had the governments' "tacit consent"[43] in a show of respect for the norm of state sovereignty, though such measures did not curb criticism. The international community also criticized the United States in the name of state sovereignty for its clear violation of the sovereignty of Pakistan when American Special Forces eliminated Osama bin Laden in Abbottabad.[44]

Mary Ellen O'Connell, an international law scholar at the University of Notre Dame, argues that "international law has a definition of war [that] refers to places where intense, protracted, organized intergroup fighting occurs. It does not refer to places merely where terrorist suspects are found."[45] She further argues that outside the narrowly defined theaters of war, spelled out in declarations of war by the nations involved, the "law of peace" should guide counterterrorist efforts.[46]

Along similar lines, other scholars maintain that it is never permissible, according to the UN Charter, to militarily infringe upon another state's territorial sovereignty in order to deal with a nonstate threat.[47]

Moreover, until the late 1980s, terrorist acts were considered to be outside the jurisdiction of the Security Council, meaning that states had little recourse in responding to transnational terrorism within the purview of international law. Still, the Security Council and General Assembly condemned the Israeli attack on the Palestine Liberation Organization headquarters in 1985[48] and the American strike against Libyan targets in 1986.[49] Both of these responses to transnational terrorism (past and expected) were deemed violations of the international norms of state sovereignty. In 2004 UNSC Resolution 1566 addressed the issue of terrorism as criminal activity, hence a matter to be handled by local law enforcement authorities, rather than as conduct associated with war.[50] And in 2006 the United Nations adopted a Global Counter-Terrorism Strategy to combat terrorism using a criminal law model.[51] The United Nations thus undermines "the possibility that states could lawfully resort to forcible measures against terrorists based in another country."[52]

As I see it, however, from a normative standpoint there are strong grounds to add the Responsibility to Prevent Transnational Terrorism (RtoPT) to the norms that nations are expected to uphold. If a state fails to honor this responsibility, it seems morally appropriate for the attacked nation to respond with counterterrorism measures within the territory of a state used as a base and launching pad by the attackers.[53] That is, sovereignty should be defined down one more notch; nations should add one more responsibility to maintaining their status as good citizens of the nascent global community.

Behind the arguments that follow in support of the RtoPT is the rather basic moral intuition that if terrorists do not respect international borders (by attacking across them), those who respond to their attacks need not do so either. This intuition is supported here by a new application of a very widely respected normative principle, the golden rule. It holds that you should expect others to treat you the same way you treat them. To test this intuition, I suggest one should apply what might be called the "uniform test." If the military of a given nation crossed a border and attacked and terrorized the people of another nation, very few would hold that these troops can hide behind claims of sovereignty for the nation from which the attack stemmed to be spared from counterattacks. If these troops took off their uniforms but engaged in the same kind of attacks, that is hardly a reason for them to be spared. Indeed, as I see it, they are entitled to fewer rights than uniformed fighters. In other words, terrorists have a lower standing than soldiers.

The main reason for this lower standing is that terrorists are violating one of the most profound rules of all armed conflicts: the rule of distinction. The rule of distinction holds that combatants should make special efforts to spare civilians when engaging in armed confrontations.[54] It is for this reason that the majority of American military aircraft involved in the fight against ISIS are returning to their bases without dropping their bombs, or only dropping them on low-value targets. This is the case because when they close in on their original targets, they often find that civilians would be hurt.[55] Responding forces often cannot effectively eliminate combatants who masquerade as civilians and hide among them without killing some innocent civilians. Thus, terrorists are entitled to less protection than soldiers because they are violating a very basic principle of armed conflicts. In this case, there seems no reason to accord terrorists any special privileges.

The main counterargument to the RtoPT vis-à-vis terrorism is that while armies are under the control of a given nation's government and hence can be held accountable for their acts, this is not the case for terrorist organizations and individual terrorists. Hence, the sovereignty of the nations from which terrorists attack should be respected. However, one should note that there are basically two different situations: one in which nations in effect have considerable control over the terrorists and one in which the terrorists act from ungoverned, undergoverned, or ill-governed parts of a country (hereafter referred to as ungoverned).

True, nations rarely admit that the terrorists they launch are their agents. However, in quite a few cases, there is considerable evidence that governments help finance terrorists; provide them with intelligence, arms, and other equipment; and, above all, signal which targets to attack and when, as well as where to refrain from attacking. In short, to a large extent, these governments control the terrorists. Iran and Hezbollah function in this way, as do Pakistan and Lashkar-e-Taiba with attacks on India. The United States' support of the Mujahideen during the Soviet War in Afghanistan can also be characterized this way. In other cases, the connection is weaker and less evident.[56] The varying degrees of control and involvement by nations in support of terrorism suggest that the response should be similarly graded. The less clear it is whether a given nation is indeed in charge, that is, whether the terrorists are state agents, the more warning said nation should be given and the more limited counterstrikes should be. For instance, the use of drones might be used in place of Special Forces because use of the latter is considered a greater violation of sovereignty. Granting concurrent notification might also be considered in such cases.

Indeed, the United States (and several other nations) designate select nations as terrorist-sponsoring states. As determined by the secretary of state, the United States currently recognizes Iran, Sudan, and Syria as "countries determined . . . to have repeatedly provided support for acts of international terrorism,"[57] pursuant to Section 6(j) of the Export Administration Act, which states that support for acts of international terrorism includes the recurring use of the land, waters, and airspace of the country as a sanctuary for terrorists (for training, financing, and recruitment) or as a transit point.[58] The government must also expressly consent to—or with knowledge, allow, tolerate, or disregard—such use of land by terrorists. As a result of this determination, these countries are subject to restrictions on US foreign assistance, a ban on defense exports and sales, certain controls over exports of dual-use items, and miscellaneous financial and other restrictions. What I am calling for is simply taking the next step: legitimizing armed responses when the measures already listed do not suffice to stop attacks.

One may argue that this step is not needed because, as of 2012, there were thirteen international conventions and protocols that required state parties to criminalize a particular manifestation of international terrorism under domestic law, cooperate in the prevention of terrorist acts, and take action to ensure that offenders are held responsible for their crime.[59] However, the enforcement of these conventions relies on international courts, which raises numerous issues that cannot be explored here. Suffice it to say, there have been no signs that this approach could curb transnational terrorism; hence, this task is left to the assaulted nations.

What about terrorists who are based in and launch their attacks from ungoverned parts of a country? The United States does not include these nations on its list of states that are sponsoring terrorism. According to the United States' Country Reports on Terrorism 2014, terrorist safe havens include "ungoverned, under-governed, or illgoverned physical areas" where terrorists can "organize, plan, raise funds, communicate, recruit, train, transit, and operate in relative security because of inadequate governance capacity, political will, or both."[60] The report goes on to exclude these territories from the determination of a state as a sponsor of terrorism. This makes sense in one way but not in another. If a nation is not in control of a given area that serves as a base for terrorists, it should not be held responsible for what is happening in this area. Thus, the United States surely should not impose sanctions or cut aid to Pakistan if it tried in good faith to gain control of the parts of Waziristan but failed. However, it does not follow that one ought to spare terrorists in such areas. Attacking terrorists in ungoverned areas is not violating a nation's sovereignty because a national government forfeits such claims by being unable or unwilling to govern these areas. After all, sovereignty is defined as having a commanding control of a given territory. If an area is ungoverned, for practical and normative purposes, it is not encompassed in the sovereignty of the government of the nation at issue, though I grant that this position is not reflected in current understanding of international law. However, these laws were changed before and ought to be changed accordingly.

The interest of the United States and its allies in what might be refashioned as the Responsibility to Prevent Transnational Terrorism is obvious. One should not overlook that as China sees it, it too suffers from Islamic driven terrorism. The Uighurs are a Muslim ethnic minority in China who reside mainly in the northwestern region of Xinjiang.[61] After the attacks of September 11, 2001, China classified its fight against Uighur separatism as part of the war on terror.[62] Uighur separatists have reportedly been behind several other attacks in China, including an incident in 2014 in which China claimed a group of 215 assailants killed 37 civilians.[63] In the same year, China accused Xinjiang separatists of the knife attack at a Chinese train station that killed 29 and wounded 143.[64] In September 2015 there was a deadly attack by the same group at a coal mine in Xinjiang.[65] Rohan Gunaratna, a scholar in Singapore, estimated that there were over two hundred attacks in Xinjiang in a twelve-month period.[66] According to China, Uighur militants have trained in Afghanistan[67] and Pakistan.[68] In 2015 Afghanistan turned over several Uighur militants to China, and according to a Pakistani Taliban leader, a group of Uighurs moved from North Waziristan to Afghanistan after the Pakistani government's 2014 commencement of an offensive in the region.[69]

In short, nations should be expected to prevent terrorists from using their territories. If nations do not or cannot live up to this responsibility, they give up the relevant part of their sovereignty claims. Hence, the international community (and, if it fails, the nations attacked by terrorists) act legitimately when they respond to terrorists with force, regardless of what side of the border these terrorists are found.

The need to foster a new norm that mandates nations to prevent transnational terrorism—and face the consequences if they do not—is a global one. There are good reasons to hold that in a world in which the United States and China work more effectively together than they currently do, China would strongly support such a norm. This is expected because China sees itself as a subject to jihadist terrorism, much as the West does.

9

FREEDOM OF NAVIGATION ASSERTIONS: THE UNITED STATES AS THE WORLD'S POLICEMAN

reedom of navigation assertions (FONA), though often carried out, receive very little public attention. Even those who closely follow foreign policy rarely include them in their analysis of international relations. However, FONA have become a major way the United States expresses its opposition to China's unilateral actions to change the status of various "islands" (some no more than rocks submerged at high sea) in order to claim rights to the sea surrounding them. FONA allow the United States to show that it does not accept the Chinese claims and disapproves of its island-building activities—without using force to stop such activities. In effect, FONA are a relatively low-risk, low-escalation response.

FONA are also supposed to reassure allies and the American public that the United States is not ignoring China's assertive actions and is "doing something" to stop them. And these assertions also reveal, we shall see, a difference in opinion between the White House and the Pentagon on how to deal with China, casting more light on the issues raised earlier in this book about the AirSea Battle plan. Last but not least, FONA play a role in maintaining American claims that it is the super power entrusted to ensure worldwide freedom of navigation. The chapter starts with a brief review of recent FONA; it mainly deals with two rather different rationales accorded to FONA—and their flaws.

FONA in the South China Sea

During a press conference at the conclusion of the US-ASEAN summit in California on February 16, 2016, President Obama stated, "We discussed the need for tangible steps in the South China Sea to lower tensions, including a halt to further reclamation, new construction and militarization of disputed areas. Freedom of navigation must be upheld and lawful commerce should not be impeded. I reiterated that the United States will continue to fly, sail, and operate wherever international law allows, and we will support the right of all countries to do the same."[1]

Since 2015 the United States has performed three FONA in the South China Sea[2] (before this, FONA had not occurred in the South China Sea for at least three years).[3] The first occurred in October 2015 and involved the USS *Lassen,* which sailed within twelve nautical miles of Subi Reef, Northeast Cay, Southwest Cay, South Reef, and Sandy Cay, located within the Spratly Islands chain.[4] The next FONA involved the USS *Curtis Wilbur* in the Paracel Islands; in January 2016 the Navy destroyer went within twelve nautical miles of Triton Island.[5] It was followed by a FONA in May 2016, when the USS *William P. Lawrence* passed within twelve nautical miles of Fiery Cross Reef in the Spratly Islands.[6]

President Obama and US naval commanders reportedly differ about how to respond to China's island building in the South China Sea. The White House downplayed the October 2015 FONA; it did not want the press to be notified or officials to comment on it. The Pentagon, however, did inform reporters.[7] As a result, Secretary of Defense Ash Carter was in an awkward position when he testified before the Senate Armed Services Committee, and he was forced to sidestep senators' questions about it.[8]

According to an April 6, 2016, article in the *Navy Times,* Admiral Harry Harris favored a more confrontational approach, whereas the Obama administration preferred a less confrontational one, in order to maintain the United States' ability to work with China. Thus, as the result of a gag order issued by National Security Advisor Susan Rice, military officers were not allowed to speak on the South China Sea issue before the summit in the spring of 2016, during which President Obama and President Xi had a private meeting.[9]

In reference to the *Navy Times* article, Michael Cohen wrote that its content "represents a troubling breach of the norms governing civil-military relations." Although he acknowledges it is unknown whether Harris leaked information included in the article, Cohen cites an instance in which Harris, contrary to the official US policy of not taking sides on the sovereignty claims, told leaders in China that the islands were not theirs.[10] Dan De Luce reports that "Pentagon officials say the military has been ready to carry out operations more frequently within 12 nautical miles of man-made islands, but the White House so far has chosen to take a more cautious approach."[11]

Admiral Scott Swift implied that China was disrupting freedom of navigation in the South China Sea. "Intimidated by the manner in which some navies, coast guards and maritime military enforce claims in contested waters, fishermen who trawled the seas freely for generations are facing threats to their livelihoods imposed by nations with unresolved and often unrecognized claims," he said in a speech at a regional security forum.[12] However, "A Pacific Fleet spokesman, asked for specific examples of commercial ships that had been forced to change their route because of orders from the Chinese Navy, said he would need time to research the answer," according to the *New York Times*.[13] That research seems to still be ongoing.

The FONA have sparked criticism from China, which has referred to the United States' actions as threatening and illegal,[14] and as "deliberate provocation."[15] The FONA have also sparked criticism from scholars for rather different reasons. The issues they raise concern the purpose and rationale of these operations. Ships are allowed "innocent passage" through territorial waters under the UN Convention of the Law of the Sea (UNCLOS). Hence FONA in effect establish very little and are mainly for show. Indeed, in 2015 when Chinese ships passed through American waters off the Alaskan coast, Pentagon spokesman Commander Bill Urban said, "This was a legal transit of U.S. territorial seas conducted in accordance with the Law of the Sea Convention."[16] Malcolm Cook notes that the Obama administration's decision "to limit the operations to innocent passage ones" was "widely criticized."[17] Julian Ku writes, "Like the two other recent U.S. freedom of navigation operations (FONOP) in the South China Sea, the most recent U.S. FONOP was designed to avoid any conflict with China's sovereignty claims. Instead, by conducting the operations under the rules of 'innocent passage,' the U.S. Navy assumed China might have sovereign rights, but simply challenged China's domestic law requirement that foreign warships give prior notification before entering what China claims is its territorial sea."[18]

One notes that although FONA are low-risk operations compared to the use of force, they are not without risks. On several occasions, Chinese vessels and planes came very close to American ships and planes. If such maneuvers cause a loss of life—as happened in 2001 when a Chinese fighter jet tailed a US spy plane and the two collided in midair—the casualties could lead to a major confrontation, even though neither side seeks it. This is, after all, the way World War I started.

Freedom of navigation operational assertions are mainly carried out by the US Navy. The mission is to ensure that when other nations impose what the United States considers excessive restrictions on the freedom of navigation in any place in the world, the Pentagon will send naval ships or aircraft to demonstrate that the United States will not accept such restrictions. The United States also publicizes these assertions at the end of each fiscal year in order to further support the international norms and laws that call for freedom of navigation, or at least the United States' view of these norms and laws (as one Navy JAG put it, "It is an 'in your face,' 'rub your nose in it' operation, that lets people know who is the boss. At least when it comes to freedom of navigation—the US does serve as the world's cop").[19] FONA is part of a larger State Department program dedicated to preserving freedom of navigation (FON), which also draws on diplomatic protests from affected states and multilateral consultations.[20]

This analysis proceeds in four parts. Part 1 of this chapter describes FONA. Part 2 briefly discusses the normative and legal justifications provided for FONA, and their assumptions about the extent to which the American public favors liberal internationalism or American unilateralism and "realist" (i.e., power-based) foreign policy. Part 3 studies what FONA reveal about the liberal, rule-based, international order that the United States claims it is seeking to uphold, of which freedom of navigation is a key element. Part 4 studies what FONA reveal about the role freedom of navigation plays in American military strategy, particularly in terms of power projection and access to littoral regions, that is, in "realist" terms. The chapter concludes by noting the "importance of being unimportant," in the sense that the limited budget, personnel, and publicity devoted to FONA make it largely invisible to the public and hence not subjected to scrutiny.

I. FONA

FONA are low-profile operations; the Defense Department itself does not currently publish a detailed description or justification of the program. Instead, it publishes only a brief yearly summary of FONA on the website of the undersecretary of defense for policy, listing the countries against which an assertion was conducted, the "excessive claims" that were protested, and whether or not multiple assertions were carried out against a given country (without going into specific details about the date or number of operations). According to these reports, the number of countries against which assertions were conducted has fluctuated over time, ranging from as few as five each in 2005 and 2006, to as many as fifteen in 2000 and twelve in 2013.[21] The countries affected include not just American rivals such as China and Iran, but also much smaller powers and nations friendly to the United States such as the Philippines, Taiwan, and Canada.

For example, the United States conducted assertions against India, a major power with which the United States has generally good relations, for requiring authorization "for military exercises or maneuvers"[22] in its exclusive economic zone (EEZ).[23] Iran was subject to assertions for the same restriction, as well as for "excessive straight baselines" and "restrictions on right of transit passage through Strait of Hormuz to signatories."[24] Oman was subject to assertions for its claim to allow only innocent passage, or the right to transit waters subject to certain restrictions,[25] for ships transiting the Strait of Hormuz.[26] The United States targeted the tiny Maldives for its restriction on military activity in its EEZ and its requirement that "nuclear-powered ships" obtain authorization before entering its territorial sea.[27] The Seychelles was on the list of operational assertions on two occasions for requiring prior permission for warships to enter its territorial sea.[28] Longtime American ally[29] the Philippines was confronted almost every year for its "claims [of] archipelagic waters as internal waters."[30] Indonesia, as another archipelagic state, has likewise been frequently targeted for "partial designation of archipelagic sea lanes," that is, for making provision only for north-south sea-lanes between its islands and not for any east-west route.[31] China was subject to assertions in 2013 for "excessive straight baselines," "security jurisdiction in [its] contiguous zone," "jurisdiction over airspace above the [EEZ]," restrictions on survey activity in the EEZ, and restrictions of innocent passage in territorial waters.[32] The United States also targeted Taiwan, Vietnam, Indonesia, and Cambodia for similar reasons. Malaysia was targeted for requiring nuclear-powered ships to gain authorization before entering territorial waters. Most assertions were carried out by US warships, and some by US bombers. For instance, following China's November 2013 declaration of an Air Defense Identification Zone in the East China Sea requiring aircraft to identify themselves, the United States sent a pair of B-52 bombers into the zone without informing China.[33]

The US State Department also has a Freedom of Navigation (FON) Program that mainly files démarches, or official protests,[34] when other nations impose excessive restrictions on the freedom of navigation, thus "stressing the need for and obligation of all States to adhere to the customary international law rules and practices reflected in the LOS Convention."[35] The Freedom of Navigation Program was instituted in 1979 during the Carter administration,[36] though it was preceded by occasional protest sailings.

For example, in response to Canada's assertion of straight baselines, or control of all water between two points on the coast rather than at a constant distance from the land, the United States in 1967 issued a protest note that it "considers the action of Canada to be without legal justification [and] contrary to established principles of international Law [and as such] does not recognize the validity of the purported lines and reserves all rights of the United States and its nationals in the waters in question."[37] In 2002 the United States issued a diplomatic note to Chile protesting a law requiring prior authorization for ships carrying nuclear or otherwise hazardous materials in territorial waters or the EEZ, asserting that unrestricted innocent passage "regardless of cargo, armament, or means of propulsion" is among the "fundamental tenets" of the Law of the Sea, noting that the United States "does not accept" the law, and requesting that Chile revise it.[38] And so on and so on.

Such operations are intended to be "routine and frequent," though operational assertions against "particularly sensitive" countries require the approval of the Joint Chiefs of Staff or the president in order to avoid excessive political risk. According to a 1979 memo issued by the commander in chief of the US Atlantic Command, following the establishment of the FON Program, US naval forces of the Atlantic Fleet "were ordered to avoid operating in a manner which might be construed as acquiescent to claims inconsistent with U.S. maritime rights," and indeed "in certain instances, U.S. forces must consider going out of their way to contest a maritime claim."[39] These operations can be carried out "at many levels in the chain of command," so while normally directed by the combatant commander or the fleet commander (e.g., of the US Pacific Fleet or the US Pacific Command), they can occur "even further down in the chain of command, or they can come from Washington D.C."[40]

More broadly, "U.S. military forces, ships and aircraft, will exercise their [navigational] right under international law wherever the U.S. thinks they are entitled to go, and it is only in special areas that they require higher approval. If it's not in a special area that requires higher approval, than a ship's commanding officer could go ahead and go through an area that might be under the claim of another country, and that would be called an FON assertion, but it's not really part of the formal FON program."[41]

In short, FONA are—as their very title reveals—assertive operations. The United States uses its military forces to undergird its positions on the nature of freedom of navigation, and what it entails. The targets of these operations include not merely potential foes such as China and Russia, but also friendly nations and allies, such as Canada. In this matter, the United States is acting unilaterally, without appeal to international institutions such as the United Nations, to multilateral institutions such as NATO, or to informal coalitions such as those composed to fight ISIS.

2. Normative and Legal Justifications

Up until World War II, foreign policy and military decisions could be made with relative inattention from the public. However, in the decades that followed, as new segments of the public acquired higher education, and as mass media developed, a growing share of the electorate became aware and interested in these decisions. Hence, decision makers have increased their efforts to gain "public support," that most widely used definition of the term *legitimation*.[42] Scholars still differ greatly in the amount of weight they assign to public opinion; some—mainly realists— see it as much less important than other factors, while idealists see it as much more consequential.[43] However, both groups see it as playing an increasing role.

The case in support of freedom of navigation, which FONA seek to buttress, has long and strong normative and legal roots. Freedom of navigation in Western thought has its origins in the work of the seventeenth-century Dutch jurist Hugo Grotius, who argued that the world's oceans were free rather than state owned. Grotius's ideas eventually prevailed, and during the height of British power, the so-called Pax Britannica (1812–1914), freedom of navigation was a key element of British naval policy, which aimed to facilitate free trade. Piracy, state sponsored (privateering) or independent, was rampant until the nineteenth century, when international antipiracy efforts were made in earnest, and the 1856 Paris Declaration Respecting Maritime Law banned privateering.

The justification for freedom of navigation never claimed it had an absolute status. Grotius recognized that maritime countries should have some sovereignty over their coastal waters.[44] From the seventeenth through the early twentieth century, the prevailing maritime norm was the three-mile territorial sea, based on the "cannon-shot rule" that a country should have control of the seas within range of its weapons.[45] By the 1930s, countries' exclusive rights to the resources within those territorial waters were widely recognized.[46] Over the twentieth century, however, coastal states expanded their maritime territorial claims; an increasing number of countries claimed a twelve-mile territorial sea.[47]

A growing disagreement among various nations concerning what freedom of navigation entailed and what it excluded created a demand for a formal international legal regime, leading to maritime law initiatives over the twentieth century with the participation of national governments and intergovernmental and nongovernmental organizations. The Hague Codification Conference of 1930 demonstrated widespread acceptance of the three-mile territorial sea, but failed to produce a formal agreement.[48] The 1958 UN Conference on the Law of the Sea (UNCLOS I) was more successful, producing four treaties that reached "a measure of agreement" on definitions and rules for territorial waters, the contiguous zone,[49] the high seas, and the continental shelf, while putting forward "principles and mechanisms" for the management of fisheries on the high seas. It reflected and codified customary international law to some extent, but also contained "pioneering" provisions on pollution as well as "very controversial" material on fisheries.[50] The United States acceded to all four treaties.[51]

These conferences failed, however, to resolve key disputes over the extent of the territorial sea and control over fisheries beyond that limit, as did the Second UN Conference on the Law of the Sea that followed it in 1960.[52] In particular, the need for four separate treaties in 1958 reflected insufficient consensus to produce a single comprehensive treaty.[53] In order to reach a compromise on these disputes, the Third UN Conference on the Law of the Sea (UNCLOS III) was held beginning in 1973. Lasting two decades, it was one of the longest international negotiations in history, but it was ultimately successful. The conference portion concluded in 1982 with the Law of the Sea Convention, which contained 320 chapters and nine annexes, and was eventually signed by more than 150 states and ratified by more than 130.[54]

Far from acting unilaterally, the United States was a leading proponent of UNCLOS III, which was viewed by State Department officials as very much in US interests.[55] During the negotiations, the United States cooperated with the Soviet Union to push for broad freedoms of negotiation and overflight,[56] and focused particularly on innocent passage by military ships through territorial waters, transit rights through straits, freedom of navigation and other noneconomic activity in the EEZ, as well as freedom for deep seabed mining.[57]

The negotiations, which involved considerable give-and-take by the participating nations and in which the United States played an important role, resolved many serious disputes between coastal and maritime states. The resulting Law of the Sea limited territorial waters to twelve nautical miles and recognized innocent passage rights within them, established a contiguous zone extending an additional twelve miles to facilitate coastal state law enforcement, and also established the EEZ, recognizing coastal states' jurisdiction over natural resources up to two hundred nautical miles off their coasts, including fisheries. It also established legal regimes for archipelagic waters, international straits, deep seabed mining, and environmental protection. In doing so, it reconciled the conflicting claims of its state parties, balanced the rights and interests of coastal and maritime states, and both supplemented and codified customary maritime law, making it "a monumental achievement in multilateral negotiations."[58] One hundred and sixty-three UN member states, including most major powers, signed and ratified the Law of the Sea, while fourteen states signed but did not ratify, and only sixteen states neither signed nor ratified.[59] The United States is one of the few countries that did not accede to the Law of the Sea.

It is important for all that follows to note that UNCLOS III (the resulting treaty of which is referred to generally as UNCLOS, or the Law of the Sea) provides mechanisms for resolving conflicting interpretations of its chapters. Part 15 of UNCLOS, entitled "Settlement of Disputes," provides four dispute resolution mechanisms. One is the International Tribunal for the Law of the Sea (ITLOS), which has jurisdiction over disputes and legal questions relating to the Law of the Sea. Since that law entered into force in 1994, ITLOS has heard twenty-two cases relating to "prompt release of [detained] vessels and crews, coastal State jurisdiction in its maritime zones, freedom of navigation, hot pursuit, marine environment, flags of convenience and conservation of fish stocks."[60]

A second dispute resolution option is the International Court of Justice, the main judicial body of the UN, to which all UN member states are parties. Third, the Law of the Sea also contains two distinct procedures for setting up temporary arbitration tribunals. Fourth, the UN

General Assembly reviews the Law of the Sea annually, issuing resolutions on pressing issues such as environmental protection and sustainable fishing.[61]

In the past, numerous differences in opinion among nations as to what FON entails have been worked out through negotiations and consultations, leading to major compromise, consensus, and treaties. Such treaties provide mechanisms for resolving any remaining issues or newly rising issues, and the United States has played a key role in these constructive developments. However, it is one of the few nations that refused to accede to the Law of the Sea treaty. Moreover, instead of the United States drawing on mechanisms for dispute resolutions regarding restrictions on FON it considers excessive, it often acts unilaterally and in an assertive manner, primarily employing its military forces.

The United States justifies FONA in two very different ways. One line of justification holds that the freedom of navigation is a global public good that the United States is called upon to protect. The second is that freedom of navigation is essential for American security, and hence it must ensure that this freedom is not eroded. Both justifications are combined in the following statement found in a number of FON-related official documents: "For over 20 years, the United States has reaffirmed its long-standing policy of exercising and asserting its freedom of navigation and overflight rights on a worldwide basis. Such assertions by the United States preserve navigational freedoms for all nations, ensure open access to the world's oceans for international trade, and preserve global mobility of U.S. armed forces."[62]

Studies of American public opinion about foreign policy differ a great deal in terms of how they assess the extent to which American society supports liberal versus realist foreign policies (or "doves" versus "hawks"). One notes first of all that significant segments of the public are neo-isolationist, in the sense that they seek a reduced US involvement overseas, whether that involvement entails support for the UN and foreign aid or military operations.[63] Second, some studies find that large segments of the American electorate favor liberal internationalist positions,[64] while others find that the majority favors realist positions.[65] It is important to note in this context that many Americans hold a mix of these positions; sometimes the majority sides with a liberal position (e.g., a large majority supports US participation in the International Criminal Court)[66] and sometimes with a realist position (e.g., Americans are more supportive of the use of force to pursue "realpolitik missions" than "humanitarian or peacekeeping" ones).[67] These facts help explain the reason that the US government seeks to legitimate FONA in both liberal and realist terms.

The chapter next turns to examine the validity of the two major legitimations that are employed simultaneously to justify FONA.

3. FONA—for Liberalism

FONA are often justified on the grounds that global order—in particular, the rule-based, liberal international order—serves all nations well, that freedom of navigation is a key element of this order, and that the United States is called upon to uphold this order.

President Woodrow Wilson was one of the first to articulate and actively promote the liberal international order.[68] "Absolute freedom of navigation upon the seas, outside territorial waters" was one of Wilson's Fourteen Points.[69] Stewart Patrick lists "freedom of the seas" among the key principles that "have underpinned the Western-dominated liberal order since 1945."[70] Christian Le Mière points out that "the global public good" of freedom of navigation, which "has been ensured by the U.S. since the end of the Second World War, and before that by the Royal Navy," has become much more widely accepted and clearly defined since being "clarified" at UNCLOS III.[71]

The liberal justification of FONA faces a major challenge. This is the case because the liberal justification goes way beyond considering freedom of navigation as a key public good—it also calls for resolving differences through diplomatic means and via international institutions. In contrast, as far as FONA are concerned, the United States decides on its own which new restrictions introduced by any nation in the world are "excessive," and what it considers the correct interpretation of international law and UNCLOS. Moreover, it unilaterally applies its military force—not UN Blue Helmets or even that of NATO or of a coalition—to enforce the rules. In short, in these matters the United States acts as accuser, judge, jury, and executioner. It knows what the law is and has taken it upon itself to enforce it. This is a very different model from that of the liberal international order; it is much more that of a unipolar hegemon.

Those who favor FONA have made several arguments in support of this American enforcement role. One argument is that excessive restrictions on the freedom of navigation are clearly illegal, and hence the

United States is merely exercising its rights in challenging them. Thus, according to J. Ashley Roach and Robert Smith, what the United States views as excessive maritime claims, or those that claim "sovereignty, sovereign rights, or jurisdiction over ocean areas" in a way that is "inconsistent with the terms of the LOS convention," are simply "illegal in international law" and moreover "threaten the rights of other States to use the oceans."[72] Hence, the United States is merely exercising its navigational rights by carrying out FONA or otherwise ignoring such rules.

Another argument in favor of the FON Program, and particularly operational assertions, is that of precedent. Roach and Smith argue that "it is accepted international law and practice that, to prevent changes in or derogations from rules of law, states must persistently object to actions by other states that seek to change those rules."[73] However, it does not follow that therefore the United States (and not, for instance, the UN) is the one called upon to act. A naval officer who carried out several FONA himself suggested to me that in order to maintain long agreed upon international norms and laws, the United States must act when some nation makes excessive claims, because otherwise it would seem to acquiesce to the changes. And it must do so toward friends and adversaries alike, in order not to seem to discriminate. All this may be true, but it does not explain why the rejection of claims must be carried out by military rather than by diplomatic means. One may say that diplomatic means are used (by filing démarches), which is indeed the case, but it does not follow why these must be followed or accompanied by naval assertions—if the goal is to indicate that the United States (as a self-appointed enforcer of the world order) does not acquiesce to the change and refuses to accept it as a legal precedent.

One may also argue that UNCLOS III reflects a contract in which interested parties have come together, expressed their differing preferences, and negotiated a mutually acceptable compromise, after which a set of rules is established to be followed until both sides agree to change them. In this view, the restrictions on military activities deemed excessive by the United States were "rejected" or "not envisioned" during the UNCLOS III negotiations and "would never have been accepted by the maritime powers."[74] However, it still does not follow that if one party holds a contract to have been violated, it can go and use force as a means of responding. Instead, the liberal order calls for the peaceful resolution of such disputes by arbitration or other such means.

There are both generic and specific arguments against FONA, which these justifications fail to take into account. For instance, the very status of international law is not as self-evident as defenders of FONA imply. Laws command respect when they are enacted by a duly elected legislature in a liberal democratic state; international laws do not command the same standing,[75] though they surely command considerable normative and prudential adherence. Differences aside, domestic and international laws alike are subject to different interpretations and to revisions (e.g., by UN Security Council resolutions or new treaties); so too are domestic and international legal frameworks subject to different and sometimes overlapping agents of enforcement. This is clear not only in general but also specifically in matters concerning the freedom of navigation. The Law of the Sea fails to define key terms,[76] leading to stark differences in interpretations of the law by those opposing or backing coastal state maritime claims.[77] Roach and Smith—whose book is considered the most comprehensive and authoritative text on the subject— state at one point that claims viewed by the United States as inconsistent with the Law of the Sea are simply "illegal under international law," yet they then spend nearly seven hundred pages demonstrating that conflicting interpretations of the Law of the Sea are widespread.

There is great room for legitimate differences of opinion as to what the law means, and concerning how multilateral mechanisms and institutions can be used to determine which interpretation should be followed. Instead, however, under FONA the United States finds itself in the odd position of claiming that it is the sole power willing and able to protect a key element of the liberal order, freedom of navigation, while still refusing to accede to the Law of the Sea treaty that enshrines this key element.

In short, freedom of navigation is indeed an important component of the rule-based, liberal international order, and it is a major public good. However, FON operational assertions cannot be justified by appealing to the value of this order, because it is centered on consensus building, diplomatic negotiations, and multilateral institutions, and not unilateral rulings and enforcement by use of the military.

4. A Realist's Assessment

The value of the freedom of navigation, as well as the need to buttress it, is also justified by the US government on the grounds that they are essential to US national security. This realist justification is provided in general terms as well as rather specific ones. The United States is a major naval power, compared to other nations that either do not have much of a navy (China has only recently launched its first aircraft carrier and has little experience in naval warfare)[78] or rely much more on their land forces (e.g., Russia). Hence, on the face of it, the unencumbered right to move forces about in the seas favor the United States.

Roach and Smith spell out this key claim in the following terms: The United States "requires maritime mobility" for its national security and "has more to lose than any other State if its maritime rights are under-cut." As the world's preeminent naval power, it is in the interest of the United States to maximize its legal right to project naval power: "even though the United States may have the military power to operate where and in the manner it believes it has the right to, any exercise of that power is significantly less costly if it is generally accepted as being law-ful."[79] More broadly, US military strategy recognizes that "joint assured access to the global commons and cyberspace constitutes a core aspect of U.S. national security and remains an enduring mission . . . the mari-time domain enables the bulk of the [US military's] forward deployment and sustainment, as well as the commerce that underpins the global eco-nomic system."[80] Likewise, Dennis Mandsager argues that without free-dom of navigation, "the ability of the United States to project military power, provide logistics support, maintain forward presence, and ac-complish missions such as disaster relief, humanitarian assistance, and noncombatant evacuations, will be severely hampered."[81] The purpose of FON is to "preserve the global mobility of US forces by avoiding ac-quiescence in excessive maritime claims of other nations,"[82] according to Jonathan Odom, the Department of Defense oceans policy advisor; James Kraska agrees.[83] More specifically, freedom of navigation was cru-cial during the Cold War for nuclear deterrence, because it served to protect the right for ballistic missile submarines to transit international straits while submerged, a right that was threatened by the expansion of the territorial sea.[84]

FON is particularly relevant to US maritime power projection in East Asia. The United States used to be able to demonstrate its commitment to defend its allies in the region merely by sending its aircraft carriers. For instance, when China seemed to threaten to use force to integrate Taiwan into the mainland in 1996, the United States ordered two carrier battle groups to transit the Taiwan Strait, and this sufficed to persuade Beijing to back down.[85] In recent years though, China has developed antiship missiles and other weapons that are viewed by the US military as greatly undermining America's ability to rely on its naval vessels to project power. Hence, as discussed in chapter 1, the United States developed the AirSea Battle plan,[86] which assumes that in case of a war with China, the United States will have to neutralize these A2/AD weapons that are on the mainland. This in turn requires accessing the Chinese mainland—via the sea, and AirSea Battle in large part "is designed to allow the U.S. military to gain access to littoral waters in the face of China's anti-access/area denial doctrine."[87]

A critical review of these arguments finds little reason to doubt that the United States has strong security reasons to favor the freedom of navigation. However, it does not follow that military assertions are the best way to ensure this freedom, especially as the first step to counter what the United States views as excessive restrictions. Instead, moves such as operational assertions should serve as a fallback option should diplomatic measures and multilateral efforts fail.

In effect, FONA add a security risk, since they can quite readily escalate into dangerous clashes between the forces of the super powers. Roach and Smith, for example, acknowledge that "demonstrations of resolve" by US operational assertions risk "the possibility of military confrontation."[88] Two major instances of such confrontation include the Black Sea bumping incident involving the Soviet Union and the Gulf of Sidra clashes with Libya.[89] While these took place decades ago, they illustrate the risks involved and parallel recent Chinese-US naval confrontations (although the latter have involved surveillance by US forces rather than outright FON assertions).[90] There might well be occasions in which security interests compel the United States to act in ways other nations consider provocative. The United States might well be justified, for example, in conducting surveillance when it has reasons to fear an attack. However, engaging in such operations to assert rights before employing less risky measures seems unjustified, even from a realist viewpoint.

Moreover, it is far from clear that all claims and assertions by any given nation should be treated in the same manner. Some deviate much less from the letter and spirit of the Law of the Sea treaty (and from customary law and precedent) than others; some seem quite reasonable on the face of it; many could be viewed as a call for renegotiation (which, as we have shown, has often been carried out, particularly through the three UNCLOS conventions) rather than rejected out of hand.

A major case in point is the perfectly reasonable requirement for military ships to identify themselves or give advance notice before entering territorial waters (not to be conflated with the right to board and search these ships). Such a requirement seems particularly justified for ships that carry nuclear weapons or otherwise hazardous materials. Thus, scholars have pointed out that customary international law "allows transit states to require notification, before such shipments can pass through their territorial seas or EEZs," although others disagree.[91] As for military affairs, in statements on acceding to the Law of the Sea, both Bangladesh and Malta have pointed out that "effective and speedy means of communication are easily available and make the prior notification of the exercise of the right of innocent passage of warships reasonable and not incompatible with the Convention."[92] These claims were made by other nations, including Djibouti, Egypt, India, Indonesia, Taiwan, Vietnam, and Yemen. Rather than trying to accommodate or negotiate these claims, the United States conducted operational assertions against them. Indeed, the United States has strong reasons to oppose restrictions that actually hinder US mobility, such as requirements for prior permission for innocent passage through territorial waters (as claimed by China and the Maldives) or through an international strait (as claimed by Oman).

Beyond the question of whether restrictions the United States deems excessive indeed harm national security, the realist defense of FONA as currently practiced raises deeper questions about America's role in the world. The United States holds that it needs to be able to project power any place in the world, and hence must be free to move its aircraft carrier battle groups and other naval assets. However, some of the restrictions that nations seek to place on freedom of navigation effectively question whether the time has come for the United States to project less power, especially in areas in which new regional powers are rising.

I addressed this issue and related concerns in chapter 5. It suffices to state here that American FONA seek to uphold a hegemonic position—but this is not the position the United States has chosen on many other fronts. For instance, the United States responded to the Russian invasion of Ukraine and even to the rise of ISIS only after it consulted and cooperated with a broad coalition of other nations. That is also the line the United States follows with regard to the Iran nuclear negotiations or in its treatment of North Korea. FONA seem like a relic from a more assertive, powerful, unilateral United States, the one that won the Cold War.

One reason that the weakness of the liberal justification for FONA and the doubt raised by the realist justification are very rarely confronted seems to be due to what economists call the "importance of being unimportant."[93] This concept holds that when a particular item, say the cost of nails, amounts to a very small fraction of the total costs of a project, say a housing development, the producers of this item can significantly increase the price of this item without the customer switching to a different producer or substituting a different item. Evidence suggests that FONA are almost unknown to the public. The *New York Times* and *Washington Post* published zero articles on FONA over the last five years, though the *New York Times* did carry a few brief updates on the subject by Reuters. If FONA came under the kind of scrutiny to which several other military assertions have been subjected, many may agree that the time has come for this Cold War relic to be scaled back in accordance with today's evolved—and still evolving—international order.

CONCLUSION

L eading political scientists find that when a new power (as China currently is) rises and the old hegemon (in this case, the United States)
does not make some significant concessions to the rising power, war
will ensue. A growing number of American public leaders and elected
officials point to changes China is making in several contested islands
and its claims to much of the South China Sea as evidence that China is
aggressive and expansionist. China is also charged with threatening the
freedom of navigation and with "bullying" its small neighbors, including US allies. The United States is called upon to stop both forms of aggression by "all necessary means."

American defense experts openly debate the best ways to attack
China in the event of a war—an invasion of the mainland (under the
AirSea Battle plan) or a maritime blockade of China. An examination
of the military budget shows acquisitions that make little sense unless
the United States is preparing for the eventuality of war with China. Select corporations that benefit from building expensive weapon systems,
which are of no use in fighting terrorists but are suitable for war with
China, are lobbying for more of their wares to be bought by the Pentagon. The United States has formed military alliances or beefed up existing ones with nations on the border of China.

China is modernizing its military, making various assertive claims,
and coping with its own array of military and corporate lobbies. It os-
cillates between feeling humiliated and beleaguered on the one hand,
and feeling entitled to more say in regional, if not in global, affairs on
the other hand. It uses "salami" tactics to advance its territorial claims,
which are difficult to stop without risking war.

In short, there are reasons to hold that the United States and China
are drifting toward war. As someone who has been to war, not as a war
correspondent or supply clerk but as a member of the Special Forces
(although in my day, these were called commandos), I strongly believe
that war is justified only when all other means for settling conflicts have

been exhausted. And even when war is thus justified,[1] it still exacts very great human and economic costs. Moreover, the outcomes are rarely those for which the warring parties hoped. See Vietnam, Iraq, Afghanistan, Libya, and Syria. I find it particularly troubling that various published proposals for how the United States should wage war with China provide no indication of what would happen after we win (they all assume we will). Will the United States follow the "you broke it; you own it" rule, meaning that we will be obligated to rebuild China? Will the United States try to install a liberal democratic government in Beijing? Will we leave, only to face a much more resentful government? One cannot have a reasonable plan for war unless one answers what it will accomplish for us and what it will do to others.

I use the phrase "drifting toward war." The book—which focuses on the United States, given that there are many other books by Americans that focus on China—shows that the White House has not conducted a systematic response to the key question at hand: How do we respond to the rise of China? A "pivot" toward China means paying more attention to the region and dedicating some more resources to it, but not what changes in the status quo, if any, the United States is willing to make in order to accommodate China. And what will the United States expect in return for such accommodations? What kind of international arrangement in the Western Pacific would the United States and its allies find satisfactory?

We did not have a public debate about these questions. Indeed, we have had much more give-and-take about various troop surges, and even about bathroom rights for transgender people, than on whether the American public is supporting the United States' gradual retreat from the Middle East and its increasing focus on the Far East. There has been even less debate about whether the American public is willing to support one more war. More than anything else, this book seeks to contribute to such a debate.

The book finds that the United States and China have a very large number of shared interests, including combating climate change, preventing the proliferation of nuclear weapons, curbing jihadist terrorism, countering piracy on the high seas, and redirecting funds from a military buildup toward urgent domestic needs. In addition to these shared interests, there are complementary interests. For example, China needs access to US markets, and the United States needs China to continue to finance a significant part of its national debt. The remaining issues, where there are conflicting interests, concern matters that have rather limited "real" value but seem of great import once they are invested with symbolic importance. Hence, this book outlines a series of measures that will allow both sides to deflate these overblown interpretations and then be able to find ways to negotiate settlements.

The book examines the argument that the way forward is for China to be "integrated" into the prevailing liberal, rule-based, international order. This is an order the United States (and its allies) formed at the end of World War II, when the United States was a full-blown global hegemon. Two elements of this order, I find, are still compelling and should be strongly undergirded. One is that no state should use force to cross borders and interfere in the internal affairs of other states. (A rare exception is to prevent genocide, under the Responsibility to Protect.) The other is that the freedom of navigation be respected. Both these rules are said to be challenged by China, the first through its use of sa-lami tactics, that is, incremental acts of aggression which are too minor to merit a response but which, cumulatively, represent significant gains. However, this book finds that China has gained very little through these tactics. Moreover, the issues concerning the various contested islands could readily be resolved through a series of bargains among the par-ties involved once the symbolic tensions were defused. As to freedom of navigation, given that China is dependent on the importation of raw material and energy sources by sea, it is hard to imagine that it would interfere in the freedom of navigation.

Blocking aggression (defined as acts that involve the use of force) is an essential part of the liberal order. The United States should con-tinue to dedicate itself to shoring up this order, drawing on its allies in the region; however, the growing influence of China should not be equated with aggression. Influence leaves the final decision on how to act to those subject to that influence. Coercion preempts such choices and forces those subject to it to abide by the preferences of those who wield force. Germany has a disproportionate measure of influence over most European affairs compared to other EU member states, but this does not make it an aggressor, let alone a regional hegemon. The same is true—for the last twenty years or so—for the United States in the West-ern hemisphere. China is likely to continue to gain more influence in the Western Pacific. Moves by the United States to block this increase, as highlighted by its attempt to urge nations not to participate in the China-led Asian Infrastructure Investment Bank, are likely to fail and lead to increased tensions. In other words, the United States and its allies should not tolerate use of force in the region, which would violate the long-standing Westphalian principle. However, when China's moves are limited to seeking to influence the course of other nations—say, through public diplomacy, trade, investment, or cultural exchanges (e.g., opening Confucius Institutes)—the United States should counter such influence with the same kind of means but not by the use of force.

In addition, this book finds that the calls for China to be integrated into the liberal international order are often combined with putting various obstacles in China's way. For instance, the United States has resisted increasing China's share of votes in the IMF and World Bank, even after it increased its contributions to both institutions. There is also a need for extending the liberal, rule-based international order by adding new rules, especially concerning cyberspace and outer space.

China is often criticized for its poor human rights record. This is a fair and valid criticism. However, the United States is not using force, or the threat of force, to promote human rights in Vietnam, Saudi Arabia, Iran, Pakistan, or elsewhere. Instead, the United States should continue to use cultural exchange, education efforts, people-to-people engagement, public diplomacy, and trade—in sum, a policy of engagement—to continue to promote human rights in China.

One may disagree with one or more of the points made in this book, although I believe that they are well supported by the evidence I have cited. However, I hold that we can all agree that we should have a vigorous, comprehensive public debate about what the United States' China policy is and what it should be. Above all, we must find a way to stop the drift toward war without compromising any of the core interests of the United States and its allies, or the values the United States is called upon to uphold.

ACKNOWLEDGMENTS

These essays appeared in earlier form as noted below. All articles have been updated and modified, some extensively. David Kroeker-Maus helped put this book to bed.

"Who Authorized Preparations for War with China?" *Yale Journal of International Affairs,* Summer 2013, 37–51. Also draws on Amitai Etzioni, "Air Sea Battle: A Case Study in Structural Inattention and Subterranean Forces," *Armed Forces & Society* 42, no. 1 (2016): 169–91.

"China: Making an Adversary?" *International Politics* 48, no. 6 (2011): 647–66.

"How Aggressive Is China?" *Korean Journal of International Studies,* forthcoming.

"Is China a Responsible Stakeholder?" *International Affairs* 87, no. 3 (2011): 539–53.

"Accommodating China." Draws on two earlier works, "Accommodating China," *Survival: Global Politics & Strategy* 55, no. 2 (2013): 45–60; and "Mutually Assured Restraint: A New Approach for United States–China Relations," *Brown Journal of World Affairs* 20, no. 11 (2014): 37–51.

"Is the United States Trying to Integrate China into the International Order?" Appeared in an earlier form as "Asian Infrastructure Investment Bank: A Case Study of Multifaceted Containment," *Asian Perspectives* 40 (2016): 173–96.

"To Contain or Not? When and Where Is the Question." Very revised version of "Rethinking the Pakistan Plan," *National Interest,* January/February 2012.

"Armed Humanitarian Interventions versus Regime Changes." Appeared in an earlier form as "Defining Down Sovereignty," *Ethics and International Affairs* 30, no. 1 (Spring 2016): 5–20.

"Freedom of Navigation Assertions: The United States as the World's Policeman." *Armed Forces & Society* 42, no. 1 (2016): 1–17.

NOTES

Introduction

1. Cited in Zachery Keck, "US-China Rivalry More Dangerous Than Cold War?," *Diplomat,* January 28, 2014, http://thediplomat.com/2014/01/us-china-rivalry-more-dangerous-than-cold-war/.

2. Timothy Garton Ash, "If US Relations with China Turn Sour, There Will Probably Be a War," *Guardian,* October 16, 2015, http://www.theguardian.com/commentisfree/2015/oct/16/us-relations-china-war-america.

3. Michael Pillsbury, "China and the United States Are Preparing for War," *Foreign Policy,* November 13, 2014, http://foreignpolicy.com/2014/11/13/china-and-the-united-states-are-preparing-for-war/.

4. Graham Allison, "The Thucydides Trap: Are the U.S. and China Headed for War?," *Atlantic,* September 24, 2015, http://www.theatlantic.com/international/archive/2015/09/united-states-china-war-thucydides-trap/406756/.

5. Ibid.

6. "Trump: US Must Get Tougher Because China Is 'Eating Our Lunch,'" *Newsmax Finance,* September 25, 2012, http://www.newsmax.com/Finance/StreetTalk/Trump-China-lunch-Apple/2012/09/25/id/457486/.

7. Hugh White, *The China Choice: Why America Should Share Power* (Collingwood, Australia: Black Inc., 2015).

8. Amitai Etzioni, *A Diary of a Commando Soldier* (Jerusalem: Achiasaf, 1952); Etzioni, *Winning without War* (Garden City, NY: Anchor Books, 1965); and Etzioni, *The Hard Way to Peace: A New Strategy* (New York: Crowler-Collier Press, 1962).

9. Lawrence Summers, "The World—Including China—Is Unprepared for the Rise of China," *Washington Post,* November 8, 2015.

1. Who Authorized Preparations for War with China?

1. Ronald O'Rourke, "China Naval Modernization: Implications for U.S. Navy Capabilities—Background and Issues for Congress," Congressional Research Service, December 10, 2012, p. 3, http://www.fas.org/sgp/crs/row/RL33153.pdf.

2. Richard Halloran, "PACAF'S 'Vision' Thing," *Air Force Magazine,* January 2009, http://www.airforce-magazine.com/MagazineArchive/Pages/2009/January%202009/0109vision.aspx.

3. Kyle D. Christensen, "Strategic Developments in the Western Pacific: Anti-Access/Area Denial and the Airsea Battle Concept," *Journal of Military and Strategic Studies* 14, no. 3 (2012): 10.

4. US Department of Defense, *Quadrennial Defense Review Report* (Washington, DC: Government Printing Office, February 2010), 32.

5. General Norton A. Schwartz, "Air-Sea Battle Doctrine: A Discussion with the Chief of Staff of the Air Force and Chief of Naval Operations," speech, Brookings Institution, May 16, 2012, transcript available at http://www.brookings .edu/~/media/events/2012/5/16%20air%20sea%20battle/20120516_air_sea _doctrine_corrected_transcript.pdf.

6. Jan Van Tol et al., *AirSea Battle: A Point-Departure Operational Concept* (Washington, DC: Center for Strategic and International Studies, 2010), 90–91.

7. Norton A. Schwartz and Jonathan W. Greenert, "Air-Sea Battle, Promoting Stability in an Era of Uncertainty," *American Interest,* February 20, 2012, http:// www.the-american-interest.com/article.cfm?piece=1212.

8. Admiral Jonathon Greenert, "Air-Sea Battle Doctrine: A Discussion with the Chief of Staff of the Air Force and Chief of Naval Operations," video, Brookings Institution, May 16, 2012, transcript available at http://www.brookings.edu/~ /media/events/2012/5/16%20air%20sea%20battle/20120516_air_sea_doctrine _corrected_transcript.pdf.

9. Elizabeth Bumiller, "Smaller Navy Ship Has a Rocky Past and Key Support," *New York Times,* April 5, 2012, http://www.nytimes.com/2012/04/06/us/politics /a-smaller-navy-ship-with-troubles-but-presidents-backing.html?pagewanted=all &_r=0.

10. O'Rourke, "China Naval Modernization," 92.

11. Harry Kazianis, "AirSea Battle's Identity Crisis," *Geopolitical Conflict Report,* September 13, 2011, http://gcreport.com/index.php/analysis/194-airsea-battles -identity-crisis.

12. Memo via USNI News, January 30, 2015, http://news.usni.org/2015/01/20 /document-air-sea-battle-name-change-memo.

13. Harry Kazianis, "Air-Sea Battle's Next Step: JAM-GC On Deck," *National Interest,* November 25, 2015.

14. James Holmes, "Redefining AirSea Battle: JAM-JC, China and the Quest for Clarity," *National Interest,* November 22, 2015, http://nationalinterest.org /feature/the-ghosts-airsea-battle-jam-gc-china-the-quest-clarity-14418.

15. Paul McLeary, "New US Concept Melds Air, Sea, and Land," *Defense News,* January 24, 2015, http://www.defensenews.com/story/defense/policy-budget /warfare/2015/01/24/air-sea-battle-china-army-navy/22229023/.

16. Jacek Bartosiak, "As Air-Sea Battle Becomes JAM-GC . . . Don't Forget Central and Eastern Europe," Potomac Foundation, November 24, 2015, www .thepotomacfoundation.org/as-air-sea-battle-becomes-jam-gc-dont-forget-central -and-eastern-europe/.

17. US Department of Defense, "Background Briefing on Air-Sea Battle by Defense Officials from the Pentagon," news brief, November 9, 2011, transcript available at http://www.defense.gov/transcripts/transcript.aspx?transcriptid =4923.

18. Philip Ewing, "The Rise and Fall of Air-Sea Battle," *DoD Buzz,* May 17, 2012, http://www.dodbuzz.com/2012/05/17/the-rise-and-fall-of-air-sea-battle/.

19. J. Noel Williams, "Air-Sea Battle: An Operational Concept Looking for a Strategy," *Armed Forces Journal,* September 2011, http://www.armedforcesjournal .com/2011/09/7558138/.

20. Greg Jaffe, "U.S. Model for a Future War Fans Tensions with China and Inside Pentagon," *Washington Post,* August 1, 2012, http://articles.washingtonpost .com/2012-08-01/world/35492126_1_china-tensions-china-threat-pentagon.

21. Jeffrey Kline and Wayne Hughes, "Between Peace and Air-Sea Battle: A War at Sea Strategy," *Naval War College Review* 65, no. 4 (2012): 36.

22. T. X. Hammes, "Strategy for an Unthinkable Conflict," *Diplomat,* July 27, 2012, http://thediplomat.com/flashpoints-blog/2012/07/27/military-strategy-for-an -unthinkable-conflict/.

23. Andrew F. Krepinevich Jr., "How to Deter China: The Case for Archipelagic Defense," *Foreign Affairs* 94 (2015): 78–86.

24. Sydney J. Freedberg Jr., "Cartwright Targets F-35, AirSea Battle; Warns of $250B More Cuts," *AOL Defense,* May 15, 2012, http://defense.aol.com/2012/05/15 /cartwright-savages-f-35-airsea-battle-warns-of-250-billion-mo/.

25. Jaffe, "U.S. Model for a Future War." (A reviewer of this chapter from a military think tank commented that "incalculable" was an overstatement, that such a war would be only "very destructive." I stand corrected.)

26. "Pentagon to Weigh Sending Extra Subs, Bombers to Asia-Pacific," Global Security Newswire, August 2, 2012, http://www.nti.org/gsn/article/pentagon -weighing-sending-extra-subs-bombers-asia-pacific/.

27. Raoul Heinrichs, "America's Dangerous Battle Plan," *Diplomat,* August 17, 2012, http://thediplomat.com/2011/08/17/america%E2%80%99s-dangerous-battle -plan/.

28. T. X. Hammes, "Offshore Control: A Proposed Strategy for an Unlikely Conflict," *Strategic Forum,* no. 258 (National Defense University Institute for National and Strategic Studies, June 2012), 2.

29. Dan Blumenthal, "The US Response to China's Military Modernization," in *Strategic Asia 2012–13: China's Military Challenge,* ed. Ashley Tellis and Travis Tanner (Washington, DC: National Bureau of Asian Research, 2013).

30. Andrew F. Krepinevich, "Strategy in a Time of Austerity: Why the Pentagon Should Focus on Assuring Access," *Center for Strategic and Budgetary Assessments,* November 1, 2012, http://www.csbaonline.org/2012/11/01/strategy-in -a-time-of-austerity-why-the-pentagon-should-focus-on-assuring-access/3/.

31. For additional discussion, see Amitai Etzioni's White House Chronicle interviews on his YouTube channel: https://www.youtube.com/channel/UC4 H32EThts7TStEIIb_Y-Ug.

32. Jeffrey A. Bader, *Obama and China's Rise: An Insider's Account of America's Asia Strategy* (Washington, DC: Brookings Institution, 2012), 7.

33. Ibid., 3.

34. Ibid., 147–50.

35. James Mann, *The Obamians: The Struggle inside the White House to Redefine American Power* (New York: Penguin Group, 2012), 245.

36. Andrew F. Krepinevich, interview with author, December 3, 2012.

37. Martin S. Indyk, *Bending History: Barack Obama's Foreign Policy* (Washington, DC: Brookings Institution, 2012), 38–41.

38. "President Obama Speaks at the University of Indonesia," *DipNote: U.S. State Department Official Blog,* November 10, 2010, http://blogs.state.gov/index .php/site/entry/obama_university_of_indonesia.

39. David E. Sanger, *Confront and Conceal: Obama's Secret Wars and Surprising Use of American Power* (New York: Random House, 2012).

40. J. Randy Forbes, Letter to Secretary of Defense Leon Panetta, November 7, 2011, http://forbes.house.gov/uploadedfiles/panetta_asb.pdf.

41. None of this prevented the two hawkish senators from championing ASB. See J. Randy Forbes, "AirSea Office Must Battle Through, or Fail," *AOL Defense,* September 13, 2012, http://defense.aol.com/2012/09/13/airsea-office-must-battle -through-or-fail-rep-j-randy-forbes/; and Joseph Lieberman, "Peace through Strength: American Leadership in Asia Pacific," speech, Heritage Foundation's Annual B. C. Lee Lecture on U.S. Policy in the Asia-Pacific, November 2, 2012, transcript available at http://www.realfijinews.com/756328456/peace-through -strength-american-leadership-in-asia-pacific/.

42. Carl Conetta, "Asia Pivot and Air-Sea Battle: Precipitating Military Competition with China?," *Defense Strategy Review Page,* March 3, 2014.

43. Thomas Barnett, "AirSea Battle: The Military-Industrial Complex's Self-Serving Fantasy," *Time,* August 8, 2012.

44. Marc Schanz, "AirSea Battle's Battle," *Air Force Magazine* 96, no. 4 (April 2013).

45. David Sills, *The Volunteers: Means and Ends in a National Organization* (Glencoe, IL: Free Press, 1957).

46. Paul Shinkman, "Obama: 'Global War on Terror' Is Over," *U.S. News and World Report,* May 23, 2013.

47. Zachary Keck, "Air-Sea Battle to Cost $524.5 Billion through 2023," *Diplomat,* December 24, 2013.

48. J. Randy Forbes and Elbridge Colby, "We're Losing Our Military Edge over China: Here's How to Get It Back," *National Interest,* March 27, 2014.

49. Jan Van Tol et al., *AirSea Battle: A Point-Departure Operational Concept* (Washington, DC: Center for Strategic and International Studies, 2010).

50. Grace Jean, "Pentagon Budget 2015: U.S. Navy Prioritizes Shipbuilding at Expense of Aviation Procurement," *IHS Jane's Defence Weekly,* March 2, 2014.

51. Van Tol et al., *AirSea Battle.*

52. Keck, "Air-Sea Battle to Cost $524.5 Billion."

53. Peter Krause, "Troop Levels in Stability Operations: What We Don't Know," Massachusetts Institute of Technology, Center for International Studies, 2007.

54. Andrew Tilghman, "Top Brass Claims Personnel Costs Are Swamping DoD, but Budget Figures Say Otherwise," *Air Force Times,* November 24, 2013 ("Gen. Ray Odierno, Army chief of staff, has repeatedly said that Army personnel costs are projected to reach '80 percent' of that service's total budget by the end of the decade," compared to 50–70 percent for the military as a whole in the same time period).

55. Philip Ewing, "Report: US Should Place Its Bets on Navy, Air Force," *DoD Buzz,* October 7, 2011.

56. Jim Royal, "Does Lockheed Martin Pass Buffett's Test?" *Daily Finance,* November 12, 2011 (updated April 30, 2013).

57. John Driessnack and David King, "An Initial Look at Technology and Institutions on Defense Industry Consolidation," *Acquisition Review Journal* 35 (2004): 63–77.

58. Otto Kreisher, "F-35 Sails through Crucial Senate Hearing; Witnesses Testify There's No Alternative," *Breaking Defense,* June 19, 2013.

59. Particularly *Citizens United v. Federal Electoral Commission,* 558 U.S. (2010).

60. Michael Rocca and Stacy Gordon, "Earmarks as a Means and an End: The Link between Earmarks and Campaign Contributions in the U.S. House of Representatives," *Journal of Politics* 75, no. 1 (2013).

61. Christopher Witko, "Campaign Contributions, Access, and Government Contracting," *Journal of Public Administration Research and Theory* 21, no. 4 (2011).

62. These sources wished to remain anonymous. Their names were disclosed to the editor of the *Armed Forces and Society Journal.*

63. David W. Barno, "Silicon, Iron, and Shadow: Three Wars That Will Define America's Future," *Foreign Policy,* March 19, 2013.

64. Robert Gates, *Duty: Memoirs of a Secretary at War* (New York: Knopf, 2014), 143, 118.

65. "Kendall Cautions against Complacency in U.S. Tech Superiority," *American Forces Press Service,* February 25, 2014.

66. "Remarks by President Obama to the Australian Parliament," White House Office of the Press Secretary, Canberra, Australia, November 17, 2011, http://www .whitehouse.gov/the-press-office/2011/11/17/remarks-president-obama-australian -parliament.

67. Ian E. Rinehart, Steven A. Hildreth, and Susan V. Lawrence, "Ballistic Missile Defense in the Asia-Pacific Region: Cooperation and Opposition," Congressional Research Service, April 3, 2015, https://www.fas.org/sgp/crs/nuke /R43116.pdf.

2. China: Making an Adversary?

1. *Economist,* December 4, 2010.

2. Michael Slackman, "Poland, Lacking External Enemies, Turns on Itself," *New York Times,* November 27, 2010.

3. Paul Kennedy, *The Rise and Fall of the Great Powers: Economic Change and Military Conflict from 1500 to 2000* (New York: Random House, 1987); Ezra F. Vogel, "Pax Nipponica?," *Foreign Affairs* 64, no. 4 (Spring 1986).

4. Ted Fishman, "The Chinese Century," *New York Times Magazine,* July 4, 2004; Michael Elliott, "The Chinese Century," *Time,* January 11, 2007; Patrick Buchanan, "The Chinese Century," *American Conservative,* April 22, 2010.

5. Martin Jacques, *When China Rules the World: The End of the Western World and the Birth of a New Global Order* (New York: Penguin Press, 2009); "The Fourth Modernization," *Economist,* December 4, 2010, 7.

6. Private communication, March 19, 2016.

7. Charles E. Osgood, "Reciprocal Initiative," in *The Liberal Papers,* ed. James Roosevelt (New York: Doubleday, 1962).

8. Geoff Dyer and Farhan Bokhari, "China-Pakistan Reactor Deal to Open Fresh US Rift," *Financial Times,* September 23, 2010.

9. Seymour M. Hersh, "The Online Threat," *New Yorker,* November 1, 2010.

10. Amitai Etzioni, *A Comparative Analysis of Complex Organizations* (New York: Free Press, 1961; rev. ed., 1975).

11. G. William Skinner and Edwin A. Winckler, "Compliance Succession in Rural Communist China: A Cyclical Theory," in *A Sociological Reader on Complex Organizations,* ed. Amitai Etzioni, 2nd ed. (New York: Holt, Rinehart, and Winston, 1969), 410–38.

12. David Lampton, *The Three Faces of Chinese Power: Might, Money, and Minds* (Berkeley: University of California Press, 2008).

13. U.S.-China Economic and Security Review Commission, "2015 Report to Congress," http://origin.www.uscc.gov/sites/default/files/annual_reports/2015 %20Annual%20Report%20to%20Congress.PDF.

14. US Department of Defense, *Annual Report to Congress on China's Military Power, Military and Security Developments Involving the People's Republic of China* (Washington, DC: Government Printing Office, 2013).

15. Elbridge Colby, "Why China's Growing Defense Budget Matters," *Real Clear Defense,* March 9, 2015, http://www.realcleardefense.com/articles/2015/03/09/why _chinas_growing_defense_budget_matters-2.html.

16. Sam Perlo-Freeman, Aude Fleurant, Pieter D. Wezeman, and Siemon T. Wezeman, *Trends in World Military Expenditure,* 2014, 2015, http://books.sipri.org /files/FS/SIPRIFS1504.pdf.

17. Ted Galen Carpenter, "China's Military Spending: No Cause for Panic," *Aspenia online,* April 4, 2013, https://www.aspeninstitute.it/aspenia-online/article /china's-military-spending-no-cause-panic.

18. Simon Denver, "China's Slowing Economy Leads to Smallest Increase in Military Spending in Years," *Washington Post,* March 4, 2016, https://www .washingtonpost.com/world/china-military-spending-growth-slows-in-line-with -economy-army-downsizing/2016/03/04/5c3686ab-b483-4f7d-86b2-77125c67dd4c _story.html.

19. Andrew S. Erickson, Abraham M. Denmark, and Gabriel Collins, "Beijing's 'Starter Carrier' and Future Steps: Alternatives and Implications," *Naval War College Review* 65, no. 1 (2012).

20. Robert Farley, "Does the US Navy Have 10 or 19 Aircraft Carriers?," *Diplomat,* April 17, 2014, http://thediplomat.com/2014/04/does-the-us-navy-have -10-or-19-aircraft-carriers/.

21. Bryan McGrath and Seth Cropsey, "The Real Reason China Wants Aircraft Carriers," *Real Clear Defense,* April 16, 2014, http://www.realcleardefense.com /articles/2014/04/16/the_real_reason_china_wants_aircraft_carriers.html.

22. Erickson, Denmark, and Collins, "Beijing's 'Starter Carrier,'" 15.

23. Ronald O'Rourke, "China Naval Modernization: Implications for US Navy

Capabilities—Background and Issues for Congress," *Congressional Research Service*, July 5, 2013; US Department of Defense, *Annual Report to Congress on China's Military Power*, 2013.

24. Robert S. Ross, "The 1995–96 Taiwan Strait Confrontation: Coercion, Credibility, and the Use of Force," *International Security* 25, no. 2 (2000): 87–123.

25. Harry Kazianis, "Is China's 'Carrier-Killer' Really a Threat to the U.S. Navy?," *National Interest*, September 2, 2015, http://nationalinterest.org/blog/the-buzz/chinas-carrier-killer-really-threat-the-us-navy-13765.

26. Shannon Tiezzi, "US Admiral: Chinese Subs Outnumber America's," *Diplomat*, February 27, 2015, http://thediplomat.com/2015/02/us-admiral-chinese-subs-outnumber-americas/.

27. Eric Heginbotham, Michael Nixon, Forrest E. Morgan, Jacob Heim, Jeff Hagen, Sheng Li, Jeffrey Engstrom, Martin C. Libicki, Paul DeLuca, David A. Shlapak, David R. Frelinger, Burgess Laird, Kyle Brady, and Lyle J. Morris, "U.S. and Chinese Air Superiority Capabilities: An Assessment of Relative Advantage, 1996–2017," RAND Corporation, 2015, http://www.rand.org/pubs/research_briefs/RB9858z3.html.

28. Jonah Friedman, "Nuclear vs. Diesel Submarines," *Center for Strategic & International Studies* 18 (2011), http://csis.org/blog/nuclear-vs-diesel-submarines.

29. John Pomfret, "Military Strength Eludes China, Which Looks Overseas for Arms," *Washington Post*, December 25, 2010.

30. Hans M. Kristensen, director of the Nuclear Information Project at the Federation of American Scientists, cited in ibid.

31. Adm. Gary Roughead, chief of naval operations, cited in Gregg Easterbrook, "Waste Land," *New Republic*, November 10, 2010, 20.

32. Drew Thompson, "Think Again: China's Military," *Foreign Policy*, no. 178 (March/April 2010): 86–90.

33. Dave Majumdar, "Warning: China's Airpower Will Equal the U.S. Air Force by 2030," *National Interest*, March 2, 2016, http://nationalinterest.org/blog/the-buzz/warning-chinas-airpower-will-equal-the-us-air-foce-by-2030-15384.

34. Michael Kofman, "An Uneasy Ménage à Trois," *Foreign Affairs*, December 4, 2014, https://www.foreignaffairs.com/articles/east-asia/2014-12-04/uneasy-m-nage-trois.

35. Jennifer Anderson, *The Limits of Sino-Russian Strategic Partnership*, Adelphi Papers, no. 315 (New York: Routledge, 2013).

36. Brendan Thomas-Noone and Rory Medcalf, "Nuclear-Armed Submarines in Indo-Pacific Asia: Stabilizer or Menace?," Lowy Institute for International Policy, September 4, 2015, http://www.lowyinstitute.org/files/nuclear-armed-submarines-in-indo-pacific-asia-stabiliser-or-menace_0.pdf.

37. Edward Wong, Jane Perlez, and Chris Buckley, "China Announces Cuts of 300,000 Troops at Military Parade Showing Its Might," *New York Times*, September 2, 2015.

38. Dean Cheng, "The Chinese People's Liberation Army and Special Operations," *Special Warfare* 25, no. 3 (July–September 2012).

39. *The Professional Bulletin of Army Special Operations* 25, no. 3 (2012),

http://www.soc.mil/swcs/swmag/archive/SW2503/SW2503TheChinesePeoples
LiberationArmy.html.

40. Roy Kamphausen, "China's Land Forces: New Priorities and Capabilities,"
National Bureau of Asian Research, October 2012, http://nbr.org/publications
/element.aspx?id=616.

41. Cary Huang, "Retired PLA General Xu Caihou: A Big Shot with Friends in
High Places," *South China Morning Post,* March 20, 2014.

42. Michael S. Chase, Jeffrey Engstrom, Tai Ming Cheung, Kristen A. Gunness,
Scott Warren Harold, Susan Puska, and Samuel K. Berkowitz, *China's Incomplete
Military Transformation: Assessing the Weaknesses of the People's Liberation Army
(PLA)* (Santa Monica: RAND Corporation, 2015).

43. Dennis J. Blasko, "Ten Reasons Why China Will Have Trouble Fighting a
Modern War," *War on the Rocks,* February 18, 2015, http://warontherocks.com/2015
/02/ten-reasons-why-china-will-have-trouble-fighting-a-modern-war/.

44. Hans M. Kristensen and Robert S. Norris, "Status of World Nuclear
Forces," Federation of American Scientists, http://fas.org/issues/nuclear-weapons
/status-world-nuclear-forces/, accessed March 4, 2016.

45. Hans M. Kristensen and Robert S. Norris, "Chinese Nuclear Forces, 2015,"
Bulletin of the Atomic Scientists 71, no. 4 (2015): 77–84.

46. Kingston Reif, "U.S. Nuclear Modernization Programs," Arms Control
Association, December 2015, https://www.armscontrol.org/factsheets/USNuclear
Modernization.

47. Fiona S. Cunningham and M. Taylor Fravel, "Assuring Assured Retaliation:
China's Nuclear Posture and US-China Strategic Stability," *International Security*
40, no. 2 (2015): 7–50.

48. T. S. Kelso, "Analysis of the 2007 Chinese ASAT Test and the Impact of Its
Debris on the Space Environment," paper presented at the 8th Advanced Maui
Optical and Space Surveillance Technologies Conference, Maui, HI, 2007.

49. Ibid.

50. Brian Weeden, "Anti-Satellite Tests in Space—The Case of China," Secure
World Foundation, August 16, 2013, http://swfound.org/media/115643/china_asat
_testing_fact_sheet_aug_2013.pdf.

51. China's state media described the launch as a "land-based anti-missile
technology experiment" rather than an ASAT weapon, but the US State
Department claimed it was a "non-destructive anti-satellite test." See Zachary
Keck, "China Conducted Anti-Satellite Missile Test," *Diplomat,* July 29, 2014,
http://thediplomat.com/2014/07/china-conducted-anti-satellite-missile-test/.

52. Michael Klein, "What You May Not Know about China and Currency
Manipulation," *Wall Street Journal,* May 22, 2015, http://blogs.wsj.com/washwire
/2015/05/22/what-you-may-not-know-about-china-and-currency-manipulation/.

53. Brian Wingfield, "China Cited by U.S. for Trade Barriers on Autos, Steel,
Beef," Bloomberg Business, April 1, 2013, http://www.bloomberg.com/news
/articles/2013-04-01/china-cited-by-u-s-for-trade-barriers-on-autos-steel-dvds.

54. US-China Business Council, "US State Exports to China (2005–2014)," 2015.

55. US-China Business Council, "Consumption: New Key to Chinese Growth,"

China Business Review, July 1, 2010, http://www.chinabusinessreview.com /consumption-new-key-to-chinese-growth/.

56. US Office of the National Counterintelligence Executive, "Foreign Spies Stealing US Economic Secrets in Cyberspace: Report to Congress on Foreign Economic Collection and Industrial Espionage, 2009–2011," October 2011, https:// www.ncsc.gov/publications/reports/fecie_all/Foreign_Economic_Collection_2011 .pdf.

57. The US assistant secretary of commerce put the estimate at nearly $24 billion a year in a 2004 statement: "US Lashes Out at Chinese Piracy," *Asia Times,* January 15, 2005, http://www.atimes.com/atimes/China/GA15Ad03.html.

58. Stefan Halper, *The Beijing Consensus: How China's Authoritarian Model Will Dominate the Twenty-first Century* (New York: Basic Books, 2010); see also Jacques, *When China Rules the World.*

59. Lamido Sanusi, "Africa Must Get Real about Chinese Ties," *Financial Times,* March 11, 2013.

60. Thomas L. Friedman, "Our One-Party Democracy," *New York Times,* September 8, 2009.

61. Stein Ringen, "Is Chinese Autocracy Outperforming Western Democracy?" *OpenDemocracy,* June 12, 2015, https://www.opendemocracy.net/stein-ringen/is -chinese-autocracy-outperforming-western-democracy.

62. Howard Chao, "China's Great Firewall Blocks Innovation and Commerce," *South China Morning Post,* July 6, 2013, http://www.scmp.com/comment/insight -opinion/article/1276177/chinas-great-firewall-blocks-innovation-and-commerce.

63. David Shambaugh, *China's Future* (London: Polity, 2016).

64. World Bank data, accessed March 29, 2016, at http://data.worldbank.org /indicator/SI.POV.GINI.

65. Leon Hadar, "Don't Fear China," *American Conservative,* December 17, 2010, http://www.amconmag.com/blog/dont-fear-china/.

66. Michael Mandelbaum, *The Frugal Superpower: America's Global Leadership in a Cash-Strapped Era* (New York: Public Affairs, 2010), 4–5.

67. Robert D. Kaplan, "The Geography of Chinese Power: How Far will Beijing Reach on Land and at Sea?," *Foreign Affairs* 89, no. 3 (May/June 2010): 22–41.

68. Kenneth G. Lieberthal, "Is China Catching Up with the United States?," *Ethos* 8 (2010): 12–16.

69. Robert Kagan, "The Illusion of 'Managing' China," *Washington Post,* May 15, 2015.

70. Clifford Krauss and Keith Bradsher, "China's Global Ambitions, Cash and String Attached," *New York Times,* July 24, 2015, http://www.nytimes.com/2015 /07/26/business/international/chinas-global-ambitions-with-loans-and-strings -attached.html?_r=0.

71. Kaplan, "The Geography of Chinese Power."

72. Andrea Ghiselli, "China's First Overseas Base in Djibouti, an Enabler of Its Middle East Policy," *China Brief* 16, no. 2 (January 25, 2016), http://www .jamestown.org/programs/chinabrief/single/?tx_ttnews%5Btt_news%5D=45017& cHash=72bded6b3552a69643f291b3afccff69#.V6H78vkrIdU.

73. Elizabeth C. Economy, "The Game Changer," *Foreign Affairs* 89, no. 6 (November 2010): 142–52.

74. Andrew J. Nathan, "China's Challenge," *Journal of Democracy* 26, no. 1 (2015): 156–70.

75. Doug Bandow, "China's Military Rise Means End of US Hegemony?," *Korea Times,* May 5, 2009.

76. Jonathan Fenby, "Does China Have a Foreign Policy? Domestic Pressures and China's Strategy," in *China's Geoeconomic Strategy,* ed. Nicholas Kitchen (London: LSE IDEAS, 2012), 12–18.

77. Katherine Morton, "China's Ambition in the South China Sea: Is a Legitimate Order Possible?" *International Affairs* 92, no. 4 (2016): 909–40.

78. Henry Kissinger, *On China* (New York: Penguin, 2011).

79. Michael D. Swaine, "The Real Challenge in the Pacific," *Foreign Affairs* 94 (2015): 148.

80. Bates Gill, "China's Evolving Regional Security Strategy," in *Power Shift: China and Asia's New Dynamics,* ed. David Shambaugh (Berkeley: University of California Press, 2005), 257.

81. Evan S. Medeiros, "Strategic Hedging and the Future of Asia-Pacific Stability," *Washington Quarterly* 29, no. 1 (Winter 2005/6): 145–67.

82. Paul Godwin, "Perspective: Asia's Dangerous Security Dilemma," *Current History,* no. 728 (September 2010): 264; see also "China's Military Power," Council on Foreign Relations, Independent Task Force on Chinese Military Power, May 2003, p. 1.

83. Robert Kaplan, "How We Would Fight China," *Atlantic* 295, no. 5 (June 2005): 49–64.

84. Ross, "The Rise of Chinese Power and the Implications for the Regional Security Order," Foreign Policy Research Institute, October 1, 2010, p. 545.

85. "Connect the World," CNN International, January 20, 2011, http://archives.cnn.com/TRANSCRIPTS/1101/20/ctw.01.html; see also Avery Goldstein, Testimony before the U.S. Economic and Security Review Commission, July, 21, 2005: "A rush to judgment about the nature of the China we are likely to face several decades from now is not only unwise, it is also unnecessary."

86. Jonathan Holslag, "Embracing Chinese Global Security Ambitions," *Washington Quarterly* 32, no. 3 (July 2009): 105–18.

87. This paradigm was advanced by the RAND Corporation and especially Andy Marshall: see Zalmay Khalilzad and John White, eds., *Strategic Appraisal: The Changing Role of Information in Warfare* (Santa Monica: RAND Corporation, 1999); see also John Nagl, "Let's Win the Wars We're In," *Joint Force Quarterly* 52 (First Quarter 2009): 20–26.

88. Mandelbaum, *The Frugal Superpower.*

89. Keith Bradsher, "Sitting Out the China Trade Battles," *New York Times,* December 23, 2010.

3. How Aggressive Is China?

1. Andrew J. Nathan and Andrew Scobell, "How China Sees America: The Sum of Beijing's Fears," *Foreign Affairs* 91, no. 5 (September/October 2012): 32–47.

2. G. William Skinner and Edwin A Winkler, "Compliance Succession in Rural Communist China: A Cyclical Theory" (1969), in *A Sociological Reader on Complex Organization,* comp. Amitai Etzioni (New York: Holt, Reinhart, and Winston, 1980), 410–38; David M. Lampton, *Three Faces of Chinese Power: Might, Money, and Minds* (Berkeley: University of California Press, 2008).

3. Joseph Nye Jr., *Soft Power: The Means to Success in World Politics* (New York: PublicAffairs, 2004).

4. Davis Brown, "Why the Crime of Aggression Will Not Reduce the Practice of Aggression," *International Politics* 51, no. 5 (2014): 649.

5. Andreas Paulas, "Second Thoughts on the Crime of Aggression," *European Journal of International Law* 20, no. 4 (2009): 111–20.

6. Carrie McDougall, "When Law and Reality Clash—the Imperative of Compromise in the Context of the Accumulated Evil of the Whole: Conditions for the Exercise of the International Criminal Court's Jurisdiction over the Crime of Aggression," *International Criminal Law Review* 7, nos. 2–3 (2007): 277–333.

7. Noah Weisbord, "Judging Aggression," *Columbia Journal of International Law* 50, no. 1 (2011): 90.

8. Keith A. Petty, "Sixty Years in the Making: The Definition of Aggression for the International Criminal Court," *Hastings International and Comparative Law Journal* 31, no. 2 (2008): 531–54; Jackson Nyamuya Maogoto, "Aggression Supreme: International Offence Still in Search of Definition," *Southern Cross University Law Review* 6, no. 1 (2002): 278–317.

9. Matthew C. Weed, "International Criminal Court and the Rome Statute: 2010 Review Conference," Congressional Research Service, 2011, https://www.fas.org/sgp/crs/row/R41682.pdf.

10. Oscar Solera, "The Definition of the Crime of Aggression: Lessons Not-Learned." *Case Western Reserve Journal of International Law* 42, no. 3 (2010): 803–4.

11. Mary Ellen O'Connell and Miralomal Niyazmatov, "What Is Aggression? Comparing the *Jus ad Bellum* and the ICC Statute," *Journal of International Criminal Justice* 10, no. 1 (2010): 189–207; Carsten Stahn, "The 'End,' the 'Beginning of the End' or the 'End of the Beginning'? Introducing Debates and Voices on the Definition of 'Aggression,'" *Leiden Journal of International Law* 23, no. 4 (2010): 875–82; Marina Mancini, "A Brand New Definition for the Crime of Aggression: The Kampala Outcome," *Nordic Journal of International Law* 81, no. 2 (2012): 227–48; Jennifer Trahan, "A Meaningful Definition of the Crime of Aggression," *University of Pennsylvania Journal of International Law* 33, no. 4 (2012): 907–69.

12. Stahn, "The 'End.'"

13. Mancini, "A Brand New Definition."

14. Harold Hongju Koh and Todd F. Buchwald, "The Crime of Aggression:

The United States Perspective," *American Journal of International Law* 109 (2015): 257–95.

15. Thomas W. Robinson and David Shambaugh, *Chinese Foreign Policy: Theory and Practice* (New York: Oxford University Press, 1994), 387.

16. M. Taylor Fravel, "Regime Insecurity and International Cooperation: Explaining China's Compromises in Territorial Disputes," *International Security* 30, no. 2 (2005): 46.

17. Harry Harding, "Has US China Policy Failed?," *Washington Quarterly* 38, no. 3 (2015): 95–122.

18. Kathleen Miles, "Robert Gates: China, Russia Are Becoming More Aggressive as They Perceive U.S. Pulling Back," *Huffington Post*, May 21, 2012, http://www.huffingtonpost.com/2014/05/21/robert-gates-china-russia_n_5361462 .html.

19. Keith Johnson, "Sand Pebbles: Why Are Superpowers Squabbling over Rocks?," *Foreign Policy*, April 2, 2015, http://foreignpolicy.com/2015/04/02 /sand-pebbles-why-are-superpowers-squabbling-over-rocks-us-china-scs-reef -reclamation/.

20. Samuel J. Locklear, "PACOM Testimony before the House Appropriations Committee: Remarks," http://www.pacom.mil/Media/SpeechesTestimony/tabid /6706/Chapter/581146/pacom-before-the-house-appropriations-committee -remarks.aspx.

21. Bonnie S. Glaser, "Armed Clash in the South China Sea," Council on Foreign Relations, 2012, http://www.cfr.org/world/armed-clash-south-china-sea /p27883; Glaser, "Conflict in the South China Sea," Council on Foreign Relations, 2015, http://www.cfr.org/asia-and-pacific/conflict-south-china-sea/p36377.

22. David Blair, "Barack Obama Calls on China to End 'Aggressive' Actions in South China Sea," *Telegraph*, June 1, 2015.

23. Associated Press, "China 'Aggressively' Expanding into South China Sea Says US," *Guardian*, February 26, 2015, http://www.theguardian.com/world/2015 /feb/27/china-aggressively-expanding-into-south-china-sea-says-us.

24. Michael Auslin, "China's Wall Crumbles," *National Review*, February 20, 2013, http://www.nationalreview.com/chapter/341066/chinas-wall-crumbles -michael-auslin.

25. This is not an exact quotation from James Lewis, but rather a quotation of the article that summarizes Lewis's statements. See Eric Geller, "Cyber Security Expert: U.S.-China Cybercrime Agreement 'a Major Step Forward,'" *Daily Dot*, September 25, 2015, http://dailydot.com/layer8/us-china-cyber-agreement-james -lewis-reaction/.

26. Sophie Brown, "Stop Spy Flights, China Warns the U.S.," CNN, August 29, 2014, http://www.cnn.com/2014/08/29/world/asia/china-us-spy-flights/.

27. Helene Cooper, "Pentagon Says Chinese Fighter Jet Confronted American Navy Plane," *New York Times*, August 22, 2014, http://www.nytimes.com/2014 /08/23/world/asia/us-says-chinese-fighter-jet-confronted-american-navy-plane .html.

28. Shannon Tiezzi, "Preventing Another 'Hainan Incident,'" *Diplomat*,

August 27, 2014, http://thediplomat.com/2014/08/preventing-another-hainan
-incident/.

29. Martin Fackler, "Japan Protests Chinese Flybys over East China Sea," *New York Times*, June 11, 2014, http://www.nytimes.com/2014/06/12/world/asia/japan
-protests-chinese-flybys-over-east-china-sea.html.

30. Anna Mulrine, "USS Cowpens: Why China Forced a Confrontation at Sea with the US Navy," *Christian Science Monitor*, December 13, 2013, http://www
.csmonitor.com/World/Security-Watch/2013/1213/USS-Cowpens-Why-China
-forced-a-confrontation-at-sea-with-US-Navy.

31. Ankit Panda, "Japan to Formally Nationalize 280 Islands," *Diplomat*, January 9, 2014, http://thediplomat.com/2014/01/japan-to-formally-nationalize
-280-islands/.

32. The Chinese ADIZ also overlaps with an ADIZ claimed by South Korea. Harry Kazianis, "China's East China Sea ADIZ Gamble: Past, Present, and South China Sea Future?," *National Interest*, June 19, 2015, http://nationalinterest.org
/feature/chinas-east-china-sea-adiz-gamble-past-present-south-china-13150.

33. Ian E. Reinhart and Bart Elias, "China's Air Defense Identification Zone (ADIZ)," Congressional Research Service, 2015, http://www.fas.org/sgp/crs/row
/R43894.pdf.

34. Jon R. Lindsay, "The Impact of China on Cybersecurity: Fiction and Friction," *International Security* 39, no. 3 (2015): 7–47.

35. Marcel A. Green, "China's Growing Cyberwar Capabilities," *Diplomat*, April 13, 2015, http://thediplomat.com/2015/04/chinas-growing-cyberwar
-capabilities/.

36. Ellen Nakashima, "Hacks of OPM Databases Compromised 22.1 Million People, Federal Authorities Say," *Washington Post*, July 9, 2015.

37. "Remarks by the President to the Business Roundtable," White House Office of the Press Secretary, September 16, 2015, https://www.whitehouse.gov/the
-press-office/2015/09/16/remarks-president-business-roundtable.

38. Lindsay, "Impact of China on Cybersecurity."

39. Max Fisher, "China's Culture of Hacking Cost the Country $873 Million in 2011," *Washington Post*, May 20, 2013.

40. Amitai Etzioni, "The Private Sector: A Reluctant Partner in Cybersecurity," in *Privacy in a Cyber Age: Policy and Practice*, by Etzioni and Christopher J. Rice (New York: Palgrave Macmillan US, 2015), 93–100.

41. U.S.-China Economic and Security Review Commission (USCC), 2010 Report to Congress, November 2010, http://www.uscc.gov/annual_report/2010
/annual_report_full_10.pdf, accessed November 17, 2010; Siobhan Gorman, "Electricity Grid in U.S. Penetrated by Spies," *Wall Street Journal*, April 8, 2009.

42. Shannon Tiezzi, "Japan Seeks Chinese Compensation over 2010 Boat Collision Incident," *Diplomat*, February 14, 2014, http://thediplomat.com/2014/02
/japan-seeks-chinese-compensation-over-2010-boat-collision-incident/.

43. J. Michael Cole, "China, Japan, Taiwan, and the East China Sea," *Diplomat*, July 13, 2012, http://thediplomat.com/2012/07/china-japan-taiwan-and-the-east
-china-sea/.

44. Zachery Keck, "China Military Trains for War against Japan," *Diplomat,* February 19, 2014, http://thediplomat.com/2014/02/chinas-military-trains-for-war-against-japan/.

45. "Chinese Ships Enter Disputed Senkaku Waters." *Telegraph,* October 25, 2012, http://www.telegraph.co.uk/news/worldnews/asia/china/9632333/Chinese-ships-enter-disputed-Senkaku-waters.html.

46. Clint Richards, "There's Been a Quiet Decline in Senkaku Confrontations," *Diplomat,* September 19, 2014, http://thediplomat.com/2014/09/theres-been-a-quiet-decline-in-senkaku-confrontations/.

47. Harry Kazianis, "Senkaku/Diaoyu Islands: A 'Core Interest' of China," *Diplomat,* April 29, 2013, http://thediplomat.com/2013/04/senkakudiaoyu-islands-a-core-interest-of-china/.

48. Allen R. Carlson, "Why Chinese Nationalism Could Impact the East and South China Seas Very Differently," *National Interest,* September 24, 2015, http://nationalinterest.org/feature/why-chinese-nationalism-could-impact-the-east-south-china-13922.

49. The 1948 atlas featured an "eleven-dash line; two of the dashes were removed in 1953." See Zhiguo Gao and Bing Bing Jia, "The Nine-Dash Line in the South China Sea: History, Status, and Implications," *American Journal of International Law* 107, no. 1 (2013): 98–124.

50. Jackson Nyamuya Maogoto, "Aggression Supreme: International Offence Still in Search of Definition," *Southern Cross University Law Review* 6, no. 1 (2002): 278–317; "Philippine Warship 'in Stand-Off' with Chinese Vessels," BBC News, April 11, 2012, http://www.bbc.com/news/world-asia-17673426; "China, Philippines Locked in Naval Standoff," CNN, April 11, 2012, http://www.cnn.com/2012/04/11/world/asia/philippines-china-naval-standoff/.

51. "Philippines: China 'Increasing Ships at Disputed Shoal,'" BBC News, May 23, 2015, http://www.bbc.com/news/world-asia-18171009.

52. M. Taylor Fravel, "China's Island Strategy: 'Redefine the Status Quo,'" *Diplomat,* November 1, 2012, http://thediplomat.com/2012/11/chinas-island-strategy-redefine-the-status-quo/.

53. Shannon Tiezzi, "Philippines Accuses China of Ramming Boats in South China Sea," *Diplomat,* February 2, 2015, http://thediplomat.com/2015/02/philippines-accuses-china-of-ramming-boats-in-south-china-sea/.

54. Scott Neumann, "Little Islands Are Big Trouble in South China Sea," NPR, September 7, 2012, http://www.npr.org/2012/09/07/160745930/little-islands-are-big-trouble-in-the-south-china-sea.

55. "Philippines Says Chinese Ship Rammed Fishing Boats in Scarborough Shoal," Reuters, February 4, 2015, http://www.reuters.com/chapter/2015/02/04/us-philippines-china-idUSKBN0L81IM20150204#lUsPxlqAR5bUsAuu.97.

56. "Sandcastles of Their Own: Vietnamese Expansion in the Spratly Islands," Asia Maritime Transparency Initiative, http://amti.csis.org/vietnam-island-building/, accessed March 29, 2016.

57. Gregory Poling, "Spratly Airstrip Update: Is Mischief Reef Next?," Asia

Maritime Transparency Initiative, https://amti.csis.org/new-imagery-release/, accessed August 3, 2016.

58. Christopher Mirasola, "What Makes an Island? Land Reclamation and the South China Sea Arbitration," Asia Maritime Transparency Initiative, 2015.

59. *Philippines v. China*, 2015, PCA Case no. 2013–19, Award of Jurisdiction and Admissibility.

60. Ankit Panda, "Russia, India, China Address South China Sea in Trilateral Statement," *Diplomat*, April 21, 2016, http://thediplomat.com/2016/04/russia-india-china-address-south-china-sea-in-trilateral-statement/.

61. Mira Rapp-Hooper and Harry Krejsa, "Reefs, Rocks, and the Rule of Law: After the Arbitration in the South China Sea," Center for a New American Society, 2016, http://www.cnas.org/sites/default/files/publications-pdf/CNASReport-AfterArbitration-FINAL.pdf.

62. Jesse Johnson, "Beijing Turns on Japanese Judge as Hague Tribunal Ruling over South China Sea Nears," *Japan Times*, July 8, 2016, http://www.japantimes.co.jp/news/2016/07/08/national/politics-diplomacy/beijing-turns-japanese-judge-hague-tribunal-ruling-south-china-sea-nears/#.V50Ts_krIdV.

63. Jane Perlez, "Tribunal Rejects Beijing's Claims in South China Sea," *New York Times*, July 12, 2016, http://www.nytimes.com/2016/07/13/world/asia/south-china-sea-hague-ruling-philippines.html.

64. Thomas C. Schelling, *Arms and Influence*, with a new preface and afterword (New Haven: Yale University Press, 2008), 68.

65. Robert Haddick, "Salami Slicing in the South China Sea," *Foreign Policy*, August 3, 2012, http://foreignpolicy.com/2012/08/03/salami-slicing-in-the-south-china-sea/.

66. Antillean Media Group, "Exxon's Guyana Oil Find Could Be Worth $40 Billion," July 22, 2015, http://www.antillean.org/exxon-guyana-oil-exploration-404/.

67. David Jessop, "Will CARICOM Stand Up to Venezuela over Its Guyana Territorial Claims?," Antillean Media Group, http://www.antillean.org/guyana-venezuela-border-dispute-286/.

68. Doug Bandow, "The Ultimate Irony: Is China the 'America' of Asia?," *National Interest*, May 27, 2015, http://nationalinterest.org/feature/the-ultimate-irony-china-the-america-asia-12976.

69. David Kilgour, "The Rule of Law and the South China Sea," *Epoch Times*, July 19, 2016, http://www.theepochtimes.com/n3/2118181-the-rule-of-law-and-the-south-china-sea/.

70. Gordon C. Chang, "China vs. Philippines: What's at Stake as the Verdict in The Hague Looms," *National Interest*, July 11, 2016, http://nationalinterest.org/feature/china-vs-philippines-whats-stake-the-verdict-the-hague-looms-16918.

71. This claim is, of course, disputable. Ret. commodore Sam Bateman of the Australian National Centre for Ocean Resources and Security writes that US FON operations around the disputed islands are based on an "unreasonably assertive interpretation of the international law of the sea." See Bateman, "Does

the US Know What It's Doing in the South China Sea?," *Australian Strategic Policy Institute*, May 19, 2015, http://www.aspistrategist.org.au/does-the-us-know-what-its-doing-in-the-south-china-sea/.

72. Ibid.

73. Graham Allison, "Of Course China, like All Great Powers, Will Ignore an International Legal Verdict," *Diplomat*, July 11, 2016, http://thediplomat.com/2016/07/of-course-china-like-all-great-powers-will-ignore-an-international-legal-verdict/.

74. Michael Forsythe, "China Deployed Missiles on Disputed Island, U.S. Says," *New York Times*, February 16, 2016, http://www.nytimes.com/2016/02/17/world/asia/china-is-arming-south-china-sea-island-us-says.html.

75. Michael Forsythe, "Possible Radar Suggests Beijing Wants 'Effective Control' in South China Sea," *New York Times*, February 23, 2016, http://www.nytimes.com/2016/02/24/world/asia/china-south-china-sea-radar.html.

76. BBC News, "China Lands Military Plane on Disputed South China Sea Reef," April 18, 2016, http://www.bbc.com/news/world-asia-china-36069615.

77. "China Able to Project 'Substantial Offensive Power' from Spratlys in Months: U.S.," Reuters, March 11, 2016, http://www.reuters.com/article/us-south chinasea-china-spratlys-idUSKCN0WC2I0.

78. "China Says U.S. 'Militarising' South China Sea," Reuters, July 30, 2015, http://uk.reuters.com/article/uk-southchinasea-china-usa-idUKKCN0Q41532015 0730.

79. Bill Gertz, "Beijing Targets US Pacific Commander as Carrier Sails South China Sea," *Asia Times*, March 7, 2016, http://atimes.com/2016/03/beijing-targets-us-pacific-commander-as-carrier-sails-south-china-sea/.

80. Kirk Spitzer, "New Garrison, Old Troubles in the South China Sea," *Time*, July 26, 2012, http://nation.time.com/2012/07/26/new-garrison-old-troubles-in-the-south-china-seas/.

81. Ibid.

82. Bonnie Glaser, "Armed Clash in the South China Sea: Contingency Planning Memorandum No. 14," Council on Foreign Relations, http://www.cfr.org/asia-and-pacific/armed-clash-south-china-sea/p27883.

83. David Larter, "4-Star Admiral Wants to Confront China: White House Says Not So Fast," *Navy Times*, April 6, 2016, http://www.navytimes.com/story/military/2016/04/06/4-star-admiral-wants-confront-china-white-house-says-not-so-fast/82472290/.

84. Peter Lee, "China Not Leaving the 'South China Sea,'" *Asia-Pacific Journal* 14, no. 6 (March 15, 2016), http://apjjf.org/2016/06/Lee.html.

85. "Shipping Unscathed as China Flights Raise South China Sea Tension," Reuters, January 13, 2016, http://www.reuters.com/article/southchinasea-shipping-idUSL8N14R17X20160114.

86. Greg Austin, "4 Reasons Why China Is No Threat to South China Sea Commerce," *Diplomat*, May 22, 2015, http://thediplomat.com/2015/05/4-reasons-why-china-is-no-threat-to-south-china-sea-commerce/.

87. Barry Wain, "Manila's Bungle in the South China Sea," *Far Eastern Economic Review* 171, no. 1 (2008): 45.

88. Chunjuan Nancy Wei, "Beijing's Formidable Strategy in the South China Sea," *Diplomat*, May 21, 2015, http://thediplomat.com/2015/05/beijings-formidable -strategy-in-the-south-china-sea/.

89. Jeremy Page and Gordon Lubold, "Chinese Navy Ships Came within 12 Nautical Miles of U.S. Coast," *Wall Street Journal*, September 4, 2015, http://www .wsj.com/chapters/chinese-navy-ships-off-alaska-passed-through-u-s-territorial -waters-1441350488.

4. Is China a Responsible Stakeholder?

1. Robert Kaplan, "Don't Panic about China," *Atlantic*, January 28, 2010.

2. John Lee, "China Won't Be a Responsible Stakeholder," *Wall Street Journal*, February 1, 2010.

3. Elizabeth C. Economy, "The Game Changer: Coping with China's Foreign Policy Revolution," *Foreign Affairs*, November/December 2010, p. 142.

4. Richard Nixon, "Asia after Viet Nam," *Foreign Affairs*, October 1967.

5. Alastair Iain Johnston, "Is China a Status Quo Power?," *International Security* 27, no. 4 (Spring 2003): 6–7.

6. Tony Blair's 1996 speech in Singapore cited in Michael Hopkins, *The Planetary Bargain: Corporate Social Responsibility Matters* (London: Earthscan Publications, 2003), 18.

7. Robert Ross, "Beijing as a Conservative Power," *Foreign Affairs*, March/April 1997.

8. Johnston, "Is China a Status Quo Power?," 28.

9. Zheng Bijian, "China's Peaceful Rise to Great-Power Status," *Foreign Affairs*, September/October 2005.

10. Yukon Huang, "China's Road to Becoming a 'Responsible' World Power," Carnegie Endowment for International Peace, March 26, 2013, http://carnegie endowment.org/2013/03/26/china-s-road-to-becoming-responsible-world-power.

11. Shannon Tiezzi, "China's $3 Billion Message to the UN: Yes, We Are a Responsible Power," *Diplomat*, September 29, 2015, http://thediplomat.com/2015 /09/chinas-3-billion-message-to-the-un-yes-we-are-a-responsible-power/.

12. Erich Follath, "China's Soft Power Is a Threat to the West," *Der Spiegel*, July 28, 2010, http://www.spiegel.de/international/world/0,1518,708645,00.html.

13. Evan A. Feigenbaum, "Beijing's Billions," *Foreign Policy*, May 20, 2010, http://www.foreignpolicy.com/articles/2010/05/19/beijings_billions, accessed October 18, 2010.

14. Srikanth Kondapalli, "Tsunami and China: Relief with Chinese Characteristics," *Asian Affairs*, January 17, 2005.

15. Drew Thompson, "Tsunami Relief Reflects China's Regional Aspirations," *China Brief*, Jamestown Foundation, January 17, 2005, http://www.jamestown.org /single/?no_cache=1&tx_ttnews[tt_news]=27394, accessed October 21, 2010.

16. Kondapalli, "Tsunami and China."

17. "China Must End UN 'Interference,'" Save Darfur, http://www.savedarfur.org/pages/press/china_must_end_un_interference/, accessed November 17, 2010.

18. Christopher Drew, "New Targets for Spies: Employers' Trade Secrets," *International Herald Tribune,* October 19, 2010.

19. USCC, 2010 Report to Congress.

20. "Chinese Cyberattacks on U.S. Companies Continue, Report Says," NBC, October 19, 2015, http://www.nbcnews.com/tech/tech-news/chinese-cyberattacks-u-s-companies-continue-report-says-n447016.

21. The US assistant secretary of commerce put the estimate at nearly $24 billion a year in a 2004 statement: "US Lashes Out at Chinese Piracy," *Asia Times,* January 15, 2005, http://www.atimes.com/atimes/China/GA15Ad03.html. See also Henry Blodget, "How to Solve China's Piracy Problem," *Slate,* April 12, 2005, http://www.slate.com/id/2116629/.

22. Frederik Balfour, "U.S. Takes Piracy Pushback to WTO," *Bloomberg Business Week,* April 10, 2007, http://www.businessweek.com/globalbiz/content/apr2007/gb20070410_466097.htm, accessed November 15, 2010.

23. *U.S. National Security and Military/Commercial Concerns with the People's Republic of China,* 106th Cong., 1st sess., 1999, 60.

24. Michael R. Crittenden and Shayndi Rice, "Chinese Firm 'Hijacked' Data," *New York Times,* November 18, 2010, A8.

25. James Lewis, "To Protect the U.S. against Cyberwar, Best Defense Is a Good Offense," *U.S. News and World Report,* March 29, 2010.

26. "Cyber War: Sabotaging the System," *60 Minutes,* November 8, 2009.

27. Ellen Nakashima, "Hacks of OPM Databases Compromised 22.1 Million People, Federal Authorities Say," *Washington Post,* July 9, 2015, https://www.washingtonpost.com/news/federal-eye/wp/2015/07/09/hack-of-security-clearance-system-affected-21-5-million-people-federal-authorities-say/.

28. Samantha Power, *A Problem from Hell* (New York: Basic Books, 2002).

29. World Bank data, accessed March 29, 2015, at http://data.worldbank.org/indicator/NY.GDP.PCAP.PP.KD.

30. Bates Gill, "China Becoming a Responsible Stakeholder," event resource, Carnegie Endowment for International Peace, June 11, 2007, http://carnegieendowment.org/files/Bates_paper.pdf, accessed October 20, 2010. See also Bates Gill, *Rising Star: China's New Security Diplomacy* (Washington, DC: Brookings Institution Press, 2007).

31. Andrew Higgins, "China Showcasing Its Softer Side," *Washington Post,* December 2, 2009.

32. Maureen Fan, "China to Aid in Fighting Somali Pirates," *Washington Post,* December 18, 2008.

33. Anne Barrowclough, "China Sends Navy to Fight Somali Pirates," *Times* (London), December 26, 2008.

34. Balfour, "U.S. Takes Piracy Pushback to WTO."

35. Jerome A. Cohen and Jon M. Van Dyke, "Finding Its Sea Legs," *South China Morning Post,* October 26, 2010.

36. "China to Buy $50 Billion of First I.M.F. Bonds," *New York Times,*

September 3, 2009. On China's economic leadership, see also David M. Lampton, *The Three Faces of Chinese Power* (Berkeley: University of California Press, 2008), 111.

37. Jackson Diehl, "Obama's National Security Strategy Is Light on Human Rights," *Washington Post*, May 31, 2010.

38. Shaun Narine, "State, Sovereignty, Political Legitimacy and Regional Institutionalism in the Asia-Pacific," *Pacific Review* 17, no. 3 (2004): 14; Lau Guan Kim, 'A Lie Repeated Often Becomes Truth,' *China Daily*, April 14, 2004, http://www.chinadaily.com.cn/english/doc/2004-04/14/content_323217.htm, accessed December 3, 2010.

39. Michael Mandelbaum, *The Frugal Superpower: America's Global Leadership in a Cash-Strapped Era* (New York: Public Affairs, 2010), 4–5.

5. Accommodating China

1. Sean Clark, "Deadly Decay: Great Power Decline and Cataclysmic War," *International Journal* 65, no. 2 (Spring 2010): 477.

2. Graham T. Allison Jr., "Obama and Xi Must Think Broadly to Avoid a Classic Trap," *New York Times*, June 6, 2013.

3. Preeti Bhattacharji, "Uighurs and China's Xinjiang Region," Council on Foreign Relations, last updated May 29, 2012, http://www.cfr.org/china/uighurs-chinas-xinjiang-region/p16870.

4. Michael D. Swaine, *America's Challenge: Engaging a Rising China in the Twenty-First Century* (Washington, DC: Carnegie Endowment for International Peace, 2011), 278.

5. On "Morning Edition," *National Public Radio*, November 17, 2016. For a more comprehensive view of potential Trump administration policy toward China, written by top advisors, see "Alexander Gray and Peter Navarro, "Donald Trump's Peace through Strength Vision for the Asia-Pacific," *Foreign Policy*, November 7, 2016, http://foreignpolicy.com/2016/11/07/donald-trumps-peace-through-strength-vision-for-the-asia-pacific/.

6. Kenneth Lieberthal and Wang Jisi, "Addressing U.S.-China Strategic Distrust," John L. Thornton China Center Monograph Series no. 4, Brookings Institution, http://www.brookings.edu/~/media/research/files/papers/2012/3/30%20us%20china%20lieberthal/0330_china_lieberthal.

7. Charles E. Osgood, *An Alternative to War or Surrender* (Urbana: University of Illinois Press, 1962); and Amitai Etzioni, *The Hard Way to Peace: A New Strategy* (New York: Collier Books, 1962).

8. Lieberthal and Jisi, "Addressing U.S.-China Strategic Distrust."

9. Hugh White, *The China Choice: Why America Should Share Power* (Melbourne: Black Inc., 2012), 118–19.

10. Zbigniew Brzezinski, "How To Stay Friends with China," *New York Times*, January 2, 2011, http://www.nytimes.com/2011/01/03/opinion/03brzezinski.html.

11. For more discussion, see Amitai Etzioni, "The Kennedy Experiment," *Western Political Quarterly* 20, no. 2 (June 1967): 361–80.

12. This group of scholars convened for a US-China relations symposium in

January 24. The outcome of the meeting, a position paper outlining the principles of mutually assured restraint, is available on the Communitarian Network website: http://communitariannetwork.org/endorse-mutually-assured-restraint -position-paper/. For an in-depth analysis of MAR, and its political prospects, see chapter 2 of Nikolas K. Gvosdev, *Communitarian Foreign Policy: Amitai Etzioni's Vision* (New Brunswick, NJ: Transaction Publishers, 2015).

13. Su Ge, "A New Relationship Model," *Beijing Review,* September 17, 2015, http://www.bjreview.com/World/201509/t20150917_800038580.html.

14. Speech by Foreign Minister Wang Yi, "Toward a New Model of Major-Country Relations between China and the United States," Ministry of Foreign Affairs of the People's Republic of China, September 20, 2013; US Department of State, "U.S.-China Cooperation in the Asia-Pacific Region," July 12, 2012.

15. Klaus Wiegrefe, "An Inside Look at the Reunification Negotiations," *Der Spiegel,* September 29, 2010.

16. "China Warns U.S., Japan, Australia Not to Gang Up in Sea Disputes," Reuters, October 6, 2013.

17. "Japan Nationalists Return after Nearing Islands Disputed with China," NBC, August 18, 2013.

18. Jerome A. Cohen and Jon M. Van Dyke, "Defusing the Bomb in the East China Sea," US-Asia Law Institute, November 10, 2010.

19. "Approaches to Solving Territorial Conflicts: Sources, Situations, Scenarios, and Suggestions," Carter Center, May 2010, 60–62.

20. Bonnie S. Glaser, "Armed Clash in the South China Sea," Council on Foreign Relations, Contingency Planning Memorandum no. 14, April 2012, http://www.cfr.org/east-asia/armed-clash-south-china-sea/p27883.

21. Shirley A. Kan, "China-U.S. Aircraft Collision Incident of April 2001: Assessments and Policy Implications," Congressional Research Service, October 10, 2001, http://www.fas.org/sgp/crs/row/RL30946.pdf.

22. Matthew Franklin, "Our 'Indispensable' Alliance: Barack Obama," *Australian,* November 17, 2011, http://www.theaustralian.com.au/national-affairs /our-indispensable-alliance-barack-obama/story-fn59niix-1226197309213.

23. Matt Siegel, "As Part of Pact, U.S. Marines Arrive in Australia, in China's Strategic Backyard," *New York Times,* April 4, 2012, http://www.nytimes.com /2012/04/05/world/asia/us-marines-arrive-darwin-australia.html?_r=0; Marcus Weisgerber, "Leon Panetta: US to Deploy 60% of Navy Fleet to Pacific," BBC, June 1, 2012, http://www.bbc.co.uk/news/world-us-canada-18305750.

24. "Agreement Calls for 4 U.S. Littoral Combat Ships to Rotate through Singapore," *Defense News,* June 2, 2012, http://rpdefense.over-blog.com/article -agreement-calls-for-4-u-s-littoral-combat-ships-to-rotate-through-singapore -106279617.html.

25. Chas W. Freeman, Intervention at the 8th Sino-US Colloquium of the Institute for Communitarian Policy Studies, George Washington University, Washington, DC, October 5, 2015, https://icps.gwu.edu/sites/icps.gwu.edu/files /downloads/Chas%20Freeman%20Intervention.doc.

26. Andrew Yo, "Will S. Korea's New Naval Base Provoke China?" *Diplomat,* July 10, 2013.

27. Tom Phillips, "China 'Seriously Concerned' after Trump Questions Taiwan Policy," *Guardian,* December 12, 2016, https://www.theguardian.com/us-news /2016/dec/12/donald-trump-questions-us-commitment-to-one-china-policy.

28. Office of the Secretary of Defense, "Annual Report to Congress: Military and Security Developments Involving the People's Republic of China 2013," Department of Defense, 2013, http://www.defense.gov/pubs/2013_china_report _final.pdf.

29. Miles Yu, "Inside China: Taiwan Invasion Exercise," *Washington Times,* October 17, 2013, http://www.washingtontimes.com/news/2013/oct/17/inside-china -taiwan-invasion-exercise/?page=all.

30. Harold Brown et al., *Chinese Military Power,* Task Force Report no. 44 (New York Council on Foreign Relations, Maurice R. Greenberg Center for Geoeconomic Studies, 2003), 34.

31. David E. Sanger, "Mutually Assured Cyberdestruction?," *New York Times,* June 2, 2012, http://www.nytimes.com/2012/06/03/sunday-review/mutually -assured-cyberdestruction.html?pagewanted=all.

32. "The Dragon's New Teeth: A Rare Look inside the World's Biggest Military Expansion," *Economist,* April 7, 2012, http://www.economist.com/node/21552193.

33. Li Yan, "Securing the Global Commons, a New Foundation for the Sino-US Relationship," *China-US Focus,* March 19, 2012, http://www.chinausfocus .com/peace-security/securing-the-global-commonsa-new-foundation-for-the -sino-us-relationship/.

34. Cheryl Pellerin, "U.S., China Must Work Together on Cyber, Panetta Says," American Forces Press Service, May 7, 2012, http://www.defense.gov/news /newsarticle.aspx?id=116235.

35. "China, Russia and Other Countries Submit the Document of International Code of Conduct for Information Security to the United Nations," Ministry of Foreign Affairs of the People's Republic of China, September 13, 2011, http://www .fmprc.gov.cn/eng/zxxx/t858978.htm.

36. Adam Segal, "China and Information vs. Cyber Security," Asia Unbound, Council on Foreign Relations, September 15, 2012, http://blogs.cfr.org/asia/2011/09 /15/china-and-information-vs-cybersecurity/.

37. David C. Gompert and Phillip C. Saunders, *The Paradox of Power: Sino- American Strategic Restraint in an Age of Vulnerability* (Washington, DC: National Defense University Press, 2011), xx.

38. Ibid., xxi.

39. "Fact Sheet: President Xi Jinping's State Visit to the United States," White House Office of the Press Secretary, September 25, 2015, https://www.whitehouse .gov/the-press-office/2015/09/25/fact-sheet-president-xi-jinpings-state-visit-united -states.

40. "China, Russia and Other Countries Submit the Document of International Code of Conduct for Information Security to the United Nations,"

Ministry of Foreign Affairs of the People's Republic of China, September 13, 2011, http://www.fmprc.gov.cn/eng/wjdt/wshd/t858978.htm.

41. Bruce W. Bennett, "Preparing for the Possibility of a North Korean Collapse," RAND Corporation, http://www.rand.org/content/dam/rand/pubs /research_reports/RR300/RR331/RAND_RR331.pdf: 96-97.

42. Ibid.

43. Wen Han, "Hu Jintao Urges Breakthrough in 'Malacca Dilemma,'" *Wen Wei Po,* January 14, 2004; "China Builds Up Strategic Sea Lanes," *Washington Times,* January 17, 2005.

44. T. X. Hammes, "Sorry, AirSea Battle Is No Strategy," *National Interest,* August 7, 2013.

45. Tim Summers, "What Exactly Is 'One Belt, One Road'?," *World Today* 71 (1): 2015, https://www.chathamhouse.org/publication/twt/what-exactly-one-belt -one-road.

46. The term "String of Pearls" was first coined in Juli A. MacDonald, Amy Donahue, and Bethany Danyluk, *Energy Futures in Asia: Final Report* (Washington, DC: Booz-Allen & Hamilton, 2004).

47. Ariel Cohen, "U.S. Interests and Central Asia Energy Security," Heritage Foundation, November 15, 2006.

48. James Steinberg and Michael E. O'Hanlon, *Strategic Reassurance and Resolve: US-China Relations in the Twenty-first Century* (Princeton: Princeton University Press, 2015).

49. "Mutually Assured Restraint: A New Approach to U.S.-China Relations," position paper available at https://communitariannetwork.org/endorse-mutually -assured-restraint-position-paper.

50. "UN Security Council Condemns Latest DPRK Missile Launches, Notes 'Flagrant Disregard' for Previous Statements," UN News Service, September 6, 2016, http://www.un.org/apps/news/story.asp?NewsID=54859#.WFgKwPkrIdV.

51. David Ignatius, "North Korea Is an Urgent Challenge for the Next American President," *Washington Post,* June 9, 2016, https://www.washingtonpost .com/opinions/north-korea-is-an-urgent-challenge-for-the-next-american -president/2016/06/09/2ba1a260–2e6f-11e6–9de3–6e6e7a14000c_story.html.

52. "Bangs and Bucks: America Is Looking for New Ways to Curb the North's Nuclear Ambitions," *Economist,* September 17, 2016, http://www.economist.com /news/asia/21707239-america-looking-new-ways-curb-norths-nuclear-ambitions -bangs-and-bucks.

53. Paul Sonne, "Ash Carter Says China Shares Responsibility for North Korea Nuclear Test," *Wall Street Journal,* September 9, 2016, http://www.wsj.com/articles /ash-carter-says-china-shares-responsibility-for-north-korea-nuclear-test -1473438718.

54. Jane Perlez, "Few Expect China to Punish North Korea for Latest Nuclear Test," *New York Times,* September 11, 2016, http://www.nytimes.com /2016/09/12/world/asia/north-korea-china-nuclear-sanctions-thaad-america .html?_r=0.

55. "Press Conference of President Obama after ASEAN Summit," White

House Office of the Press Secretary, September 8, 2016, https://www.whitehouse
.gov/the-press-office/2016/09/08/press-conference-president-obama-after-asean
-summit.

56. Pieter D. Wezeman and Siemon T. Wezeman, *Trends in International Arms Transfers, 2014* (Stockholm: Stockholm International Peace Research Institute, 2015), http://books.sipri.org/files/FS/SIPRIFS1503.pdf.

57. "U.S. Relations with Taiwan," US Department of State, last updated August 20, 2012, http://www.state.gov/r/pa/ei/bgn/35855.htm.

58. Amitai Etzioni, "Cooler Heads in the South China Sea," *National Interest,* September 26, 2012, http://nationalinterest.org/commentary/cooler-heads-the
-south-china-sea-7520.

59. Zachary Fillingham, "Arctic Ownership Claims," Geopolitical Monitor, April 21, 2012, http://www.geopoliticalmonitor.com/arctic-ownership-claims.

60. Amitai Etzioni, "Point of Order," *Foreign Affairs,* November/December 2011, http://www.foreignaffairs.com/articles/136548/amitai-etzioni-g-john
-ikenberry/point-of-order.

61. Zbigniew Brzezinski, "The Group of Two that Could Change the World," *Financial Times,* January 13, 2009, http://www.ft.com/intl/cms/s/0/d99369b8-e178
-11dd-afa0-0000779fd2ac.html#axzz2AzHiT8ac.

62. Henry Kissinger, *On China* (New York: Penguin Group, 2011); Michiko Kakutani, "An Insider Views China, Past and Future," *New York Times,* May 9, 2011, http://www.nytimes.com/2011/05/10/books/on-china-by-henry-kissinger
-review.html?pagewanted=all.

63. White, *The China Choice.*

64. Michael Haas, "A MARred Alternative: Offense, Defense and U.S.-China Relations," *Diplomat,* October 8, 2013.

6. Is the United States Trying to Integrate China into the International Order?

1. G. John Ikenberry, *Liberal Leviathan: The Origins, Crisis, and Transformation of the American World Order* (Princeton: Princeton University Press, 2012).

2. Robert Keatley, "China's AIIB Challenge: How Should America Respond?," *National Interest,* April 18, 2015, http://nationalinterest.org/feature/americas-big
-strategic-blunder-not-joining-chinas-aiib-12666.

3. Matthew P. Goodmn, Daniel F. Runde, Connor M. Savoy, and Amy Jean Studdart, "The Asian Infrastructure Investment Bank," Center for Strategic & International Studies, March 20, 2015, http://csis.org/publication/asian
-infrastructure-investment-bank; Helmut Reisen, "How the New AIIB Dwarfs the Asian Development Bank," *Globalist,* April 2015, http://www.theglobalist.com/aiib
-to-dwarf-adb-loan-portfolio/.

4. "21 Asian Countries Sign MOU on Establishing Asian Infrastructure Investment Bank," Xinhuanet, October 24, 2014, http://news.xinhuanet.com
/english/business/2014-10/24/c_133740149.htm.

5. "China-led AIIB Development Bank Holds Signing Ceremony," BBC News, June 29, 2015, http://www.bbc.com/news/world-asia-33307314.

6. Another scholar estimates that China expects to hold a 44 percent stake in the bank (Yonhap News Agency, 2015).

7. "The Infrastructure Gap," *Economist,* March 21, 2015, http://www.economist .com/news/asia/21646740-development-finance-helps-china-win-friends-and -influence-american-allies-infrastructure-gap.

8. Shannon Tiezzi, "China's AIIB: The Final Tally," *Diplomat,* April 17, 2015, http://thediplomat.com/2015/04/chinas-aiib-the-final-tally/.

9. Henry Sender, "Japan Expected to Join Asian Infrastructure Investment Bank," *Financial Times,* March 30, 2015, http://www.ft.com/intl/cms/s/0/40b0fff8 -d6ae-11e4-97c3-00144feab7de.html#axzz43w2iJSg1.

10. "G7 wish Asian Infrastructure Investment Bank Success," Xinhuanet, May 29, 2015, http://news.xinhuanet.com/english/2015-05/29/c_134282485.htm.

11. Ian Talley, "U.S. Looks to Work with China-Led Infrastructure Fund," *Wall Street Journal,* March 22, 2015, http://www.wsj.com/articles/u-s-to-seek -collaboration-with-china-led-asian-infrastructure-investment-bank-1427057486.

12. "Reversion to the Mean," *Economist,* September 26, 2015, http://www .economist.com/news/asia/21667964-chinas-new-infrastructure-bank-has-gained -wide-support-lending-will-be-tougher-reversion.

13. Robert Zoellick, "Shunning Beijing's Infrastructure Bank Was a Mistake for the US," *Financial Times,* June 7, 2015, http://www.ft.com/intl/cms/s/0/c870c090 -0a0c-11e5-a6a8-00144feabdc0.html#axzz43w2iJSg1.

14. Hugh White, "China Outsmarts US Diplomacy on Asia Bank," *The Age,* March 31, 2015, http://www.theage.com.au/comment/aiib-china-outsmarts-us -diplomacy-on-asia-bank-20150329-1ma0q7.html.

15. Lawrence Summers, "Time US Leadership Woke Up to New Economic Era," *Financial Times,* April 5, 2015, http://www.ft.com/intl/cms/s/2/a0a01306-d887 -11e4-ba53-00144feab7de.html#axzz3WX4sXQ7O.

16. See also Thomas Wright, "A Special Argument: The U.S., U.K., and the AIIB 2015," Brookings Institution, March 13, 2015; Benn Steil and Dinah Walker, "Should the United States Encourage Japan to Join the AIIB?," Council on Foreign Relations, April 20, 2015, http://blogs.cfr.org.

17. Patrick Chovanec, Zha Daojing, Scott Kennedy, and Stephen S. Roach, "What Went Wrong with U.S. Strategy on China's New Bank and What Should Washington Do Now?," ChinaFile, March 24, 2015, https://www.chinafile.com /conversation/what-went-wrong-us-strategy-chinas-new-bank-and-what-should -washington-do-now.

18. Dong Leshou and Lia Zhu, "US 'Miscalculated' on AIIB: Albright," *China Daily,* April 1, 2015.

19. Chovanec et al., "What Went Wrong with U.S. Strategy."

20. Tania Branigan, Paul Lewis, and Nicholas Watt, "US Anger at Britain Joining Chinese-Led Investment Bank AIIB," *Guardian,* March 12, 2015, http:// www.theguardian.com/us-news/2015/mar/13/white-house-pointedly-asks-uk-to -use-its-voice-as-part-of-chinese-led-bank.

21. Talley, "U.S. Looks to Work."

22. Bhaskar Chakravorti, "China's New Development Bank Is a Wake-Up Call

for Washington," *Harvard Business Review,* April 20, 2015, https://hbr.org/2015/04 /chinas-new-development-bank-is-a-wake-up-call-for-washington.

23. Mercy A. Kuo and Angie O. Tang, "China's AIIB and the US Reputation Risk," *Diplomat,* April 16, 2015, http://thediplomat.com/category/the-rebalance /page/3/; Don Rodney Ong Junio, "Asian Infrastructure Investment Bank: An Idea Whose Time Has Come?," *Diplomat,* December 4, 2014.

24. Robert Keatley, "China AIIB Challenge: How Should American Respond?" *Glocal,* April 29, 2015, http://www.glocal.org.hk/archives/42190.

25. Talley, "U.S. Looks to Work."

26. Branigan, Lewis, and Watt, "US Anger at Britain."

27. Matthew Yglesias, "How a Chinese Infrastructure Bank Turned into a Diplomatic Fiasco for America," *Vox,* April 1, 2015, http://www.vox.com/2015/4/1 /8311921/asian-infrastructure-investment-bank.

28. Eleanor Albert and Robert Kahn, "A Bank Too Far?" Council on Foreign Relations, March 17, 2015, http://www.cfr.org/global-governance/bank-too-far /p36290; Chakravorti, "China's New Development Bank."

29. Bob Davis and Lingling Wei, "China Forgoes Veto Power at New Bank to Win Key European Nations' Support," *Wall Street Journal,* March 23, 2015, http://www.wsj.com/articles/china-forgoes-veto-power-at-new-bank-to-win-key -european-nations-support-1427131055.

30. "IMF Says Ukraine Debt Deal Needed Soon," Sky News Australia, May 1, 2015, http://www.skynews.com.au/business/business/world/2015/05/01/imf-says -ukraine-debt-deal-needed-soon.html.

31. "IMF Rule Change Keeps Ukraine Support; Russia Complains," Reuters, December 8, 2015, http://www.reuters.com/article/us-ukraine-crisis-imf -idUSKBN0TR28Q20151208.

32. Larry Hanauer and Lyle J. Morris, *Chinese Engagement in Africa: Drivers, Reactions, and Implications for US Policy* (Santa Monica: RAND Corporation, 2014).

33. Albert and Kahn, "A Bank Too Far?"

34. Fareed Zakaria, "China's Growing Clout," *Washington Post,* November 13, 2014, https://www.washingtonpost.com/opinions/fareed-zakaria-chinas-growing -clout/2014/11/13/fe0481f6-6b74-11e4-a31c-77759fc1eacc_story.html.

35. G. John Ikenberry, "The Rise of China and the Future of the West: Can the Liberal System Survive," *Foreign Affairs,* January/February 2008, https://www .foreignaffairs.com/articles/asia/2008-01-01/rise-china-and-future-west; Robert B. Zoellick, "Whither China: From Membership to Responsibility?," US Department of State, September 21, 2005, http://2001-2009.state.gov/s/d/former/zoellick/rem /53682.htm.

36. Greg Mastel, "China, Taiwan, and the World Trade Organization," *Washington Quarterly* 24, no. 3 (2001): 45–56, https://muse.jhu.edu/journals /washington_quarterly/v024/24.3mastel.html.

37. Henry Gao, "China on the World Stage: A Trade Law Perspective," in *Proceedings of the 104th Annual Meeting of the American Society for International Law* (Washington, DC: American Society for International Law, 2010), 532–35.

38. T. P. Bhat, "Assessing China's Compliance with WTO Commitments," *India Quarterly: A Journal of International Affairs* 65, no. 3 (2009): 215–35.

39. Nicholas R. Lardy, "Issues in China's WTO Accession, US-China Security Review Commission," Brookings Institution, May 9, 2001.

40. Bhat, "Assessing China's Compliance."

41. Timothy Webster, "Paper Compliance: How China Implements WTO Decisions," *Michigan Journal of International Law* 35 (2014): 525.

42. Gerald Chan, "China and the WTO: The Theory and Practice of Compliance," *International Relations of the Asia-Pacific* 4, no. 1 (2004): 47–72.

43. Ian Jeffries, *China: A Guide to Economic and Political Developments* (London: Routledge, 2007).

44. Natalie Laura Bridgeman, "World Bank Reform in the 'Post-Policy' Era," *Georgetown International Environmental Law Review* 13 (2000): 1013.

45. Chris Simms, "Good Governance at the World Bank," *Lancet* 371, no. 9608 (2008): 202–3.

46. Catherine Weaver, "The World's Bank and the Bank's World," *Global Governance: A Review of Multilateralism and International Organizations* 13, no. 4 (2007): 493–512.

47. Mario Stumm, "More Responsibility for Developing Countries," World Bank, 2011, http://www.dandc.eu/en/article/how-voice-reform-came-about-world-bank.

48. Eric A. Posner and Alan O. Sykes, "Voting Rules in International Organizations," *Chicago Journal of International Law* 15 (2014): 195.

49. Lesley Wroughton, "China Gains Clout in the World Bank Vote Shift," Reuters, April 25, 2015, http://www.reuters.com/article/2010/04/25/us-worldbank-idUSTRE63O1RQ20100425.

50. "China's Voting Power in the World Bank Ascends to Third Place," Xinhuanet, April 26, 2010, http://news.xinhuanet.com/english2010/china/2010-04/26/c_13266890.htm.

51. "Analysis of World Bank Voting Reforms," Bretton Woods Project, April 30, 2010, http://www.brettonwoodsproject.org/2010/04/art-566281/.

52. Ying Ma, "An Influential Voice Slams U.S. Handling of New China-Led Infrastructure Bank," *Wall Street Journal,* March 19, 2015, http://blogs.wsj.com/chinarealtime/2015/03/19/an-influential-voice-slams-u-s-handling-of-new-china-led-infrastructure-bank/.

53. Walden Bello, "China's Offering a World Bank Alternative—and U.S. Allies Are Signing Up," *Foreign Policy in Focus,* April 23, 2015, http://fpif.org/chinas-offering-a-world-bank-alternative-and-u-s-allies-are-signing-up/.

54. David P. Rapkin and Jonathan R. Strand, "Reforming the IMF's Weighted Voting System," *World Economy* 29, no. 3 (2006).

55. Ibid.

56. Ibid.

57. Ibid.

58. See, e.g., Rebecca M. Nelson and Martin A. Weiss, "IMF Reforms: Issues for Congress," Congressional Research Service, April 9, 2015, https://www.fas.org/sgp/crs/misc/R42844.pdf; and Anna Yukhananov, "U.S. Congress Will Not Pass

IMF Reforms This Year," Reuters, December 10, 2014, http://www.reuters.com
/article/2014/12/10/us-usa-congress-imf-idUSKBN0JO1UC20141210.

59. The voting share losses would be borne by European countries. See Jeffrey
Frankel, "IMF Reform and Isolationism in the US Congress," East Asia Forum,
January 29, 2014.

60. "IMF Executive Board Approves 4-Year US$17.5 Billion Extended Fund
Facility for Ukraine; US$5 Billion for Immediate Disbursement," International
Monetary Fund, March 11, 2015, http://www.imf.org/external/np/sec/pr/2015
/pr15107.htm.

61. Nelson and Weiss, "IMF Reforms."

62. Mike Callaghan, "G20 Gives US an Ultimatum on IMF Reform: But Is It a
Bluff?," Lowy Interpreter, April 15, 2014, http://www.lowyinterpreter.org/post/2014
/04/15/G20-US-ultimatum-IMF-reform.aspx?COLLCC=2937502547&.

63. Posner and Sykes, "Voting Rules in International Organizations."

64. Bernard K. Gordon, "Bring China into TPP," National Interest, April 11,
2014, http://nationalinterest.org/commentary/bring-china-tpp-10227.

65. Antonio C. Hsiang, "TPP as Grand Strategy: Latin American Perspectives,"
FLACSO-ISA Joint International Conference, July 2014, http://web.isanet.org/Web
/Conferences/FLACSO-ISA%20BuenosAires%202014/Archive/d6eac132-1985-441c
-9491-1ae088f4cfaa.pdf.

66. "TPP: What's at Stake with the Trade Deal?" BBC News, April 22, 2014,
http://www.bbc.com/news/business-27107349.

67. Shuaihua Cheng, "TPP, China and the Future of the Global Trade Order,"
Yale Global Online, October 14, 2014.

68. "China Considers Economic Benefit to Joining Trans-Pacific Partnership,"
Asia Briefing, June 27, 2014, http://www.asiabriefing.com/news/2014/06/china
-considers-economic-benefit-joining-trans-pacific-partnership/.

69. "PBOC's Ma Urges Joining TPP to Boost Growth, Report Shows,"
Bloomberg Business, June 25, 2014, http://www.bloomberg.com/news/articles
/2014-06-24/pboc-s-ma-urges-joining-tpp-to-boost-growth-report-shows.

70. Zachary Keck, "China May Join US-led Trans-Pacific Partnership Talks,"
Diplomat, May 31, 2013, http://thediplomat.com/2013/05/china-may-join-us-led
-trans-pacific-partnershi-talks/.

71. Gordon, "Bring China into TPP."

72. Susan Rice, "Remarks as Prepared for Delivery by National Security
Advisor Susan E. Rice," speech given at Georgetown University, November 20,
2013, https://www.whitehouse.gov/the-press-office/2013/11/21/remarks-prepared
-delivery-national-security-advisor-susan-e-rice.

73. Jake Tapper et al., "45 Times Secretary Clinton Pushed the Trade Bill She
Now Opposes," CNN, June 15, 2015, http://www.cnn.com/2015/06/15/politics/45
-times-secretary-clinton-pushed-the-trade-bill-she-now-opposes/.

74. Katie Holliday, "China Must Meet 'High Standards' to Join TPP: US Trade
Rep," CNBC, March 20, 2013, http://www.cnbc.com/id/100575526.

75. Keith Bradsher, "Once Concerned, China Is Quiet about Trans-Pacific
Trade Deal," New York Times, April 28, 2015.

76. Shannon Tiezzi, "Will China Join the Trans-Pacific Partnership?," *Diplomat,* October 10, 2014, http://thediplomat.com/2014/10/will-china-join-the-trans-pacific-partnership/.

77. David Pilling, "It Won't be Easy to Build an 'Anyone but China' Club," *Financial Times,* May 22, 2013, http://www.ft.com/intl/cms/s/0/08cf74f6-c216-11e2-8992-00144feab7de.html#axzz3Yo3SyY34.

78. See, e.g., Wen Jin Yuan, "The Trans-Pacific Partnership and China's Corresponding Strategies," Center for Strategic and International Studies, 2012, http://csis.org/files/publication/120620_Freeman_Brief.pdf; and Robert D. Blackwill and Ashley J. Tellis, "Revising U.S. Grand Strategy toward China," Council on Foreign Relations, 2015, http://carnegieendowment.org/files/Tellis_Blackwill.pdf.

79. Bradsher, "Once Concerned, China Is Quiet."

80. David Nakamura, "Obama Working to Make Vietnam an Ally in Dealing with China's Rise," *Washington Post,* July 6, 2015.

81. Ashley J. Tellis, "Balancing without Containment: A U.S. Strategy for Confronting China's Rise," *Washington Quarterly,* December 2013.

82. Chas W. Freeman, "Arguments for TPP Don't Make Sense," *Boston Globe,* May 31, 2015.

83. Henry Kissinger, *World Order* (New York: Penguin Press, 2014).

84. "When a latecomer acquires sufficient power, it may be expected to challenge the status quo. When this challenger is resisted by the dominant state, war ensues. The two sides desire to contest the status quo presumably because it confers uneven benefits on them." The established power can offer "pay-offs" to the challenger to peaceably reach a new division of benefits. See Steve Chan, *China, the U.S. and the Power-Transition Theory: A Critique* (New York: Routledge, 2008).

85. G. John Ikenberry, "A World of Our Making," *Democracy* 21, no. 1 (2011).

86. Michael D. Swaine, *America's Challenge: Engaging a Rising China in the Twenty-first Century* (Washington, DC: Carnegie Endowment for International Peace, 2011).

87. Amitai Etzioni, "Air Sea Battle: A Case Study in Structural Inattention and Subterranean Forces," *Armed Forces & Society,* September 2014.

88. Ted Galen Carpenter, "Washington's Clumsy China Containment Policy," *National Interest,* November 30, 2011, http://nationalinterest.org/blog/the-skeptics/washington%E2%80%99s-clumsy-china-containment-policy-6202.

89. Thomas Manesca, "Obama: Goal is Not to 'Contain' China," *USA Today,* April 28, 2014.

90. "John Kerry: 'The United States Does Not Seek to Contain China,'" BBC News, July 9, 2014, http://www.bbc.com/news/world-asia-28223494.

91. Chovanec et al., "What Went Wrong with U.S. Strategy."

92. John Mearsheimer, *The Tragedy of Great Power Politics* (New York: W. W. Norton, 2014).

93. Barry R. Posen, "Pull Back: The Case for a Less Activist Foreign Policy," *Foreign Affairs,* January/February 2013.

94. Amitai Etzioni, *Winning without War* (Garden City, NY: Doubleday, 1964).

95. Amitai Etzioni, "The Kennedy Experiment Revisited," *Political Research Quarterly* 61, no. 1 (2008).

96. Bob Davis, "U.S. Blocks China Efforts to Promote Asia Trade Pact," *Wall Street Journal*, November 2, 2014.

97. Veasna Var, "Cambodia: Between China and the United States," *Diplomat*, May 20, 2015, http://thediplomat.com/2015/05/cambodia-between-china-and-the-united-states/.

98. Yun Sun and Jane Olin-Ammentorp, "The US and China in Africa: Competition or Cooperation?," Brookings Institution, April 28, 2014, www.brookings.edu/blogs/africa-in-focus/posts/2014/04/28-us-china-africa-policy-sun.

99. Nele Noesselt and Ana Soliz Landivar, "China in Latin America: Competition in the United States' 'Strategic Backyard,'" German Institute of Global and Area Studies, 2013, http://www.giga-hamburg.de/en/publication/china-in-latin-america-competition-in-the-united-states%E2%80%99-%E2%80%9Cstrategic-backyard%E2%80%9D.

100. Julian E. Barnes, "China Rejects Multilateral Intervention in South China Sea Disputes," *Wall Street Journal*, August 29, 2013.

101. Huy Duong, "Negotiating the South China Sea," *Diplomat*, July 20, 2011, http://thediplomat.com/2011/07/negotiating-the-south-china-sea/.

102. Katie Bo Williams, "US, China Conclude Cybersecurity Discussions," *The Hill*, September 14, 2015, http://thehill.com/policy/cybersecurity/253523-us-china-conclude-cybersecurity-discussions.

103. "US, China Strike Deal, Set to Hold Joint Military Drills," Reuters, June 15, 2015, https://www.rt.com/news/267241-china-us-drills-agreement/.

104. "China Heads to Joint Naval Exercises with U.S.," CBS, June 10, 2014, http://www.cbsnews.com/news/china-heads-to-joint-naval-exercises-with-america/.

105. David Dollar and Wei Wang, "S&ED: Chinese and American Media Tell Two Tales," Brookings Institution, June 29, 2015, www.brookings.edu/blogs/order-from-chaos/posts/2015/06/29-sed-chinese-american-media-dollar-wang.

106. James Clad and Ron Wahid, "The Real New Type of U.S.-China Relations," *National Interest*, July 14, 2015, http://nationalinterest.org/feature/the-real-new-type-us-china-relations-13323.

107. Ralph A. Cossa, "Track Two Diplomacy: Promoting Regional Peace, Stability," *U.S. Foreign Policy Agenda* 3, no. 1 (1998).

108. Charles Homans, "Track II Diplomacy: A Short History," *Foreign Policy*, June 20, 2011.

109. Michael O. Wheeler, "Track 1.5/2 Security Dialogues with China: Nuclear Lessons Learned," Institute for Defense Analyses, 2014, https://www.ida.org/~/media/Corporate/Files/Publications/IDA_Documents/SFRD/2014/P-5135.pdf.

110. Edward Wong, "Inner Circle of China's President Gives Cold Shoulder to Western Officials," *New York Times*, September 27, 2015.

111. Ibid.

112. Glenn E. Schweitzer, *Scientists, Engineers, and Track-Two Diplomacy:*

A Half-Century of U.S.-Russian Interacademy Cooperation (Washington, DC: National Academies Press, 2004).

7. To Contain or Not? When and Where Is the Question

1. White House Office of the Press Secretary, "Remarks by President Obama and President Xi of the People's Republic of China before Bilateral Meeting," March 31, 2016, http://www.whitehouse.gov/the-press-office/2016/03/31/remarks -president-obama-and-president-xi-peoples-republic-china.

2. Shaun Gregory, "The Terrorist Threat to Pakistan's Nuclear Weapons," *CTC Sentinel* 2, no. 7 (2009): 1–4, https://www.ctc.usma.edu/posts/the-terrorist-threat -to-pakistan%E2%80%99s-nuclear-weapons.

3. Jane Perlez, "64 in Pakistan Die in Bombing at Arms Plant," *New York Times,* August 21, 2008, http://www.nytimes.com/2008/08/22/world/asia/22pstan .html.

4. Ariel Zirulnick, "Pakistani Militants Infiltrate Naval Base Just 15 Miles from Suspected Nuclear Site," *Christian Science Monitor,* May 23, 2011, http://www .csmonitor.com/World/terrorism-security/2011/0523/Pakistani-militants-infiltrate -naval-base-just-15-miles-from-suspected-nuclear-site.

5. Declan Walsh, "Militants Attack Pakistani Air Force Base," *New York Times,* August 16, 2012, http://www.nytimes.com/2012/08/17/world/asia/pakistani-air -force-base-with-nuclear-ties-is-attacked.html.

6. Mark Hibbs, "Moving Forward on the U.S.-India Nuclear Deal," Carnegie Endowment for International Peace, April 5, 2010, http://www .carnegieendowment.org/publications/?fa=view&id=40491.

7. Paul Richter, "In Deal With India, Bush Has Eye on China," *Los Angeles Times,* March 4, 2006, http://articles.latimes.com/2006/mar/04/world/fg-usindia4.

8. Jayshree Bajoria, "U.S.-India Relations Face Serious Challenges," Council on Foreign Relations, October 17, 2007, http://www.cfr.org/india/us-india-relations -face-serious-challenges/p14544.

9. Terrence P. Smith, "Pakistan Joins the Nuclear 100 Club," *CSIS,* February 1, 2011, http://csis.org/blog/pakistan-joins-nuclear-100-club.

10. Paul K. Kerr and Mary Beth Nikitin, "Pakistan's Nuclear Weapons," Congressional Research Service, August 1, 2016, https://www.fas.org/sgp/crs/nuke /RL34248.pdf.

11. Usman Ansari, "Fourth Pakistani Reactor Meets Long-Term Goal," *Defense News,* January 19, 2015, http://www.defensenews.com/story/defense/policy-budget /warfare/2015/01/19/pakistan-reactor-nuclear-plutonium-fourth-isis-deterrent /22006509/.

12. Rodney W. Jones, "Pakistan's Nuclear Poker Bet," *Foreign Policy,* May 27, 2011, http://foreignpolicy.com/2011/05/27/pakistans-nuclear-poker-bet/.

13. Saurav Jha, "India's Undersea Deterrent," *Diplomat,* March 30, 2016, http:// thediplomat.com/2016/03/indias-undersea-deterrent/.

14. Jeffrey Lin and Peter W. Singer, "New Chinese Submarines to Pakistan," *Popular Science,* April 7, 2015, http://www.popsci.com/new-chinese-submarines -pakistan.

15. Iskander Rehman, "Murky Waters: Naval Nuclear Dynamics in the Indian Ocean," Carnegie Endowment for International Peace, 2015, http://carnegie endowment.org/files/murky_waters.pdf.

16. Amit R. Saksena, "Can India Accommodate the INS Arihant?," *Diplomat,* January 26, 2015, http://thediplomat.com/2015/01/can-india-accommodate-the-ins -arihant/.

17. Ted Galen Carpenter, "Fading Hopes for India as a Strategic Counterweight to China," *China-US Focus,* October 4, 2013, http://www.cato.org/publications /commentary/fading-hopes-india-strategic-counterweight-china.

18. Dingding Chen, "Why China Doesn't See India as a Threat," *Diplomat,* February 2, 2015, http://thediplomat.com/2015/02/why-china-doesnt-see-india-as -a-threat/.

19. Mark Mazzetti, "Should (Could) America and Pakistan's Bond Be Broken?," *New York Times,* June 4, 2011.

20. Franz-Stefan Gady, "Pakistan Moves East," *National Interest,* June 3, 2011, http://nationalinterest.org/commentary/the-china-pakistan-alliance-5400.

21. "China to Sell 50 Fighter Jets to Pakistan," Associated Press, May 20, 2011, http://www.thenational.ae/news/worldwide/south-asia/china-to-sell-50-fighter -jets-to-pakistan.

22. Salman Masood and Chris Buckley, "Pakistan Breaks Ground on Nuclear Plant Project with China," *New York Times,* November 26, 2013, http://www .nytimes.com/2013/11/27/world/asia/pakistan-breaks-ground-on-nuclear-power -plant-project-with-china.html?_r=0.

23. Benjamin David Baker, "Revealed: Why China Is Selling Submarines to Pakistan," *Diplomat,* September 28, 2015, http://thediplomat.com/2015/09/revealed -why-china-is-selling-submarines-to-pakistan/.

24. Franz-Stefan Gady, "China and Pakistan Air Forces Launch Joint Training Exercise," *Diplomat,* April 12, 2016, http://thediplomat.com/2016/04/china-and -pakistan-air-forces-launch-joint-training-exercise/.

25. Gady, "Pakistan Moves East."

26. Gady, "China and Pakistan Air Forces."

27. Griff Witte, "Pakistan Courts China as Relations with the U.S. Grow Strained," *Washington Post,* June 22, 2011, http://www.washingtonpost.com/world /asia-pacific/pakistan-courts-china-as-relations-with-us-grow-strained/2011/06 /19/AGDCyWfH_story.html.

28. Daniel Markey and James West, "Behind China's Gambit in Pakistan," Council on Foreign Relations, May 12, 2016, http://www.cfr.org/pakistan/behind -chinas-gambit-pakistan/p37855.

8. Armed Humanitarian Interventions versus Regime Changes

1. G. John Ikenberry, "The Future of the Liberal World Order," *Foreign Affairs,* May/June 2011.

2. The historical question whether this conception of sovereignty arose out of the Treaty of Westphalia is the subject of significant debate within the literature. For a concurring view, see Daniel Philpott, *Revolutions in Sovereignty: How Ideas*

Shaped Modern International Relations (Princeton: Princeton University Press, 2001), 76. For dissenting views, see Daniel Nexon, "Zeitgeist? Neo-idealism and International Political Change," *Review of International Political Economy* 12 (2005): 700–719; and Stephen Krasner, *Sovereignty: Organized Hypocrisy* (Princeton: Princeton University Press, 1999), 20–25.

3. For a recent example, see Romit Guha and Brian Spegele, "China-India Border Tensions Rise," *Wall Street Journal*, April 26, 2013, http://online.wsj.com /article/SB10001424127887323789704578446970130137416.html.

4. Some scholars (e.g., John Ikenberry) hold that the international order centered on Westphalian sovereignty is a decidedly liberal order, while others (e.g., Anne Marie Slaughter) associate the Westphalian model of sovereignty with realism as distinct from a liberal notion of sovereignty under which states have responsibilities, especially to protect their citizens, as well as rights. For Ikenberry's view, see G. John Ikenberry, *Liberal Leviathan* (Princeton: Princeton University Press, 2011). For Slaughter's, see Anne Marie Slaughter, "Sovereignty and Power in a Networked World Order," *Stanford Law Review* 40 (2004): 283–329; and Slaughter, "Intervention, Libya, and the Future of Sovereignty," *Atlantic*, September 4, 2011, http://www.theatlantic.com/international/archive/2011/09 /intervention-libya-and-the-future-of-sovereignty/244537/, accessed July 16, 2015.

5. Daniel Philpott, "Sovereignty," *Stanford Encyclopedia of Philosophy* (summer 2010 ed.), ed. E. N. Zalta, http://plato.stanford.edu/cgi-bin/encyclopedia/archinfo .cgi?entry=sovereignty; see also Jack Goldsmith and Daryl Levinson, "Law for States: International Law, Constitutional Law, Public Law," *Harvard Law Review* 122 (2009): 1844.

6. The Rome Statute of the International Criminal Court, December 31, 2000.

7. Charter of the United Nations, June 26, 1945.

8. Philpott, "Sovereignty."

9. J. Maritain, *Man and the State* (Chicago: University of Chicago Press, 1951).

10. Krasner, *Sovereignty*, 85–86, 108, 163–75, 180–82, 202–17.

11. Bertrand de Jouvenel, *Sovereignty: An Inquiry into the Political Good* (Cambridge: Cambridge University Press, 1957).

12. One might observe a certain similarity between this view and Kant's idea proposed in his essay "Perpetual Peace: A Philosophical Sketch."

13. See 2005 World Summit Outcome (draft resolution referred to the High-Level Plenary Meeting of the General Assembly by the General Assembly at its fifty-ninth session), September 15, 2005, http://www.who.int/hiv/universalaccess 2010/worldsummit.pdf.

14. Francis M. Deng, Sadikiel Kimaro, Terrence Lyons, Donald Rothchild, and I. William Zartman, *Sovereignty as Responsibility: Conflict Management in Africa* (Washington, DC: Brookings Institution Press, 1996).

15. Ibid., xvii.

16. Gareth Evans, Mohamed Sahnoun, et al., *The Responsibility to Protect: Report of the International Commission on Intervention and State Sovereignty* (Ottawa: International Development Research Centre, 2001), 13.

17. UN Department of Public Information, *A More Secure World: Our Shared Responsibility* (New York: United Nations, 2004), 17.

18. Ibid.

19. Security Council Resolution 1674, S/RES/1674 (April 28, 2006).

20. Luke Glanville, "The Responsibility to Protect beyond Borders," *Human Rights Law Review* 12 (2012): 1.

21. B. Ackerman, "Obama's Unconstitutional War," *Foreign Policy,* March/April 2011; R. Norton-Taylor, "Libya Campaign 'Has Made UN Missions to Protect Civilians Less Likely,'" *Guardian,* March 18, 2012, http://www.guardian.co.uk /world/2012/mar/19/libya-un-missions-civilians.

22. Quoted in Luke Glanville, "Darfur and the Responsibilities of Sovereignty," *International Journal of Human Rights* 15 (2011): 465.

23. Commission on Global Governance, *Our Global Neighborhood: Report of the Commission on Global Governance* (New York: Oxford University Press, 1995).

24. A. P. V. Rogers, "Humanitarian Intervention and International Law," *Harvard Journal of Law and Policy* 27 (2004): 728. See also Fernando R. Teson, "Collective Humanitarian Intervention," *Michigan Journal of International Law* 17 (1996): 324; and Jack Donnelly, "Genocide and Humanitarian Intervention," *Journal of Human Rights* 1 (2002): 100, 101.

25. B. S. Chimni, "Forum Replies: A New Humanitarian Council for Humanitarian Interventions?," *International Journal of Human Rights* 6 (2002): 107.

26. Evans, Sahnoun, et al., *The Responsibility to Protect,* 31, 32.

27. Amitai Etzioni, "The Democratization Mirage," *Survival: Global Politics and Strategy* 57, no. 4 (2015): 139–56.

28. Ikenberry, *Liberal Leviathan,* 250.

29. For example, both China and Russia have endorsed the "Responsibility to Protect," and the two nations (reluctantly) permitted the intervention in Libya by declining to veto the UN Security Council's authorization of the use of force in the country. See D. Bilefsky and M. Landler, "As U.N. Backs Military Action in Libya, U.S. Role Is Unclear," *New York Times,* March 17, 2011, http://www.nytimes.com /2011/03/18/world/africa/18nations.html?pagewanted=all.

30. Sarah Teitt, "The Responsibility to Protect and China's Peacekeeping Policy," *International Peacekeeping* 18, no. 3 (2011).

31. Ramesh Thakur, "Law, Legitimacy and United Nations," *Melbourne Journal of International Law* 11 (2010).

32. UN General Assembly Official Records, 63rd Sess., 98th mtg. at 23–24, U.N. Doc. A/63/PV.98 (2009).

33. Andrew Garwood-Gowers, "China's 'Responsible Protection' Concept: Reinterpreting the Responsibility to Protect (R2P) and Military Intervention for Humanitarian Purposes," *Asian Journal of International Law* 6, no. 1 (2016).

34. UNSC 6531st mtg. at 20, U.N. Doc. S/PV.6531 (2011).

35. Garwood-Gowers, "China's 'Responsible Protection' Concept."

36. Ibid.; Tiewa Liu and Haibin Zhang, "Debates in China about the

Responsibility to Protect as a Developing International Norm: A General Assessment," *Conflict, Security & Development* 14, no. 4 (2014): 403–27.

37. Anne Barnard, "New Diplomacy Seen on U.S.-Russian Efforts to End Syrian Civil War," *New York Times,* August 11, 2015, http://www.nytimes.com /2015/08/12/world/middleeast/new-diplomacy-seen-on-us-russian-efforts-to-end -syrian-civil-war.html?_r=0.

38. Former senior White House advisor Phil Gordon has said that "to maintain [Assad's departure] as a precondition for de-escalating the conflict . . . is a recipe for continuing the conflict." Hannah Allam, "'Assad Must Go' Demand Should Go, ex-White House Official Says," *McClatchy DC,* May 12, 2016, http://www .mcclatchydc.com/news/nation-world/national/national-security/article77313747 .html; for more discussion, see Etzioni, "The Democratization Mirage."

39. Paul Harris, Martin Chulov, David Batty, and Damian Pearse, "Syria Resolution Vetoed by Russia and China at United Nations," *Guardian,* February 4, 2012, https://www.theguardian.com/world/2012/feb/04/assad-obama-resign-un -resolution.

40. Etzioni, "The Democratization Mirage."

41. Gerald Seib, "Listen Closely: Donald Trump Proposes Big Mideast Strategy Shift," *Wall Street Journal,* December 12, 2016, http://www.wsj.com/articles/listen -closely-donald-trump-proposes-big-mideast-strategy-shift-1481561492?.

42. Akbar Nasir Khan, "Legality of Targeted Killings by Drone Attacks in Pakistan," *Pak Institute for Peace Studies* 1 (2011).

43. *Rise of the Drones II: Examining the Legacy of Unmanned Targeting: Hearing before the Subcommittee on National Security and Foreign Affairs, United States House of Representatives,* 111th Congress (2010), statement of Mary Ellen O'Connell (Robert and Marion Short Chair in Law, University of Notre Dame, South Bend, IN), https://fas.org/irp/congress/2010_hr/042810oconnell.pdf; see also Dana Priest, "Foreign Network at Front of CIA's Terror Fight," *Washington Post,* November 18, 2005, http://www.washingtonpost.com/wp-dyn/content/article /2005/11/17/AR2005111702070_3.html.

44. Chris Woods, "CIA Drone Strikes Violate Pakistan's Sovereignty, Says Senior Diplomat," *Guardian,* August 2, 2012, http://www.guardian.co.uk/world /2012/aug/03/cia-drone-strikes-violate-pakistan.

45. Mary Ellen O'Connell, "When Is a War Not a War? The Myth of the Global War on Terror," *ILSA Journal of International & Comparative Law* 12 (2005): 5.

46. This assumes sovereignty in the Westphalian sense. In an influential book, Stephen Krasner identifies three further notions of sovereignty: international legal sovereignty, which is a property of independent territorial entities that have rights, like entering into contracts; interdependence sovereignty; and domestic sovereignty. On Krasner's view, Westphalian sovereignty captures the idea that states can organize their domestic affairs any way they wish and other states may not intervene in these domestic affairs, which he considers a misnomer and argues has never truly been practiced in international relations. See Krasner, *Sovereignty: Organized Hypocrisy* (Princeton: Princeton University Press, 1999).

47. It is important to note that the Rome Statute of the International Criminal

Court authorizes the ICC to prosecute individuals of nonstate but state-like entities who commit crimes against humanity. Because the ICC does not have a police force but relies on states to apprehend and arrest individuals suspected of such crimes, this practice does not raise concerns with violations of territorial sovereignty.

48. Security Council Resolution 573, S/RES/573 (October 4, 1985).

49. General Assembly Resolution 41/38, A/RES/41/38 (November 20, 1986).

50. Security Council Resolution 1566, S/RES/1566 (October 8, 2004).

51. General Assembly Resolution 60/288, A/RES/60/288 (September 8, 2006).

52. Christian J. Tams, "The Use of Force against Terrorists," *European Journal of International Law* 20 (2009): 359–97.

53. A Justice Department white paper states that a targeted killing in a foreign nation would be "consistent with legal principles of sovereignty and neutrality if it were conducted, for example, with the consent of the host nation's government or after a determination that the host nation is unable or unwilling to suppress the threat posed by the individual targeted." Department of Justice, *Lawfulness of a Lethal Operation Directed against a U.S. Citizen Who Is a Senior Operational Leader of Al-Qa'ida or an Associated Force,* Washington, DC, http://msnbcmedia .msn.com/i/msnbc/sections/news/020413_DOJ_White_Paper.pdf.

54. Amitai Etzioni, "A Liberal Communitarian Paradigm for Counterterrorism," *Stanford Journal of International Law* 49, no. 2 (2013): 356.

55. Eric Schmitt, "U.S. Caution in Strikes Gives ISIS an Edge, Many Iraqis Say," *New York Times,* May 26, 2015, http://www.nytimes.com/2015/05/27/world /middleeast/with-isis-in-crosshairs-us-holds-back-to-protect-civilians.html?_r=0.

56. See, e.g., Renée De Nevers, "Sovereignty and Ethical Argument in the Struggle against State Sponsors of Terrorism," *Journal of Military Ethics* 6, no. 1 (2007): 1–18; and Daniel Byman, "Passive Sponsors of Terrorism," *Survival* 47, no. 4 (2005): 119.

57. US Department of State, *State Sponsors of Terrorism,* http://www.state.gov/j /ct/list/c14151.htm, accessed September 16, 2015.

58. Section 2405 Foreign Policy Controls, Cornell University Law School, https://www.law.cornell.edu/uscode/html/uscode50a/usc_sec_50a _00002405----000-.html.

59. Kimberley N. Trapp, "Holding States Responsible for Terrorism before the International Court of Justice," *Journal of International Dispute Settlement* 3, no. 2 (2012): 279–98.

60. US Department of State, *Country Reports on Terrorism 2014,* June 2015, http://www.state.gov/documents/organization/239631.pdf.

61. *Britannica Academic,* s.v. "Uighur," accessed July 27, 2016, http://academic .eb.com/levels/collegiate/article/74113, accessed July 27, 2016.

62. Chien-peng Cheung, "China's 'War on Terror': September 11 and Uighur Separatism," *Foreign Affairs,* July/August 2002, http://www.cfr.org/china/chinas -war-terror-september-11-uighur-separatism/p4765.

63. "Xinjiang Violence: China Says 'Gang' Killed 37 Last Week," August 3, 2014, http://www.bbc.com/news/world-asia-china-28628332.

64. Andrew Jacobs and Chris Buckley, "China Blames Xinjiang Separatists for Stabbing Rampage at Train Station," *New York Times*, March 2, 2014, http://www.nytimes.com/2014/03/03/world/asia/china.html.

65. Javier C. Hernandez, "China Acknowledges Killing 28 People: Accuses Them of Role in Mine Attack," *New York Times*, November 20, 2015, http://www.nytimes.com/2015/11/21/world/asia/china-xinjiang-uighurs-raid-coal-mine-attack.html.

66. Jacobs and Buckley, "China Blames Xinjiang Separatists."

67. Elisabeth Rosenthal, "A Nation Challenged: Asian Terror; Beijing Says Chinese Muslims Were Trained as Terrorists with Money from bin Laden, *New York Times*, January 22, 2002, http://www.nytimes.com/2002/01/22/world/nation-challenged-asian-terror-beijing-says-chinese-muslims-were-trained.html.

68. Michael Wines, "China Blames Foreign-Trained Separatists for Attacks in Xinjiang," *New York Times*, August 1, 2011, http://www.nytimes.com/2011/08/02/world/asia/02china.html.

69. Hamid Shalizi, "Afghans Arrested Chinese Uighurs to Aid Taliban Talks Bid: Officials," Reuters, February 20, 2015, http://www.reuters.com/article/us-afghanistan-taliban-china-idUSKBN0LO18020150220.

9. Freedom of Navigation Assertions: The United States as the World's Policeman

1. "Remarks by President Obama at US-ASEAN Press Conference," White House Office of the Press Secretary, February 16, 2016, https://www.whitehouse.gov/the-press-office/2016/02/16/remarks-president-obama-us-asean-press-conference.

2. Jane Perlez, "U.S. Sails Warship Near Island in South China Sea, Challenging Chinese Claims," *New York Times*, May 10, 2016, http://www.nytimes.com/2016/05/11/world/asia/south-china-sea-us-warship.html; Julian G. Ku, M. Taylor Fravel, and Malcolm Cook, "Freedom of Navigation Operations in the South China Sea Are Not Enough," *Foreign Policy*, May 16, 2016, http://foreignpolicy.com/2016/05/16/freedom-of-navigation-operations-in-the-south-china-sea-arent-enough-unclos-fonop-philippines-tribunal/.

3. Lynn Kuok, "The U.S. FON Program in the South China Sea: A Lawful and Necessary Response to China's Strategic Ambiguity," Center for East Asia Policy Studies at Brookings, East Asia Policy Paper 9, June 2016, http://www.brookings.edu/~/media/research/files/papers/2016/06/07-kuok-fon-south-china-sea/the-us-fon-program-in-the-south-china-sea.pdf.

4. "Document: SECDEF Carter Letter to McCain on South China Sea Freedom of Navigation Operation," *USNI News*, January 5, 2016, https://news.usni.org/2016/01/05/document-secdef-carter-letter-to-mccain-on-south-china-sea-freedom-of-navigation-operation; Helene Cooper and Jane Perlez, "White House Moves to Reassure Allies with South China Sea Patrol, But Quietly," *New York Times*, October 27, 2015, http://www.nytimes.com/2015/10/28/world/asia/south-china-sea-uss-lassen-spratly-islands.html.

5. See "South China Sea FONOP 2.0: A Step in the Right Direction," *Asia Maritime Transparency Initiative*. https://amti.csis.org/south-china-sea-fonop-2-0-a-step-in-the-right-direction/.

6. Perlez, "U.S. Sails Warship."

7. Cooper and Perlez, "White House Moves to Reassure Allies."

8. Ibid.

9. David Larter, "4-Star Admiral Wants to Confront China: White House Says Not So Fast," *Navy Times,* April 6, 2016, http://www.navytimes.com/story/military /2016/04/06/4-star-admiral-wants-confront-china-white-house-says-not-so-fast /82472290/.

10. Michael A. Cohen, "The Military Must Follow the White House's Lead on South China Sea Policy," *World Politics Review,* April 13, 2016, http://www .worldpoliticsreview.com/articles/18480/the-military-must-follow-the-white -house-s-lead-on-south-china-sea-policy.

11. Dan de Luce, "Lawmakers to White House: Get Tough with China over South China Sea," *Foreign Policy,* April 27, 2016, http://foreignpolicy.com/2016/04 /27/lawmakers-to-white-house-get-tough-with-beijing-over-south-china-sea/.

12. Jane Perlez, "US. Commanders Implies China Has Eroded Safety of South China Sea," *New York Times,* December 15, 2015, http://www.nytimes.com/2015/12 /16/world/asia/us-navy-commander-implies-china-has-eroded-safety-of-south -china-sea.html.

13. Ibid.

14. Perlez, "U.S. Sails Warship."

15. Cooper and Perlez, "White House Moves to Reassure Allies."

16. Jeremy Page and Gordon Lubold, "Chinese Navy Ships Came within 12 Nautical Miles of U.S. Coast," *Wall Street Journal,* September 4, 2015, http://www .wsj.com/articles/chinese-navy-ships-off-alaska-passed-through-u-s-territorial -waters-1441350488.

17. Ku, Fravel, and Cook, "Freedom of Navigation Operations."

18. Ibid.

19. Off-the-record briefing under Chatham House rules, in Washington, DC, February 2, 2012.

20. "Maritime Security and Navigation," US Department of State, http://www .state.gov/e/oes/ocns/opa/maritimesecurity/, accessed January 9, 2015.

21. "DoD Annual Freedom of Navigation (FON) Reports," Undersecretary of Defense for Policy, US Department of Defense, updated March 6, 2014, http:// policy.defense.gov/OUSDPOffices/FON.aspx.

22. "Declarations and Statements," UN Division for Ocean Affairs and the Law of the Sea, updated October 29, 2013, http://www.un.org/depts/los/convention _agreements/convention_declarations.htm.

23. The Exclusive Economic Zone, or EEZ, is defined as "an area beyond and adjacent to the territorial sea," typically 200 nautical miles in breadth, in which states have "sovereign rights for the purpose of exploring and exploiting, conserving and managing the natural resources." See the UN Convention on the Law of the Sea, part V.

24. "Freedom of Navigation (FON) Report for Fiscal Year (FY) 2013," Department of Defense, March 6, 2014, http://policy.defense.gov/OUSDPOffices /FON.aspx; "Declarations and Statements."

25. Innocent passage is defined by the Law of the Sea as "continuous and expeditious" navigation "through the territorial sea" that "is not prejudicial to the peace, good order or security of the coastal State [and] shall take place in conformity with this Convention and with other rules of international law."

26. "Freedom of Navigation (FON) Report for Fiscal Year (FY) 2013."

27. Robert W. Smith and Sarah Morison, "Maldives Maritime Claims and Boundaries," Bureau of Oceans and International Environmental and Scientific Affairs, Department of State, September 8, 2005, http://www.state.gov/documents /organization/57678.pdf.

28. Steven Groves, "Accession to the U.N. Convention on the Law of the Sea Is Unnecessary to Secure U.S. Navigational Rights and Freedoms," Heritage Foundation, August 24, 2011.

29. "U.S. Collective Defense Arrangements," Department of State, http://www .state.gov/s/l/treaty/collectivedefense/, accessed January 16, 2015; "Bush 'Upgrades' Philippines," CNN, May 20, 2003.

30. "DoD Annual Freedom of Navigation (FON) Reports," Undersecretary of Defense for Policy, US Department of Defense, updated March 6, 2014.

31. Groves, "Accession to the U.N. Convention."

32. See n. 29.

33. Zachary Keck, "US Bombers Challenge China's Air Defense Identification Zone," *Diplomat*, November 27, 2013.

34. A wide array of the associated démarches may be found in J. Ashley Roach and Robert W. Smith, *Excessive Maritime Claims*, 3rd ed. (Leiden: Koninklijke Brill NV, 2012).

35. "Maritime Security and Navigation," Department of State, http://www.state .gov/e/oes/ocns/opa/maritimesecurity/, accessed January 16, 2015.

36. Roach and Smith, *Excessive Maritime Claims*, 8.

37. Ibid., 95.

38. Ibid., 409.

39. W. J. Aceves, "Freedom of Navigation Program: A Study of the Relationship between Law and Politics," *Hastings International and Comparative Law Review* 19 (1995): 281–82.

40. Private Communication, December 2, 2014.

41. Private Communication, December 2, 2014.

42. See, e.g., Martin E. Spencer, "Weber on Legitimate Norms and Authority," *British Journal of Sociology* 21, no. 2 (1970): 123–34 ("By a legitimate order is meant a normative system which is upheld by the belief in the actors of its binding quality or rightness"); Amitai Etzioni, "On Communitarian and Global Sources of Legitimacy," *Review of Politics* 73, no. 1 (2011): 105.

43. See Scott Burchill et al., *Theories of International Relations*, 3rd ed. (New York: Palgrave Macmillan, 2005), 60 ("Some liberals emphasize the institutional constraints on liberal-democratic states, such as public opinion, the rule of law, and representative government"). For example, Joseph Nye argues, "Another problem for those who urge that we accept the idea of an American empire is that they misunderstand the underlying nature of American public opinion and

institutions. Even if it were true that unilateral occupation and transformation of undemocratic regimes in the Middle East and elsewhere would reduce some of the sources of transnational terrorism, the question is whether the American public would tolerate an imperial role for its government." See Nye Jr., "Soft Power and American Foreign Policy," *Political Science Quarterly* 119, no. 2 (2004): 255, 263.

44. "Law of the Sea," Office of Coast Survey, National Oceanic and Atmospheric Administration, accessed January 16, 2015, http://www.nautical charts.noaa.gov/staff/law_of_sea.html.

45. Sayre Swarztrauber, *Three-Mile Limit of Territorial Seas: A Brief History* (Annapolis: Naval Institute Press, 1972), 46.

46. "Law of the Sea," Office of Coast Survey.

47. Roach and Smith, *Excessive Maritime Claims*, 136.

48. Hunter Miller, "The Hague Codification Conference," *American Journal of International Law* 24, no. 4 (October 1930): 674–93.

49. An area extending beyond a coastal state's territorial waters in which, under the Law of the Sea, that state, "may exercise the control necessary" to prevent and punish "infringement of its customs, fiscal, immigration or sanitary laws and regulations within its territory or territorial sea." See the UN Convention on the Law of the Sea 4:33.

50. Tullio Treves, "1958 Geneva Conventions on the Law of the Sea," UN Audiovisual Library of International Law, 2013, http://legal.un.org/avl/ha/gclos /gclos.html, accessed January 12, 2015.

51. Ronald O'Rourke, "Changes in the Arctic: Background and Issues for Congress," Congressional Research Service, August 4, 2014, 11.

52. Peter Prows, "Tough Love: The Dramatic Birth and Looming Demise of UNCLOS Property Law," *Texas International Law Journal* 42 (2006): 241, 255.

53. Treves, "1958 Geneva Conventions on the Law of the Sea."

54. Mark Rosen, "Challenges to Public Order and the Seas," CNA China Studies, March 2014, https://www.cna.org/sites/default/files/research/DPP-2013 -U-006302-1Rev.pdf.

55. John Norton Moore, "Briefing Memorandum to the Deputy Secretary of State," September 25, 1975, http://www.fordlibrarymuseum.gov/library/document /0067/1563044.pdf.

56. John Norton Moore, "The Regime of Straits and the Third United Nations Conference on the Law of the Sea," *American Journal of International Law* 74 (1980): 77, 82–83.

57. George Galdorisi and Alan Kaufman, "Military Activities in the Exclusive Economic Zone: Preventing Uncertainty and Defusing Conflict," *California Western School of Law Scholarly Commons* 32, no. 2 (2001).

58. Aceves, "Freedom of Navigation Program," 268.

59. "Chronological Lists of Ratifications of, Accessions and Successions to the Convention and the Related Agreements as at 3 October 2014," UN Division for Ocean Affairs and the Law of the Sea, http://www.un.org/Depts/los/reference_files /chronological_lists_of_ratifications.htm.

60. "General Information," International Tribunal for the Law of the Sea, http://www.itlos.org/index.php?id=8, accessed January 16, 2015.

61. "General Assembly Resolutions and Decisions," Oceans and the Law of the Sea in the General Assembly of the United Nations, http://www.un.org/depts/los /general_assembly/general_assembly_resolutions.htm, accessed January 16, 2015.

62. These include "The Commander's Handbook on the Law of Naval Operations, Edition July 2007," Department of the Navy, Office of the Chief of Naval Operations, July 2007, https://www.usnwc.edu/getattachment/a9b8e92d -2c8d-4779-9925-0defea93325c/; and the Freedom of Navigation appendices to the secretary of defense's annual reports to the president and the Congress in 1998, 1999, 2000, and 2001, at "DoD Annual Freedom of Navigation (FON) Reports," Undersecretary of Defense for Policy, US Department of Defense, http://policy .defense.gov/OUSDPOffices/FON.aspx, accessed January 12, 2015.

63. Charles Glaser, "Will China's Rise Lead to War? Why Realism Does Not Mean Pessimism," *Foreign Affairs* 90, no. 2 (2011): 80–91 ("Arguing . . . that the United States can be secure simply by taking advantage of its power, geography, and nuclear arsenal, so-called neo-isolationists conclude that the United States should end its alliances in Europe and Asia because they are unnecessary and risky. If the United States can deter attacks against its homeland, they ask, why belong to alliances that promise to engage the United States in large wars on distant continents?"). For a more expansive and critical view of this trend, see Bret Stephens, *America in Retreat: The New Isolationism and the Coming Global Disorder* (New York: Sentinel, 2014).

64. See, e.g., "Public Opinion on Global Issues: World Order" and "Public Opinion on Global Issues: International Institutions," Council on Foreign Relations, 2012, http://www.cfr.org/thinktank/iigg/pop/, accessed April 14, 2015.

65. Daniel W. Drezner, "The Realist Tradition in American Public Opinion," *Perspectives on Politics* 6, no. 1 (2008): 51–70.

66. Dina Smeltz, *Foreign Policy in the New Millennium: Results of the 2012 Chicago Council Survey of American Public Opinion and U.S. Foreign Policy* (Chicago: Chicago Council on Global Affairs, 2012), 23.

67. Drezner, "The Realist Tradition."

68. See, e.g., G. John Ikenberry, "Liberal Internationalism 3.0: America and the Dilemmas of Liberal World Order," *Perspectives on Politics* 7, no. 1 (March 2009): 71–87.

69. Woodrow Wilson, "President Woodrow Wilson's Fourteen Points," speech, Washington DC, January 8, 1918.

70. Stewart M. Patrick, "Obama's Message: An 'Atlantic Charter' for a Pacific Century," Council on Foreign Relations, November 21, 2011.

71. Christian Le Mière, *Maritime Diplomacy in the 21st Century* (New York: Routledge, 2014), 89.

72. Roach and Smith, *Excessive Maritime Claims,* 19.

73. Ibid., 9.

74. Raul Pedrozo, "Preserving Navigational Rights and Freedoms: The Right to

Conduct Military Activities in China's Exclusive Economic Zone," *Chinese Journal of International Law* 9, no. 1 (2010), http://chinesejil.oxfordjournals.org/content/9/1/31.full.pdf.

75. See, e.g., Jack L. Goldsmith and Eric A. Posner, *The Limits of International Law* (Oxford: Oxford University Press, 2006).

76. Roach and Smith, *Excessive Maritime Claims*, 30, 414.

77. See, e.g., Pedrozo, "Preserving Navigational Rights and Freedoms," debating Zhang Haiwen on military activities in the EEZ.

78. See, e.g., Seth Robson, "Perception Outweighs Ability as China Builds Blue-Water Fleet," *Stars and Stripes*, February 4, 2014; Ronald O'Rourke, "China Naval Modernization: Implications for U.S. Navy Capabilities," Congressional Research Service, December 23, 2014.

79. Roach and Smith, *Excessive Maritime Claims*, 9.

80. Joint Chiefs of Staff, "The National Military Strategy of the United States of America 2011," February 2011, at 3 and 9, http://www.isn.ethz.ch/Digital-Library/Publications/Detail/?id=154942.

81. Dennis Mandsager, "The U.S. Freedom of Navigation Program: Policy, Procedure, and Future," *International Law Studies* 72 (1997): 116.

82. Jonathan Odom, "Current Oceans Law & Policy Issues in East Asia," Georgetown University Law Center, May 20, 2014, http://www.armfor.uscourts.gov/newcaaf/ConfHandout/2014ConfHandout/2014JonathanOdom.pdf.

83. James Kraska, *Maritime Power and the Law of the Sea* (Oxford: Oxford University Press, 2011), 1–2.

84. Steven Groves, "Accession to the U.N. Convention on the Law of the Sea Is Unnecessary to Secure U.S. Navigational Rights and Freedoms," Heritage Foundation, August 24, 2011. Dennis Mandsager adds a whole slew of other and current US security needs that require freedom of navigation: these include the ability of "military forces to engage in flight operations, exercises, surveillance and intelligence activities, and weapons testing," as well as "other lawful uses of the oceans important to U.S. military interests, albeit not directly related to navigation, include[ing] laying submarine cables, hydrographic surveys, telecommunications activities, and the collection of marine weather and oceanographic data." See Mandsager, "U.S. Freedom of Navigation Program," 113.

85. Vasilis Trigkas, "Aircraft Carriers in the Taiwan Strait," *Diplomat*, December 29, 2014, http://thediplomat.com/2014/12/aircraft-carriers-in-the-taiwan-strait/.

86. Amitai Etzioni, "Air Sea Battle: A Case Study in Structural Inattention and Subterranean Forces," *Armed Forces & Society* (2014); Etzioni, "Who Authorized Preparations for War with China?" *Yale Journal of International Affairs* 37 (Summer 2013), http://ssrn.com/abstract=2273837.

87. Zachary Keck, "Is Air Sea Battle Useless?," *National Interest*, May 16, 2014, http://nationalinterest.org/feature/air-sea-battle-useless-10473.

88. Roach and Smith, *Excessive Maritime Claims*, 643.

89. John Rolph, "Freedom of Navigation and the Black Sea Bumping Incident:

How 'Innocent' Must Innocent Passage Be?," *Military Law Review* 135 (1992): 137; Robert Pear, "U.S. Downs 2 Libyan Fighters, Citing Their Hostile Intent," *New York Times,* January 5, 1989.

90. Ann Tyson, "Navy Sends Destroyer to Protect Surveillance Ship after Incident in South China Sea," *Washington Post,* March 13, 2009; Bill Gertz, "Pentagon Says Chinese Jet Carried Out 'Aggressive' and 'Dangerous' Intercept of Navy Intelligence Jet," *Washington Free Beacon,* August 21, 2014.

91. David B. Dixon, "Transnational Shipments of Nuclear Materials by Sea: Do Current Safeguards Provide Coastal States a Right to Deny Innocent Passage?," *Journal of Transnational Law and Policy* 16, no. 1 (2006).

92. "United Nations Convention on the Law of the Sea: Declarations Made upon Signature, Ratification, Accession or Succession or Anytime Thereafter," UN Division for Ocean Affairs and the Law of the Sea, updated October 29, 2013, http://www.un.org/depts/los/convention_agreements/convention_declarations .htm.

93. Karl E. Case et al., *Principles of Economics,* 10th ed. (Upper Saddle River, NJ: Prentice Hall, 2011), 107.

Conclusion

1. For a thorough review of current debates in Just War theory, see Mark Evans, ed., *Just War Theory: A Reappraisal* (Edinburgh: Edinburgh University Press, 2005).

INDEX